D0772553

Local, Corporational, and
International Administration

By the same author

An Introduction to Public Administration (Staples Press)
The Essentials of Public Administration (Staples Press)
British Public Service Administration (Staples Press)
Approach to Public Administration (Staples Press)
Civil Services of the United Kingdom, 1855–1970 (Cass)
A History of Public Administration (Cass)
Ypres, 1917 (Kimber)
Across the Piave (HMSO for Imperial War Museum)

Contents of Volume One

E N Gladden MSc PhD

Local, Corporational and International Administration

A Student's Guide to Public Administration

Volume Two

Staples Press   London

Granada Publishing Limited
First published in Great Britain 1972 by Staples Press
3 Upper James Street London W1R 4BP

Copyright © 1972 by E N Gladden

ISBN 0 286 11002 4 (boards)
ISBN 0 286 11006 7 (paper)
Printed in Great Britain by
Richard Clay (The Chaucer Press) Ltd
Bungay, Suffolk

Contents

Part Three: Administration Abroad

Part Four: Public Administration and the Public

Charts, Schedules, and diagrams

Author's Note

Each of the broad spheres of public administration dealt with in this present volume, local, corporational, and international, is linked in varying degree with *Central Government Administration* which is the main topic of Volume I. Introductory matter on Local and Corporational Administration will be found in Chapter 2 of Volume I. On the other hand the final Part Three, in the present volume, on 'Public Administration and the Public', is germane to all branches of the subject.

In conclusion, it is again emphasized that, at this introductory stage, Public Administration is being approached as a whole and that in the division of the work into two volumes is one of convenience and not of principle.

Preface

This *Student's Guide*, although closely following the aim and design of the same author's *An Introduction to Public Administration*, is a completely new work planned to meet the needs of both enquiring reader and student in the seventies.

Since the first edition of the earlier work an administrative revolution has been in progress. In the period immediately following the Second World War there was no general acceptance in Britain, even in the universities or by the official training establishments then beginning to operate, of public administration as a subject for study in its own right. Few could have foreseen the great expansion in administration as a vital activity of the new technological society, inaugurated during the Second World War, and of the Welfare State, whose development had been under such eager discussion since the appearance of the Beveridge Report in 1942. Even fewer could foresee the dynamic extension of interest in the study of, and research into, public administration which was to take place as a result of developments in the international sphere, and in particular in the new nations which were to emerge during the 'fifties and 'sixties.

As its title indicates the work concentrates upon the administrative aspects of the public sphere. It is designed to supplement, and not to examine all over again the ground covered by the many admirable treatises on government, which rightly concentrate upon such subjects as political theory and policy, the constitution, franchise, law-making, the judiciary, and so forth. It is concerned primarily with the administrative, as distinct from the political and legal aspects of government, although of course the latter will not be ignored where they vitally affect the administration.

The work is introductory in the sense that it does not assume preliminary knowledge of the system of public administration, but its level has been raised well above that of the early editions of the previous work to take due account of the substantial advances in the techniques of the subject and of its teaching during the quarter century since the Second World War. It is important to emphasize that administration is a universal activity, all pervading in its operation and influence, and that, within its reasonable compass, this new *Student's Guide* takes a broad and expansive view of its subject. It is concerned with Public Administration in the United Kingdom as a whole, in the separate national and other administrative areas within the United Kingdom, extending over the spheres of central and local government, nationalized industries and other public enterprises, and the numerous public activities on the fringes of the public–private sphere. It is also concerned, though in less detail for want of space, with the links between the several national administrative spheres and their extensions in the international field. It aims at presenting the picture as a whole. Having achieved this the reader will be in a better position to fit his own particular interest into its proper context.

As in the earlier work, special attention has been given to providing supplementary visual aids in the form of charts and schedules, which it is hoped, will help to co-ordinate the more detailed information. Attention is specially drawn to the *Key to Change in Title of Government Departments*, immediately following the present general Preface, listing in detail the changes in departmental titles which, during the period, have become so numerous and incoherent as to add greatly to the difficulty of understanding what is already a difficult subject, and unnecessarily to confuse the citizen about a sphere in which his interests are actively and continuously involved.

The Further Reading notes, which were a special feature of the earlier work, have been completely revised, and each is now divided into an Introductory section and an Historical and Advanced section.

The *Student's Guide* is divided into seven Parts and for convenience in handling has been printed as two volumes, covering respectively:

    I. Central Government Administration. Three Parts
    II. Local, Corporational and International Administration. Four
    Parts

    Parts and Chapters are numbered separately in each volume, but in view of the essential wholeness of the subject there are a substantial number of overlaps, to which reference is made in the Notes preceding the Prefaces of the individual volumes.

    A feature of *Part One: Introduction* is Chapter Two which briefly describes the system of government in the early forties with reference to the administrative factors. *Part Two: Central Government Administration* pays special attention to the Civil Service, and in Chapter Nine provides a summary of the changes that are taking place, following the issue of the Fulton Report. *Part Three: General Control and Co-ordination* is designed to relate the central administration to the other main branches of government, and, with Chapters Three and Seven, Volume II, in the two following parts, to link it with Local Government and the Public Corporations and thus provide a co-ordinated picture of the entire system. Chapter Sixteen describes the machinery of planning as it had developed up to 1969.

    Local Government Administration (Part One of Volume II) pays special attention to the several reports which are influencing the changes at present in contemplation. *Other British Public Administration*, the next Part, is not confined to the important sphere of the Nationalized Industries to which Chapters Five and Seven of this volume are specially devoted, but also to other public bodies which proliferate on the fringes of public administration, with some references in Chapter Six to the voluntary field. *Administration Abroad* must suffice to place in due perspective the many important fields of international administration and *Public Administration and the Public* rounds off the study, somewhat summarily, it is feared, by emphasizing the importance of the citizen in all that has previously been examined.

    Since the author has written other works to elucidate the subject of Public Administration it may not be out of place to indicate how three of these titles (also from Staples Press) bear upon the present work. *The Essentials of Public Administration*, which first appeared in 1953, deals with the theoretical aspects of the subject. *British Public Service Administration* provides a picture of the development and structure of public administration in Britain in its several branches as they existed in 1960. An elementary is offered in *Approach to Public Administration*, first published in 1966, which introduces the subject broadly through a short summary of general principles and techniques, supplemented by an appendix summarizing on a comparative basis the government structure of the United Kingdom, the United States, France, Switzerland, and the USSR.

Acknowledgements

My sincere thanks are due to Dr D. Menhennet and Kenneth Bradshaw, Esq, members of the House of Commons staff, for their invaluable assistance in bringing up to date the Progress Chart of Statute Making and related information. Special acknowledgement is due to HM Stationery Office for permission to reprint numerous extracts from official publications; to the United Nations for up-to-date information about their organization, and to the Royal Institute of Public Administration for access to their excellent specialized library.

E. N. GLADDEN

New Barnet, 1972

Key to Changes in Titles of Government Departments, 1945/71

Frequent changes in departmental titles during recent decades (usually, though not always, indicative of an important redistribution of functions) have tended to confuse students of British Government and Administration and to render the understanding of texts more difficult than need be. The following list of titles of the more important Government Departments operating during the post-war period is designed to aid the reader throughout the present work whenever superseded titles are mentioned. It should also prove useful in their wider readings of the subject. The position seems unlikely to remain static, and the reader is therefore advised to ascertain what changes, if any, have been made since our date of publication. Current titles are marked *.

Abbreviations: Bd (Board); Dept (Department); Min. (Ministry)

Admiralty, Bd of—1690, Lord High Admiral replaced by Board; 1964, Board absorbed into Min. of Defence, q.v.

*Agriculture, Fisheries and Food, Min. of—1919, former Bd of Agriculture and Fisheries reconstituted as Ministry; 1955, Min. of Food, q.v., absorbed and present title assumed.

Air Ministry—1918, established; 1964, absorbed into Min. of Defence, q.v.

Aircraft Production, Min. of—1942, hived off from Air Min. q.v.; 1946, merged with Min. of Supply, q.v.

Assistance Board—1940, scope of Unemployment Assistance Board broadened and title changed; 1948, renamed 'National Assistance Board', q.v.

Aviation, Min. of—1959, hived off from Min. of Transport and Civil Aviation, q.v., and Min. of Supply, q.v.: 1966, civil aviation functions to Bd of Trade, q.v.; 1967, remaining functions to Min. of Technology, q.v.

Aviation Supply, Min. of—1970, hived off from Ministry of Technology, q.v.; 1971, abolished (functions to Min. of Defence and Dept of Trade and Industry).

Board of Trade, 1786, reconstituted; 1970 merged with Min. of Technology, q.v., to form Dept of Trade and Industry, q.v.

Burma Office—1937 separated from India Office, q.v.; 1948 abolished.

*Cabinet Office—1916, established during First World War.

Central Africa Office—1962 hived off from Colonial and Commonwealth Relations Offices, q.v.; 1964, returned to latter.

Central Land Board—1947, set up; 1959 abolished.

*Central Office of Information—1946, superseded Min. of Information, q.v.; 1967, Social Survey becomes Government Social Survey Dept, q.v.

Civil Aviation, Min. of—1945, hived off from Air Min.; 1953, combined with Min. of Transport to form Min. of Transport and Civil Aviation, q.v.

Civil Service Commission—1855, first appointed; 1968, merged into new Civil Service Department, q.v., but maintains its identity.

*Civil Service Department—1968, created mainly from Establishments side of Treasury, q.v., and the Civil Service Commission, q.v.

Colonial Office—1812, separated from War and Colonial Dept; 1966, merged with Commonwealth Relations Office, q.v., to form Commonwealth Office, q.v.

Commonwealth Office—1966, formed out of Colonial Office, q.v., and Commonwealth Relations Office, q.v.; 1968, merged with Foreign Office, q.v., to form Foreign and Commonwealth Office, q.v.

Commonwealth Relations Office—1947, new title for existing Dominions Office, q.v.; 1966 combined with Colonial Office, q.v. to form Commonwealth Office, q.v.

*Crown Estate Commission—1956, superseded former Crown Lands Commission, q.v.

Crown Lands Commission—1760, established; 1956, replaced by Crown Estate Commission, q.v.

*Customs and Excise, Bd of—1909, Excise Duties to existing Customs Bd, from Board of Inland Revenue.

* Defence, Min. of—1946, took over functions of Minister of Defence previously associated with prime ministership; 1964 absorbed Admiralty, q.v., War Office, q.v., and Air Min., q.v.

Dominions Office—1925, hived off from Colonial Office, q.v.; 1947 absorbed India Office, q.v., and renamed 'Commonwealth Relations Office', q.v.

* Duchy of Lancaster, Office of—Medieval origins.

Economic Affairs, Dept of—1964, hived off mainly from Treasury; 1968, productivity functions to Dept of Employment and Productivity, q.v.; 1969 merged back into Treasury, q.v.

Economic Warfare, Min. of—1939, set up; 1945 merged into Foreign Office.

Education, Min. of—1944, replaced Bd of Education; 1964, Office of Minister of Science (introduced 1959) absorbed and Ministry becomes Dept of Education and Science, q.v.

*Education and Science, Dept of—1964 formed by combining Ministry of Education, q.v., with Office of Minister of Science, q.v.

*Employment, Dept of—1970, replaced Dept of Employment and Productivity, q.v.

Employment and Productivity, Dept of—1968, formed by transferring productivity functions of Dept of Economic Affairs, q.v., to Min. of Labour, q.v.; 1970, with further redistribution of those functions title changed to 'Department of Employment'. q.v.

*Environment, Dept of the—1970, formed by merging Min. of Housing and Local Government, q.v.; Min. of Public Building and Works, q.v.; and Min. of Transport, q.v.

*Exchequer and Audit Dept—1866, formed to support Comptroller and Auditor General, as servant of Parliament.

Food, Min. of—1939, established; 1955, merged with Min. of Agriculture and Fisheries to form Min. of Agriculture, Fisheries and Food, q.v.

*Foreign and Commonwealth Office—1968, formed by merging Foreign Office, q.v. and Commonwealth Office, q.v.; 1970, absorbed Min. of Overseas Development, q.v.

Foreign Office—1782, home and foreign functions of Secretary of

State separated; 1968 merged with Commonwealth Office, q.v.,
to form Foreign and Commonwealth Office, q.v.

Fuel and Power, Min. of—1942, hived off from Bd of Trade; 1957,
title changed to 'Ministry of Power', q.v.; 1969, merged into Min.
of Technology, q.v.

General Register Office—1837, established; 1970, combined with
Government Social Survey Dept, q.v., to form Office of Population
Censuses and Surveys, q.v.

Government Social Survey Dept—1967, separated from Central
Office of Information, q.v.; 1970 combined with General Register
Office, q.v., to form Office of Population Censuses and Surveys,
q.v.

Government Social Survey Dept—1967, separated from Central
Office of Information, q.v.; 1970 combined with General Register
Office, q.v., to form Office of Population Censuses and Surveys,
q.v.

Health, Min. of—1919, formed mainly out of Local Government
Board; 1951, local government functions to new Min. of Housing
and Local Government, q.v. (briefly known as 'Ministry of Local
Government and Planning'); 1968, combined with Min. of Social
Security, q.v., to form Dept of Health and Social Security, q.v.

*Health and Social Security, Dept of—1968, formed by merging
Ministries of Health, q.v., and of Social Security, q.v.

*Home Office—1782, home and foreign functions of Secretary of
State separated.

Home Security, Min. of—1945 wartime department merged back into
Home Office.

Housing and Local Government, Min. of—1951, local government
functions from Min. of Health, q.v., combined with Min. of Town
and Country Planning, q.v., to form new Ministry (for a few
months known as 'Local Government and Planning'); 1970,
merged into new Dept of the Environment, q.v.

India Office—1858, set up; 1947, merged into Dominions Office, q.v.

Information, Central Office of—See 'Central Office of Information'.

Information, Min. of—1939, wartime innovation; 1946, replaced by
Central Office of Information, q.v.

*Inland Revenue, Bd of—1849, established (included Excise up to
1909, see 'Customs and Excise').

Labour, Min. of—1939, assumed wartime duties and title changed to
'Labour and National Service'; 1959, original title restored; 1968,

productivity functions transferred from Dept of Economic Affairs, q.v., and renamed 'Dept of Employment and Productivity', q.v.

Labour and National Service, Min. of—See 'Labour, Min. of'.

Land and Natural Resources, Min. of—1964, set up; 1967, merged into Min. of Housing and Local Government, q.v.

Land Commission—1967, set up; 1971, abolished.

*Law Officers' Dept—1893, replaced ancient offices.

Local Government and Planning, Min. of—1951, title held for a few months by new Min. of Housing and Local Government, q.v.

*Lord Chancellor's Office—Medieval origins; now includes a number of distinct subordinate offices—e.g. Public Record Office (1938), HM Land Registry (1863), and Public Trustee's Office (1908).

Materials, Min. of—1951, set up; 1954, merged into Bd of Trade, q.v.

National Assistance Board—1948, new title of Assistance Bd, q.v.; 1966, merged with Min. of Pensions and National Insurance, q.v., to form Min. of Social Security, q.v.

National Insurance, Min. of—1946, set up with functions from several bodies; 1953, merged with Min. of Pensions, q.v., to form Min. of Pensions and National Insurance, q.v.

*National Savings, Dept for—1969, hived off from Post Office, q.v., and associated with Savings Committees, National and Scottish, q.v.

Overseas Development, Min. of—1964, replaced Dept of Technical Co-operation, q.v.; 1970 merged into Foreign and Commonwealth Office, q.v.

Overseas Trade, Dept of—1917, set up during First World War; 1946, merged into Bd of Trade, q.v.

*Paymaster General's Office—1836, amalgamated earlier Paymaster Offices.

Pensions, Min. of—1916, set up during First World War; 1953, merged with Min. of National Insurance, q.v., to form Min. of Pensions and National Insurance, q.v.

Pensions and National Insurance, Min. of—1953, merging Min. of Pensions, q.v., with Min. of National Insurance, q.v.; 1966, combined with National Assistance Bd, q.v., to form Min. of Social Security, q.v.

*Population, Censuses and Surveys, Office of—1970, merging of General Register Office, q.v., with Government Social Survey Department, q.v.

Post Office—1660, General Letter Office established; 1969, converted into public corporation, except savings business to new Dept for National Savings, q.v., and supervision to new Ministry of Posts and Telecommunications, q.v.

Posts and Telecommunications, Min. of—1969, set up on conversion of Post Office, q.v., into public corporation.

Power, Min. of—1957, new title replacing earlier 'Fuel and Power', q.v.; 1969, merged into Min. of Technology, q.v.

Privy Council Office—Medieval origins.

Production, Min. of—1942, set up during Second World War; 1945, merged into Bd of Trade, q.v.

Public Building and Works, Min. of—1962, former Min. of Works, q.v., reorganized and renamed; 1970, merged into new Dept of the Environment, q.v.

Savings Committees, National/Scottish—1916, set up during First World War; 1969, associated with new Dept for National Savings, q.v.

Science, Office of Minister of—1959, Minister appointed; 1964, transferred to Min. of Education, renamed 'Dept of Education and Science', q.v.

Scientific and Industrial Research, Dept of—1916, set up as Committee of Privy Council; 1964, merged into new Min. of Technology, q.v.

Scottish Office—1885, established.

Social Security, Min. of—1966, combining Min. of Pensions and National Insurance, q.v., and National Assistance Bd, q.v.; 1968, merged with Min. of Health to form Dept of Health and Social Security, q.v.

Stationery Office, HM's—1786, set up.

Supply, Min. of—1939, set up; 1946, absorbed Min. of Aircraft Production, q.v.; 1959, superseded by Min. of Aviation, q.v.

Technical Co-Operation, Dept of—1961, set up; 1964, superseded by Min. of Overseas Development, q.v.

Technology, Min. of—1964, set up and absorbed Dept of Scientific and Industrial Research, q.v.; 1969, absorbed Min. of Power, q.v.; 1970, merged with Bd of Trade, q.v., to form Dept of Trade and Industry, q.v., except functions taken over by new Min. of Aviation Supply, q.v.

Town and Country Planning, Min. of—1943, hived off from Min. of Health; 1951, received local government functions from Min. of Health, q.v., and renamed 'Local Government and Planning,' which was shortly changed to 'Housing and Local Government', q.v.

Trade, Board of—1786, reconstructed as Committee of Privy Council; 1945, absorbed Min. of Production, q.v.; 1946, absorbed Dept of Overseas Trade, q.v.; 1951, hived off, partly, Min. of Materials, q.v.; 1954, absorbed Min. of Materials; 1970, merged with Min. of Technology to form Dept of Trade and Industry, q.v.

*Trade and Industry, *Dept of*—1970, established by combining Bd of Trade, q.v., and Min. of Technology, q.v.

Transport, Min. of—1946, Min. of War Transport, q.v., reassumes earlier title; 1953, absorbs Min. of Civil Aviation, and changes title to 'Transport and Civil Aviation', q.v.; 1959, again reverts to earlier title with setting up of separate Min. of Aviation, q.v.; 1970, merged into new Dept of the Environment, q.v.

Transport and Civil Aviation, Min. of—1953–9, title carried by Min. of Transport, q.v.

*Treasury, *Her Majesty's*—1612, Office of Lord High Treasurer first placed in Commission (see also 'Department of Economic Affairs' and 'Civil Service Department').

War Office—1854, separated from Colonies; 1964, merged into Min. of Defence, q.v.

War Transport, Min. of—1941–46, wartime title of Min. of Transport, q.v.

Welsh Office—1964, separate office established.

Works, Min. of—1943, former Office of Works reconstituted; 1962, renamed 'Public Building and Works', q.v.

PART ONE

Local Government

CHAPTER ONE

Local Government: Functions, Structure, and Powers

Traditions of local *self*-government, which go back to the time when central government was too distant to be able to help very much, even if it wanted to and when the assumptions of feudalism still permeated the parishes and townships, were strongly reinforced after 1835. During that expanding age the application of a widened franchise to the newly created local authorities greatly extended the participation of the ordinary citizen. The things that could best be provided and the activities best carried on locally were clearly distinguishable from those more remote matters that were best left to the central government, and there was a general awareness of the distinction between the two spheres of government activity. But with the advance of technology and the consequent broadening of the scope of administration, impelling and enabling the State to take responsibility for social services hitherto left to voluntary effort—if they were provided at all—the two spheres of government came to share the administration of a number of important services, with the result that the line between the two has become more and more difficult to draw. The problem of distinguishing between the two spheres has been complicated by the continuance of change in the general situation, the emergence of other public bodies with functions overlapping the two fields of activity, and the diversion of citizens' interest into other channels.

The structure of local government in England and Wales (as it

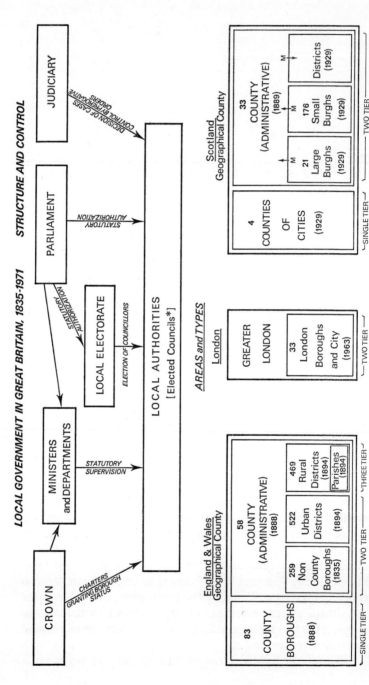

LOCAL GOVERNMENT IN GREAT BRITAIN, 1835-1971   STRUCTURE AND CONTROL

CROWN

MINISTERS and DEPARTMENTS

PARLIAMENT

JUDICIARY

LOCAL ELECTORATE

LOCAL AUTHORITIES
[Elected Councils*]

CHARTERS GRANTING BOROUGH STATUS

STATUTORY AUTHORIZATION

STATUTORY SUPERVISION

STATUTORY AUTHORIZATION

ELECTION OF COUNCILLORS

DECISION OF CASES

CONTROL BY PREROGATIVE ORDERS

AREAS and TYPES

England & Wales
Geographical County

83 COUNTY BOROUGHS (1888)	58 COUNTY (ADMINISTRATIVE) (1888)

259 Non County Boroughs (1835)

522 Urban Districts (1894)

469 Rural Districts (1894)

Parishes (1894)

SINGLE TIER — TWO TIER — THREE TIER

London

GREATER LONDON

33 London Boroughs and City (1963)

TWO TIER

Scotland
Geographical County

4 COUNTIES OF CITIES (1929)	33 COUNTY (ADMINISTRATIVE) (1889)

21 Large Burghs (1929)   M

176 Small Burghs (1929)   M

Districts (1929)   M

SINGLE TIER — TWO TIER

NB IN NORTHERN IRELAND THE SYSTEM WAS SIMILAR TO THAT OF ENGLAND AND WALES BUT IS NOW BEING REORGANIZED.

still exists in 1971) has already been summarized in Chapter two of Volume I. Excluding London, which has its own pattern, there were six main types of authority, respectively for the Counties, County Boroughs, Non-County (or Municipal) Boroughs, Urban Districts, Rural Districts, and Parishes. There were distinct arrangements for Northern Ireland. The general pattern is indicated on the Chart—Local Government in Great Britain, 1835–71, opposite page.

PRESENT FUNCTIONS

The functions of local government are numerous and can be classified in a number of ways, though none is completely satisfactory. A grouping of the various services under the headings: (1) Protective, (2) Communal, (3) Social, or Welfare, (4) Trading, and (5) Miscellaneous and Ancillary,[1] provides a broad idea of the variety and scope of local government activities. Some services are clearly the concern of, and best carried out in, the localities, especially personal services and such matters as lighting and cleansing, environmental health and amenities, prevention of offences and nuisances, allotments and footpaths, control of trading, drugs, entertainments, and so forth (although even in some of these the advance of technology may render larger areas necessary, as in the case of water supply, sewage, and waste disposal). There are other matters of vital local concern which nevertheless require a larger administrative basis, such as main roads, environmental planning, hospital services, and education, and in some cases it is not easy to decide whether the balance is in favour of local government or central administration.

Owing to changes in population and varying legislatory approaches since the Municipal Corporations were reformed in 1835, the several categories of local authority mentioned above do not clearly indicate the actual and even relative scope and functions of the individual authorities.

While of course population is not the only factor determining the scope and status of local government divisions, the following figures, indicating the population range both within and between the several types of local authority (as quoted in the *Municipal Handbook* for

[1] Formerly used in J. H. Warren's *The English Local Government System*, now replaced by P. G. Richards *The New Local Government System* (Allen & Unwin 1968) which charts the 'Distribution of Functions' in an Appendix.

1970), are sufficiently illustrative to indicate that the present patterning is hopelessly unrealistic. In England and Wales the populations
of County Boroughs range between 1,074,940 in Birmingham and
32,790 in Canterbury; of Counties between 2,428,040 in Lancashire
and 18,210 in Radnor; of Non-County Boroughs between 100,470 in
Cambridge and 980 in Montgomery; of Urban Districts between
123,230 in Thurrock and 510 in Llanwrtyd Wells; and of Rural
Districts between 86,390 in Easington and 1590 in Colwyn. In
Scotland the populations of the Counties of a City range between
945,134 in Glasgow and 181,336 in Aberdeen; of Large Burghs
between 95,059 in Paisley and 21,168 in Arbroath; and of Small
Burghs between 24,380 in Cumbernauld and 333 in New Galloway.

Failing a complete reallocation of services a tidying up process
has been going on since 1945, mainly through legislation transferring
certain services to other public bodies, e.g. electricity, gas, and
transport to Public Corporations; and public assistance, hospital
services, and rating assessment to Government Departments. In a
number of fields (e.g. education, town and country planning, health,
and police) the trend in this legislation has been to concentrate local
government responsibilities in the two largest types of authority, the
Counties and County Boroughs; or even, as in the case of police, in
combinations of these. Some local authorities have acquired other
functions through private bill legislation, so that the distribution of
functions is far from uniform, and this is further influenced by the
delegation of functions by the Counties, which is referred to below.

In an age of increasing administrative complexity it would be a
mistake to overlook the local authorities' tasks in running their own
administration, in the form of management services of various
types—servicing the Council and its committees; personnel management; financing, including the special techniques of rating; pur-
chasing and supply; information and public relations services;
computer and other office machinery; statistics, and so forth. The
organization of some of these on a common service basis to serve
all or a number of authorities, a development neglected in the past, is
becoming more and more necessary.

STRUCTURE

All the local authorities, with the exception of the smaller Parishes,
have an elected Council. Legally the authorities have the status and

responsibilities at law of corporations. They are incorporated under Acts of Parliament, which have from time to time determined the status and structure of local government, except the Boroughs (County and Non-County) which are incorporated individually by Royal Charter. In the case of the Boroughs the corporation includes the burgesses, or electors, but in all cases the Council acts as the corporation. There are special arrangements for small Parishes, which act through a Parish Meeting.

The Councils consist of Councillors, elected by universal franchise, but the Counties, County Boroughs, and Non-County Boroughs also have Aldermen, to the number of one third (or in the case of London Boroughs one sixth) of the Councillors, elected by the Councillors. Councillors are elected for three years, either annually or a third each year, and the Aldermen for six years, one half retiring every three years. Aldermen are usually selected from among the Councillors, more or less as an honour or reward for past services, but anyone eligible for election as a councillor may be chosen.

The present local government pattern is based largely upon the geographical counties, whose areas are normally divided between the administrative County and the County Boroughs within the geographical boundaries. The few exceptions are those geographical counties which, because of their size, were divided into more than one administrative County (namely Yorkshire and Lincolnshire into three, and Cambridgeshire, Hampshire, Northamptonshire, Suffolk, and Sussex each into two). Thus the administrative Counties cover the whole area within their boundaries excluding the areas of County Boroughs, which stand on their own. Within the administrative Counties there are Non-County Boroughs, Urban Districts, and Rural Districts, which are generally classified as County Districts. The widespreading Rural Districts are further divided into Parishes. Boroughs and Urban Districts are divided into Wards, but this is a purely internal arrangement for electoral purposes.

All these local authorities are multi-purpose or omnibus bodies, since they provide a range of services within their areas. Only the County Boroughs are all-purpose, i.e. responsible for all the services within their areas. This is known as the single-tier system. In the Counties, outside the County Boroughs within their areas, administration is carried out at two levels by the County Councils and County District Councils each having its own range of functions. This is known as the two-tier system, which, as we have seen, is to some

B

extent modified in the Rural Districts by the existence, in the shape of the Parishes, of a third tier. The system has grown up empirically, largely through the development of existing areas and authorities, sometimes of considerable antiquity. The single tier-system provides the most concentrated and coherent administration and is eminently suitable for large urban areas. The two-tier system is suitable for the larger rural areas where, at the expense of division of administrative responsibility between two authorities operating concurrently within the areas, it has the advantage, through the more numerous basic tier, of providing more intimate administration for the more personal, social, and neighbourhood services. Even the larger conurbations soon reach a stage when a two-tier arrangement becomes desirable to provide adequately for those services that are most effectively administered by more compact communities. As different services ideally call for differing bases to achieve efficient administration it is clear that in all systems of multi-purpose authorities there has to be a certain element of compromise. Much of the argument that goes on regarding the respective merits of the single-tier and two-tier system of organization rests upon this factor and a balanced solution is not easily achieved. Moreover, continuing changes in the technical bases of many of the services of modern public administration means that the balanced solution differs appreciably with time and place. This is one of the reasons why, especially since the Second World War, the implementation of comprehensive local government reform has been so difficult.

It will be noted that the pattern that has emerged provides for a division of local administration as between the urban and the predominantly rural areas, which in the simpler administrative conditions of the nineteenth century certainly called for different types of service, but again technical changes have tended to iron out these differences and advantages are seen in dividing the country into local government areas that combine both rural and urban localities, though this object is hardly attainable in the large conurbations.

It must be emphasized that the present structure of local authorities is geographic and not hierarchic. The County Boroughs of course stand on their own, but, while the Counties have certain superior powers and responsibilities with regard to specific duties and services, the County Districts operating within the same areas are not subject to, or agents of, the County, except where definite delegation has been arranged. Each local authority operates as an independent elected corporation whose duties and functions are assigned directly by Act of Parliament. This fact needs to be emphasized, for it is widely misunderstood.

In some cases, notably in education and town and country planning, delegation of functions by the County to the County Districts has been based upon a definite organizational pattern. In education, for example, under the Education Act of 1944 the Counties were required to submit schemes partitioning their areas into suitable divisions under committees, to which functions could be delegated. Normally these committees would constitute Divisional Executives, acting for the County Council, but in urban areas of at least 60,000 population the existing authority had the right to claim to be an Excepted District, whose committees would report to the District Council and thus enable it to enjoy a popular mandate for its decisions not available to the Divisional Executive. While the Executives work through the County officials, the Excepted Districts largely use the Borough or Urban District Councils' staffs. The actual pattern of such delegation and the resultant administration depends upon the Delegation Scheme which the County Council has drawn up and had approved by the Minister, and the extent to which such powers are exercised varies widely between county and county, some of which have made greater use of the arrangements than others. In the administration of town and country planning similar arrangements exist, with County Districts of 60,000 population, as excepted councils, entitled to delegated powers and others able to obtain such powers in special circumstances.

The Counties also have wide general powers to delegate functions to County Districts, and the extent to which these powers have been used again varies considerably. Two basic conditions have to be provided for in the delegation schemes, which have to receive ministerial approval: the County Council must (1) retain the right to decide major questions of policy, and (2) control expenditure falling on the County, through approval of annual estimates submitted by the Borough or District Council. Such delegation has clear administrative advantages, but has not been fully developed, due partly no doubt to clashes of interest between the two types of authority.

Existing local authorities can co-operate in the administration of services, and thus widen the area of administration of such services, by the formation of Joint Committees or Joint Boards to run the specific service. Joint Committees are usually constituted by

agreement between the authorities concerned, who maintain ultimate control and may terminate the arrangement. Such committees
are made up of members of the constituent authorities. The functions
delegated cannot include the power to levy a rate, to issue a precept,
or to borrow money. A Joint Board really falls into the category of
ad hoc authority referred to in the next section. Local authorities
have no general power to set up Joint Boards. These are created by
ministerial order, which in some cases requires the approval of
Parliament. Authority to transfer specific powers to Joint Boards is
contained in a number of statutes which set out the terms on which
the specific board must be constituted. A Joint Board is a corporate
body, which cannot be dissolved by agreement as in the case of the
Joint Committee, and exercises its own financial powers. It obtains
the money it requires from the constituent authorities by means of
precepts. Joint Boards have been set up under the provisions of the
relative statutes for *inter alia* public health, water, planning, and
education. (However, special rules apply to Joint Boards authorized
in connection with special review areas under the Local Government
Act, 1958.)

The system just outlined operates only in England and Wales,
with the exception of the London area, where there is a two-tier
system, consisting of the Greater London Council, which, under the
London Government Act, 1963, is responsible for metropolitan
roads, traffic management, main drainage, fire protection, the
ambulance service, and certain general services, and shares planning
and housing with the other London authorities. These consist of
thirty-two London Boroughs Councils and the City of London Corporation, an ancient body with its own historic constitution, which
has managed to survive largely unaffected by the various reforming
acts from 1835 to date. These second-tier authorities are responsible
for all other functions, and under the 1963 Act have been raised
nearer to the power of the County Boroughs elsewhere. For the
central area, covering the City of London and twelve Inner London
Boroughs, education has been consolidated under a special committee
of the Greater London Council, which operates as the Inner London
Education Authority. The outer London Boroughs are local education authorities. The local government system in Northern Ireland
is separate but similar to that of England and Wales, with certain
modifications. While the general principles are the same, local
government in Scotland embodies some interesting differences.

These have been briefly summarized in Chapter Two, Volume One.

The several systems of local government in the United Kingdom are under vigorous and widespread review and individual proposals have been made for reform in England, Northern Ireland, Scotland, and Wales respectively. These proposals and the changes so far introduced are summarized in Chapter Four of this volume.

'AD HOC' AUTHORITIES

As we have already seen, in the earlier stages of the development of the modern system of local government, in which the omnibus, or multi-purpose, type of authority was to predominate, there were strong trends towards the adoption of the single-purpose, usually known as the *ad hoc*, type of local authority. These were exemplified in the Boards of Guardians, introduced under the Poor Law Amendment Act of 1834, and the School Boards, introduced under the Education Act of 1870. The great advantage of this type is that it can be tailored to the unit area that is most suitable for meeting economically the technical requirement of the particular service and achieving the effective representation and maximum co-operation of the citizens concerned. Since this ideal area varies widely from service to service and changes with developing techniques and other requirements and conditions, a consistent application of the *ad hoc* principle would lead to a complicated proliferation of geographically overlapping authorities, and the cost in resources would more than offset the advantages of specialization. While the multi-purpose type calls for a number of compromises as to the proper bases of the various services or functions, its convenience and economy in administration normally outweigh the advantages of the *ad hoc* type. To incorporate the advantages of both types the celebrated social reformer and authority of local government, Sidney Webb (later Lord Passfield), proffered an ingenious solution in his less known work *A Constitution for the Socialist Commonwealth of Great Britain* (1920). Under his plan local government would have been based upon a series of viable neighbourhood units, each with its own elected representative. These units would have been linked up into a number of groupings varying according to the needs of the particular service to be administered. Ingenious but hopelessly impractical, such a system, had it been seriously tried, would inevitably have become too complicated to cope with the strains accompanying the dynamic changes of the next half century, strains which the erudite Webbs could not have been expected to foresee, but which the existing system of local government, despite well grounded criticisms, has managed to survive.

Yet the *ad hoc* type still has its uses and even thrives in some spheres. It contributes a basic principle to the public corporation which supplies the administrative framework of a non-government sphere of public activity, which has grown so vigorously in the middle decades of the present century, particularly as an instrument of administration for nationalized industries. This will be dealt with in Part Two of the present volume.

The *ad hoc* type also continues appropriately in some spheres that can properly be claimed as pertaining to local government: for example, in the form of Water Boards, Harbour Boards, Port Sanitary Authorities, and River Authorities. The latter are of particular interest.

Under the River Boards Act of 1948, certain bodies then operating in the several catchment areas of England and Wales (based upon the main river basins) were reconstituted as a series of River Boards, responsible for water resources, land drainage, inland fisheries, and prevention of water pollution. A further development of the system was introduced, under the Water Resources Act, 1963, which aimed to deal more comprehensively with the use of water resources. The existing boards were replaced by twenty-seven River Authorities with extended responsibilities, and a general Water Resources Board was established to advise the responsible Minister (the Minister of Housing and Local Government) as well as the individual River Authorities. The membership of these authorities, which normally varies between twenty-one and thirty, consists of a majority appointed by, or on behalf of, the County and County Borough Councils in the area; the remainder being selected, partly by the responsible Minister, and partly by the Minister of Agriculture, Fisheries, and Food.

NEW TOWNS

A local activity, which Parliament considered it desirable for the time being to take out of the control of local government, was inaugurated by the passing of the New Towns Act, 1946. By their nature the New Town Development Corporations should properly be discussed in Part Two of this volume, but their functions are so closely involved in local government matters that, in order to complete the picture, it seems desirable to include a brief discussion of the New Towns here.

With the object of moving population out of congested areas and slowing down their growth, it was decided to establish a series of satellite towns at suitable points, to which the excess populations could be attracted. Under the new legislation the Minister of Town and Country Planning (later 'of Housing and Local Government') and the Secretary of State for Scotland were empowered to designate suitable sites and to appoint Development Corporations to acquire land and to provide buildings for industrial, commercial, and residential purposes, together with roads, sewers, and such amenity services as are essential to a living community. These new Corporations are therefore planning authorities with constructional functions, but they do not replace the ordinary local government institutions. Their membership consists of a chairman and up to eight other persons with appropriate experience. By 1970 twenty-eight New Towns were in various stages of development in Great Britain, apart from those in Northern Ireland, authorized under more recent legislation (see below).

Pending receipt of sufficient income from their own properties the New Town Development Corporations are financed by loans from the Exchequer, under Treasury authority and control, and their accounts are subject to the scrutiny, on behalf of Parliament, by the Comptroller and Auditor General. It was originally intended that, when the initial task of building the New Town and establishing the new community had been completed the Corporation's powers and properties should be handed over to the established local authority for the area. But it came to be felt, particularly in view of the success of the new arrangements, that it would be invidious to hand over such resources to individual local authorities, and under the New Towns Act, 1959 new financial arrangements were introduced. A central body, known as the Commission for New Towns, was established to take over the assets of the corporations as and when their main tasks have been fulfilled. So far (1970) the assets of the New Towns of Crawley, Hemel Hempstead, Welwyn Garden City, and Hatfield (four in all) have been made over to the Commission, and future policy remains to be decided.

The New Towns system was extended to Northern Ireland in 1965, the Minister of Development being made responsible, and to date four New Towns have been planned there.

POWERS

The local authorities derive their responsibilities and powers from a diversity of statutes passed by Parliament at different times to cope with changing needs. There is a series of basic Acts—notably those of 1835, 1888, and 1895—that lay down the general pattern by authorizing the establishment of the several types of authority, and many others, including the important consolidating Local Government Act of 1933, that introduce new, or modify existing, services and procedures, and determine, albeit with numerous variations, which types of authority shall be responsible for which service, and many other matters, particularly finance. There is no settled code and the result is a chaos of law which is difficult to interpret. When it is remembered that there are also the many regulations of different types issued by branches of the Central Administration under many of these statutes, it is not surprising that local government councillors and officials are constantly dependent upon expert interpretation of the law which they are required to operate and conform to.

These statutory powers may be either mandatory or adoptive. The latter, are applicable only when adopted by resolution of the Council, a method which, particularly in the early stages of a new development, allows a good deal of flexibility and experiment and, in view of the varying financial resources of the different authorities, has often been an essential method unless the State was to bear the entire cost. Two notable, though rather special, examples of services acquired through adoptive legislation are the Birmingham Municipal Bank and the telephone system in Hull, both of which are run by the local authority.

Local authorities desiring special powers may seek them through the promotion of a Private Bill. The procedure is, however, expensive and beset with uncertainties. Consequently, for purposes likely to be of interest to a number of authorities, other means, including the adoptive methods already mentioned, were gradually devised; for example, Clauses Acts which provide sets of standardized clauses for inclusion in, and to facilitate, private legislation; Provisional Orders subject to ministerial approval and to confirmation by Act of Parliament, which have been superseded by Statutory Orders requiring ministerial approval and laying before Parliament; and scheme making under major general statutes. A detailed explanation of these administrative aids would be out of place in a brief outline, but the mere variety of ways in which local authorities can be endowed with powers, coupled with their varying size and resources, reinforces the impossibility of deducing an authority's functions merely by reference to its statutory grading. Only in the case of the County Boroughs, as single-tier authorities, is the answer reasonably clear, but even with them there are the specially acquired functions to be taken into account.

It has to be remembered that the local authorities can only operate such services as the law specifically assigns to them, since, according to the ruling of the Courts, any other activities—however legal they may be to the ordinary citizen—are *ultra vires*, i.e. outside their powers. On appeal to the Courts, therefore, any action adjudged *ultra vires* will be quashed and any expense involved or damage arising may be charged against the responsible councillors or officials. It is true that activities under Royal Charter (required to form Boroughs) are not subject to this rule but the scope of such Charters is usually so limited and the relative legal rulings difficult to apply, that this distinction does not apparently amount to much. See C. A. Cross *Principles of Local Government Law* (Sweet & Maxwell, 1966), pp. 10–17 for an interesting discussion.

Subject to the law, a local authority's power is concentrated in the Council, which may delegate a good deal of responsibility to committees except that it must retain full responsibility for the levy of a rate, the issue of a precept, borrowing money, signing contracts, and empowering a committee to delegate to a sub-committee. The Council determines the pattern of committees to be appointed (except that under statute for a few services—e.g. education, health, and social services—specific committees have to be appointed) and decides what powers shall thus be delegated. Non-members of Council may be co-opted to a committee (except to a finance committee) to the limit of one third of its membership. A few committees, including those for allotments and education, must include outsiders, but in the main co-option is not popular among councillors. Committees do frequently set up sub-committees under the Council's sanction.

Local authorities exercise certain legislatory powers through the issue of by-laws, but these relate only to a limited sphere and are all subject to confirmation by the Privy Council or the responsible Minister. Since the Councils' policy-making powers are delimited by the broad policies laid down by Parliament in the authorizing statutes, as modified by the specific policies of the government-of-the-day, it is reasonable to regard the major part of the Councils' activities as falling within the executive and administrative spheres. The important subject of internal management and external control will be dealt with in the two following chapters.

FURTHER READING

Introductory

The literature of Local Government is voluminous and there are so many works of high standard that it is invidious to select. In view of the changing situation up-to-dateness is highly important and from this angle P. G. Richards's *The New Local Government System* (Allen & Unwin, 1968), already mentioned in the text, is highly recommended. This may be supplemented by the latest editions of W. Eric Jackson's *Local Government in England and Wales* (Pelican, 1961) and R. M. Jackson's *The Machinery of Local Government* (Macmillan, 1965). J. Stanyer's short study of *County Government in England and Wales* (Routledge, 1967) provides a useful discussion.

The regional aspects of local governments in England and Wales are traced, with helpful explanatory maps, in T. W. Freeman's *Geography and Regional Administration* (Hutchinson, 1968).

An authoritative and first-rate survey of the New Towns development is now available in Frank Schaffer's *The New Town Story* (Macgibbon & Kee, 1970).

Historical and Advanced

K. B. Smellie's *A History of Local Government* (Allen & Unwin, 1968) covers a wide field in a brief text. The historical part of J. Redlich and F. W. Hirst's classic *Local Government in England* (1903), has been published separately as *The History of Local Government in England* (1958) under the editorship of B. Keith Lucas. The development of the system of local democracy is clearly described, with much illuminating detail, by

B. Keith Lucas in his *The English Local Government Franchise* (Blackwell, 1952). Local government in Scotland is excellently summarized in *A Source Book and History of Administrative Law in Scotland* by various authors (William Hodge, 1956).

A good deal of valuable information is to be gleaned from *A Century of Municipal Progress, 1835–1935* (Allen & Unwin, 1936) notably edited by W. A. Robson, H. J. Laski, and W. I. Jennings. V. D. Lipman's specialized treatise on *Local Government Areas 1834–1945* (Blackwell, 1949) will repay study. Two works on London government are also recommended: the officially sponsored *The Corporation of London: Its Origin, Constitution, Powers and Duties* (Oxford, 1956) and W. Eric Jackson's *Achievement: A Short History of the LCC* (Longmans, 1965). An excellent survey of recent developments in London Government is provided by Gerald Rhodes (for London School of Economics) in *The Government of London: the Struggle for Reform* (Weidenfeld & Nicolson, 1970).

Much invaluable information on current local government problems is to be gleaned from supplementary volumes to the Maud Report on *Management in Local Government* (HMSO, 1967), namely Volume 2 on *The Local Government Councillor*, Volume 3 on *The Local Government Elector* and Volume 5 more generally on *Local Government Administration in England and Wales*.

Every student of local government needs to have access to a comprehensive work on local government law which, in contrast to the central government sphere, delineates the subject comprehensively. Much to be recommended are C. A. Cross's *Principles of Local Government Law* (Sweet & Maxwell, 3rd edn. 1966) and the latest edition of *Hart's Introduction to the Law of Local Government and Administration* (Butterworth).

Comparative studies are not numerous and information about the local government systems of individual countries is to be sought in the more general treatises on government in those countries. G. M. Harris's *Comparative Local Government* (Hutchinson, 1948) is still useful from the historical viewpoint, but a most useful work is undoubtedly Volume 4 of the Report on Management of Local Government, which covers *Local Government Administration Abroad* and contains sections on the Republic of Ireland, Sweden, The United States and Canada, the Netherlands, and the German Federal Republic.

CHAPTER TWO

Local Government: Resources and Management

The resources of local government can be looked at generally in terms of finance—of capital and income—and of personnel, the two being deployed through management in accordance with existing law and the wishes of the local electorate.

FINANCE

It is not easy to understand the working of local government without some knowledge of its finance, although it is probable that few people, outside the local finance offices and the central audit staffs, fully comprehend the intricacies of this elusive subject. Fortunately only a broad survey is called for here and the reader wishing to delve deeper will be wise to give special attention to the more specialized works referred to in the Further Reading list at the end of the chapter.

As owners of extensive properties in the form of land, buildings, and public works, and as disbursers of large sums in the running of local government services, it is not surprising that finance is a local authority Council's most constant and vital concern. Supervised usually through a Finance Committee finance is the responsibility, under the Council, of the Chief Finance Officer, who may also have the statutory title of Treasurer and usually operates through a

Finance Department. Responsibility for the servicing of the authority's property assets will rest with other committees and departments.

Local authorities derive their income mainly from four sources, in ascending order of importance: trading, property, rates, and government grants. There are also the sums borrowed on capital account, which of course have to be repaid, covering such items as schools, houses, roads, police stations, swimming baths, and so forth. Trading income is of diminishing importance, due partly to the general policy that trading services should normally be run without profit or loss and partly to the trend since 1945 to transfer responsibility for such services, notably in power and transport, to public corporations. Income from property is important but straightforward, and it is over rating and grants-in-aid by the Government that controversy mainly arises.

RATING

Local taxation in Britain has been largely achieved through the imposition of a rate, levied on the occupier of real property (or a 'hereditament' as it is called) at so much in the £ on the net annual value of the property, unless it has been specifically derated. Until 1966 occupation of the property had to be beneficial, but by the Local Government Act of that year rating authorities were given the option of imposing rates on premises unoccupied for three months (or six months in the case of newly built properties). There are certain special exemptions, such as schools and places of worship; and allowances, particularly on property used for charity purposes. Agricultural hereditaments are exempted, but former exemptions of industrial and freight-transport hereditaments have now been withdrawn.

Until their abolition from 1 April 1927 (under the Rating and Valuation Act, 1925) the chief rating authorities were the Overseers of the Poor, to whom, for reasons of administrative convenience, the levying of rates, not only for the Poor Law, which was their particular concern, but for other purposes, had been assigned. Under the new arrangement, which still operates, the local authorities themselves raise the revenues needed for their own purposes, except that the actual collection is confined to the County Boroughs and the several County Districts. The County Councils and the Parish authorities obtain their rates through the rating authorities responsible for their areas, on whom they issue precepts for the amount needed and, calculated at so much in the £, this has to be included in the total rate collected from ratepayers. This arrangement removes the drawback of confronting the citizen in the two- or three-tier areas with more than one rate demand.

Before the rate can be levied the net annual rateable values of properties have to be ascertained. Difficulties are bound to arise here unless equitable standards are generally applied and accepted as such. Furthermore valuation of property is an expert's job that cannot be safely left to the lay representative or official. Objectivity has somehow to be achieved in a sphere where varying local conditions are unavoidable. Under the Rating and Valuation Act, 1925 a system was introduced whereby the rating authorities, working through special Assessment Committees exercising quasi-judicial functions, made individual assessments, which were subject to appeal to the magistrates in Quarter Sessions. The improvement that followed still fell short of ensuring the standardization of valuation on a national basis that was aimed at. Changes in the system, through supplementation of the rates by grants from the Exchequer, rendered such standardization even more necessary and therefore, in 1948, responsibility for valuation was transferred from the local to the national sphere and given to the Board of Inland Revenue, a Department which had already acquired skill and experience of such work in connection with the levying of property taxes. At the same time a number of Local Valuation Courts were established to hear and determine appeals against rating assessments, with further appeal to the Land Tribunal. On a point of law an appeal is available to the Court of Appeal and, by leave, to the House of Lords. It was laid down that the new valuation lists should be drawn up at five-year intervals, but the magnitude of the task, coupled with pressure of work from other directions has led to this arrangement being modified.

The modern general rate emerged in 1929 when the original poor law rate of 1601, together with a number of specific rates subsequently associated with its collection, were consolidated. Despite the technical difficulties of valuation the rate has the advantage of simplicity, cheapness in collection, and of being easily understood by the public, an important virtue in any form of taxation. It provides the local authorities with a stable source of income over which they have complete control, within the limits set, not by law, but by the property resources available in the area and the degree of acquiescence forthcoming from the local electorate (although the latter is somewhat modified by the fact that the franchise extends beyond the rate-paying group). Thus the rating system ensures a degree of financial independence of the central government, although this is weakened by the rate supplementation now provided through the block grant, to be explained in the following section.

The rate suffers from the natural disfavour in which all direct taxation is held, but does not have the advantage of fairness that can be claimed for a well devised system of income tax. Rates are not assessed according to ability to pay, since they fall relatively more heavily upon the small income family, especially when its accommodation requirement is heavy, and are therefore regressive. Moreover there is no direct connection between the amount paid and the local government services received by the ratepayer.

The search for an alternative means of local taxation, either to replace or to supplement the ordinary rate, has been pursued with more enthusiasm than success. Among the proposals that have been advocated are the changing of the basis of the rate from property values to land values, the levying of a local sales tax, the adding of a percentage for local purposes to existing national taxes, as is adopted in some other countries, or by assigning to the local authorities specific taxes levied nationally. The latter method was adopted in a limited way in Britain in 1888 when certain taxes, including those on beer and spirits, were paid into a Local Taxation Account, as Assigned Revenues for distribution to the County and County Boroughs, but the system was not popular, failed to develop and was abolished in 1929.

The most favoured alternative is a local income tax, although there would be obvious difficulties in levying this at a time when income tax has risen abnormally high and a local tax could therefore be levied only at the expense of the existing income tax. Apart from this the tax is not likely to commend itself to Chancellors of the Exchequer, because it would inevitably reduce the flexibility of the national tax system. There is also the organizational disadvantage that a local income tax would have to be collected in conjunction with the national tax, since the introduction of separate machinery would be unnecessarily costly, and, apart from technical difficulties, it would not be easy to ensure that the allocation of the tax and expense of collection fulfilled the localities' taxational requirements as approved by their councils. Thus a tax so closely involved with the central machinery of government would have little to commend it over grants-in-aid. See also page 75.

GOVERNMENT GRANTS

Grants-in-aid have for long been made from the Exchequer, either to lighten the cost of a local service or to encourage and help local authorities to bear the cost of a service which, while considered of national importance, is best administered locally. Such grants are usually fixed as a percentage of the total cost of the service, normally 50 per cent or less, although there were instances of a higher percentage, as for example for the upkeep of principal roads. The process began with the early nineteenth-century reforms and the number of grants authorized by Parliament gradually expanded until, in 1888, the introduction of the system of Assigned Revenues, already mentioned, enabled the existing grants to be curtailed. But the grant method was too useful to be discarded and percentage grants continued to be authorized.

With the introduction, in 1927, of derating of agriculture and industry a block grant from the Exchequer was introduced to make up for the revenues thus lost by the local authorities. By an ingenious formula—which unfortunately was too complicated and not easily understood—this block grant was apportioned to the several authorities in such a way as to take into account the derating loss, and weighted on the basis of local need, taking into account differences in population, the numbers of children and unemployed, and the population per mile of road. New specific grants continued to be introduced, and by 1948 a further revision was called for. The Exchequer Equalisation Grant replaced the existing block grant, now confining aid to the poorer authorities and again weighted according to population. Its aim was to bring the rate income of poorer authorities up to the average rateable level of the more prosperous ones.

On 1 April 1959 (under the Local Government Act, 1958) the system was again revised. (1) by substituting for the Exchequer Equalisation Grant a Rate Deficiency Grant, calculated on a new formula, payable to those authorities where the actual product of a rate of one penny in the £ for the area of the authority was less than the standard penny rate product for the area, and (2) a general grant to all Counties and County Boroughs in place of a number of existing specific grants, including the important and predominating education grant with many others. This change was widely challenged at the time on the grounds that it would cause authorities to economize or transfer sums to other services at the expense of education, but this does not appear to have happened. However, certain specific grants continued also to be paid, covering such important items as police, housing, highways and bridges, and certain education services not included in the general grant, i.e. for school meals and milk.

With the introduction of relief for the domestic ratepayer under the Local Government Act, 1966 a further revision of the general grant was found necessary. The new grant had three parts (1) a *needs element*, replacing the previous general grant, (2) a *resources element*, replacing the Rate Deficiency Grant, and (3) a *domestic element* to cover the cost of reducing the rate poundages of domestic ratepayers.

The original objections to the block grant, and particularly to the application of a somewhat complicated formula, are no longer widespread in a world used to administrative methods that become more and more sophisticated. But the problem of devising an appropriate formula has not been solved and probably cannot be solved in a fluid situation that calls for constant review of the formula's bases. The general grant method certainly has its advantages as a means of taking into account the varying needs of the different areas, of allowing local authorities more flexibility in deciding the extent of their expenditure on specific services, and of cutting out a good deal of the administrative detail called for, both at the centre and in the localities, in administering a number of specific percentage grants.

The financial business of the local authority has many more facets, including, on the receipt side, the problem of borrowing and on the payments side, the audit of accounts, both involved in central control, a matter to be discussed in the next chapter.

THE HUMAN RESOURCES

While good organization and sufficient, effectively deployed, finance are vital factors in the achievement of an efficient system of local government, they are of little avail without the services of willing and highly skilled workers, whose accomplishments add the seal of quality that every public service needs, but often fails to achieve. In local government, as in central government, the work is divided between a political and a professional element, the unpaid members of the Council and the paid staffs of the Council. As we have already seen, Councillors are elected on a universal franchise, but the membership of County and Borough Councils has a proportion of Aldermen, chosen by the councillors, usually from among their own members (thus creating vacancies for the election of further councillors) although outsiders are eligible, provided they would qualify for election as councillor. The Aldermen, who have something of the status of elder statesmen, exercise no special duties and enjoy no special privileges (except that in Boroughs they act as returning officers for the councillors at elections). The aldermanic system is widely criticized as antiquated, undemocratic, and privileged. The Chairman (or Mayor, who acts as such in Boroughs) is also elected by the Council and may be chosen from outside, although this is unusual. He represents the authority during his year of office and if his powers are limited, influential rather than compulsive, his prestige and dignity are considerable, especially in the case of a Mayor. He is the community's ceremonial figurehead. The Chairman or Mayor is the only member of the Council who may receive a salary, but this does not apply to the Chairman of a Parish Council.

As membership of a local council consumes a good deal of time, it is hardly surprising that certain occupational groups figure prominently among the membership: trade union officials, local employers, housewives, teachers, and retired persons, mostly middle-class people who can spare the time. Usually the majority are elected as members of one of the main political parties (sometimes masked by a different label). No doubt some become members of the Council to further personal interests (though there are strict rules against councillors participating when matters in which they have a financial interest are under discussion) but, despite all that can be alleged to the contrary, a considerable amount of effective and devoted service is forthcoming from these unpaid servants of the people. The root problem is one of achieving through such amateur instruments adequate levels of technical accomplishment in a sphere that gets more and more complicated year by year. Councillors, as ordinary citizens, are expected to know all about the responsibilities and problems of governing, a subject in which their briefing, as the educational system works at present, is almost bound to be defective. Improved training for representatives is the prime priority of any democratic system of local government. Without adequate knowledge and experience the councillors would be completely in the hands of their officials, who supply the expertise needed to run the machine and administer the numerous services.

THE LOCAL GOVERNMENT SERVICE

Local government officials are the servants of the Councils, who appoint them and pay them, decide their conditions of service, discipline and dismiss or retire them. It is only since the re-establishment in 1944 of the local government National Joint Council of the Whitley type, after an unsuccessful attempt to build up an effective consultative system between the wars, that the way was opened to the drawing up of a charter laying down a national scheme of salaries and general conditions of service. The charter, which received approval of authorities and staffs in 1946, for the first time laid the foundations of a real Local Government Service. Yet the individual Councils remained a law unto themselves and, while the majority saw the manifest advantages of a rationalized staffing basis and standardization of conditions of service, there were many who were not enthusiastic, some because of insufficient resources, to accept straight away the obligations of the new code. By the very nature of their serving a collection of autonomous employing bodies the members of the Local Government Service seem bound to lack the coherence of the Civil Service, with its centralized controls, though even there the doctrine of ministerial responsibility as applied to the political Heads of Departments, gives the Civil Service a much less consolidated form than its public image usually suggests.

The Local Government Service differs from the Civil Service in the relative proportions of administrative and technical work in the two spheres. In central government administration is the key activity and the generalist administrator is the key official: in local government, which is so much concerned with executive activities mostly of a highly technical nature, it is the qualified professional who occupies the predominant position, although not in the unified sense of the Civil Service, since in local government the several branches are under the control of different experts who form a diversity rather than a unity. Latterly the Civil Service, with its acquirement of responsibility for more and more technical functions, has been rapidly increasing its professional-technical elements, but local government, despite recent efforts to improve its over-all administrative accomplishment, is still weak in the administrative sphere, and current reforms are directed to its improvement.

Generally, the Councils decide upon the actual make up of their staffs, subject of course to the normal pattern and practices, but there are a limited number of posts that must be filled. Thus, except in the Parishes, there have to be a Clerk, a Treasurer, a Medical Officer of Health, a Surveyor (except also in Rural Districts), and a Public Health Inspector (except also in Counties). There must be a Chief Education Officer for each Local Education Authority, a Director of Social Services for each County and County Borough, and a Chief Constable for each Police Authority. The main staffs are organized into the Clerical Division (of four grades) which includes non-clerical workers formerly organized as the General Division. Above this basic division there is a Trainee Grade, consisting of suitably qualified entrants in training for the various Administrative and Professional Posts, which are organized in AP Grades 1 to 5, the Senior Officers' Grade, and the Principal Officer's Grade. There is also the Technicians and Technical Staffs Division, made up of T Grades 1 to 6. In addition there are a number of separately organized specialist grades, such as those for librarians, youth employment officers, and child care officers, as well as typists, and machine operators. To each of these grades an appropriate salary scale is assigned.

Appropriate qualifications are required of candidates for any of the professional and other specialist grades, while it is increasingly the practice to expect prescribed GCE and other educational qualifications for clerical appointments. With a view to improving both the image and the quality of the clerical-administrative field steps were taken immediately after the Second World War, largely on staff initiative through the new Whitley machinery, to introduce suitable qualifications in administration and to set up the Local Government Examinations Board to supervise the examinations. Thus the Diploma in Municipal Administration (with intermediate and final stages and equivalent to degree standard) was established as the required qualification for promotion to the Administrative Division, although actual promotion continues to depend upon selection for an actual vacancy for which the candidate is suitable and not merely upon the holding of the diploma.

Vacancies in middle range and senior posts are not normally reserved for promotees from within the authority having the vacancy, but are advertised, and Councils are willing to appoint suitably qualified and experienced officers from other authorities. In this way the inherent separatist nature of the local government system has been substantially modified and a career system provided for those, usually the more enterprising, who are prepared to uproot themselves for advancement. Only the larger concentrated authorities can provide careers within their own organizations, and even these benefit from the interchange of staff with other authorities.

The widely different history and experience of the local authorities, compared with the Civil Service, have ensured that the former have for long been more sympathetic than the latter towards the acceptance of examinations as tests of competence. On the other hand, after a traditionally slow start, the Civil Service have been ahead of local government in recognizing the importance of in-service training, which in the local government field has again been held back by its disintegrated nature. Only the largest local authorities have been able to organize effective training schemes of their own and, apart from certain local initiatives, the organization of such training across the boundaries has had to await the setting up of centralized machinery for the purpose. One of the first-fruits of the proposals in 1967 of the Mallaby Committee on *Staffing of Local Government* (to be summarized in Chapter Four of this volume) has been the setting up of the Local Government Training Board to serve the general needs of the Councils in this field. It has incorporated the existing Local Government Examinations Board.

Apart from the numerous gradings, already discussed as forming the Local Government Service, local authorities are responsible for the employment of a large number of manual workers of various types, and of teachers and members of the police and fire services.

MANAGEMENT

The Council is responsible for running the show, and for this end, as we have seen, it is empowered to appoint a competent staff. It is the accredited policy- and decision-making body which, through the appointment of committees selected mainly from among its own membership, maintains an intimate participation in the actual management of its services. Except for the financial and legal powers already mentioned, the Council has wide scope to decide what functions it shall delegate and the extent of such delegation, which in consequence varies widely from council to council. Where delegation is most complete this means that the committees' actions are subject to little more than report to the Council.

The work of the local authority is organized by the Council in a series of departments, each under its own qualified chief officer. There is no set pattern of departments, their number and scope depending upon volume of work, size of staff, the authority's traditions and special local needs, and of course upon specific statutory requirements for certain services. Normally there is likely to be a Clerk's, a Treasurer's, an Engineer and Surveyor's, and a Public Health department; while the larger authorities will need Education, Housing, Social Services, Fire, Police, Transport, and other departments, averaging some fifteen and in some cases running to over thirty departments. Such a proliferation of departments creates special problems of co-ordination and inevitably increases the impact of inter-departmental jealousies and friction. In theory most local government institutions could be streamlined with advantages in both economy and efficiency, but in practice such changes are held back by the existence of incompatible professional groupings and structural inflexibilities that cannot easily be overcome merely by internal initiative.

The committees are also numerous, which means that council members serve on more than one committee, perhaps on quite a number. The membership is usually distributed proportionately to the party groupings on the Council. The chairmanships, being of key importance, may be controlled by the majority party or shared with the other groups on an agreed basis. Their responsibilities may be shared out on a service or functional pattern, reflecting though not necessarily coinciding with the departmental pattern; that is to say dividing the work vertically on the principle advocated in the Haldane Report, or they may deal with matters that operate horizontally across the departments, such as: general purposes, finance, staffing, organization and methods, and so forth. Both forms are freely employed. Committees may also be set up to deal with specific subjects on an *ad hoc* or temporary basis.

Apart from certain statutory exceptions, namely those authorities responsible for education, health, and social services which are called upon to set up specific committees, the Councils determine their own committee pattern. Membership of the committees may be supplemented by the co-option of suitably experienced persons from outside the Council, up to one third of the membership, except in the case of finance committees. Such co-option is statutorily imposed in the case of education and allotments (in the former case the upper limit being less than one-half of the total membership). Outside these co-option is not widespread. Elected councillors do not like bringing in people who have not run the gauntlet of the polls, and naturally officials feel that they already have enough amateurs to deal with and consider themselves the proved experts in the respective fields. This is true of course, but only up to a point. Co-option can be supported as a means of achieving the maximum local co-operation and making use of the store of uncommitted and unprejudiced expertise that exists in society, the harnessing of which is essential to the administration of an expanding system.

Broadly the committees are responsible for decisions on policy and for supervision of administration, but not for actual execution and detailed administration, which are the proper responsibility of local government officials equipped with the essential competence to conduct the local authority's business. However, the amount of initiative left to the officials varies considerably as between Councils, and some committees assume executive responsibilities, but the powers delegated to them are attached to the committee as a whole and not to individual members. Nevertheless, committee chairmen come to acquire a special status which enables them to speak for the committee between meetings, especially when urgent matters need an early decision. Such members in any case need to devote more time to local government affairs than the ordinary member, who may be available only in the evening or with difficulty at other times. As enthusiasts, the committee chairmen tend to accumulate specialized knowledge of the committee's sphere of activity and this is enhanced by the practice of allowing such chairmanships to continue so long as as the chairman's party maintains control of the Council. Such councillors tend to be listened to with respect by officials, and are well able to speak for their colleagues on the committee in their absence. The committee system, though a unique element of the British system of local government which has its special virtues, has for long been under criticism, and more will be said about this later in Chapter Four.

TOWN CLERK

Thus, at the political level, management is concentrated in the hands of the elected Council, working through a series of committees, among which the finance committee or possibly a general purposes committee, can, in virtue of its functions, contribute an important co-ordinating element to the conduct of the Council's business. At administrative levels, however, co-ordination can be less satisfactory, for the professional sectors are not subject to a senior administrator with the general authority of a Permanent Secretary of a Government Department.

The Council's chief administrator is the Town Clerk, or Clerk of Council, who is responsible for the secretarial work of the Council and usually acts as its legal adviser. Because of the latter practice the office is generally held by a qualified lawyer, although this rests upon custom, arising from history and convenience, and not upon law. There is no reason, certainly in the larger authorities, why the Council's important legal business should not be given to a qualified specialist, either working with the Clerk or through his own legal department. It has become increasingly recognized that, in the modern phase local authorities need a skilled administrator at the head of their permanent staffs.

As secretary to the Council, the Clerk is in a good position to exert a beneficial influence in co-ordinating the work of the departments, an influence that is currently being reinforced by the development of new management services under his charge. This influence can be considerable where the post is held by a dominating personality with skill as a leader, but the Clerk cannot override the heads of the other departments, who, as specialists, are directly responsible to the Council. To improve this management situation a good deal of attention has been paid to the idea of introducing a professional manager on the lines of the City Manager, widely adopted by American cities and successfully copied in the Irish Republic. A few modest experiments on similar lines have been tried in Britain, so far, it would appear, with but moderate success. On this important subject interesting proposals were made by the Committee on the

Management of Local Government which reported in 1967. This matter will also be followed up in Chapter Four.

FURTHER READING

Introductory

Finance and personnel are covered in reasonable detail in most of the general works on local government. Finance is dealt with more comprehensively in J. M. Drummond's *The Finance of Local Government* (Allen & Unwin, 2nd edn. revised by W. A. C. Kitching, 1962) and A. H. Marshall's *Financial Administration in Local Government* (Allen & Unwin, for RIPA, 1960).

The personnel aspects of local government are covered in J. H. Warren's *The Local Government Service* (Allen & Unwin, 1952) and T. E. Headrick's *The Town Clerk in English Local Government* (Allen & Unwin, for RIPA, 1962).

The practical aspects of local government administration are dealt with in W. Eric Jackson's *The Secretarial Practice of Local Authorities* (Heffer, 1953).

Historical and Advanced

Improvements in the system of local taxation were proposed and discussed in *New Sources of Local Revenue* (Allen & Unwin, 1956) which embodied the findings of a Study Group set up by RIPA. This study was supplemented by a duplicated report on *Local Revenues in Eleven Overseas Countries* (RIPA, 1956) containing interesting material on the subject for Australia, Canada, Denmark, France, Germany, Netherlands, New Zealand, Norway, South Africa, Switzerland, and the United States.

E. Cannan's *History of Local Rates in England* (P. S. King, 1927) is well worth reading on the historical aspects and recent developments have been covered in a series of official publications, e.g. *Report of the Committee appointed to investigate the Operation of the Exchequer Equalization Grants in England and Wales* (1953), *Local Government Finance England and Wales*) Cmnd. 209 (1957), *Local Government Finance in Scotland*, Cmnd. 208 (1957), *Local Government Finance Scotland* Cmnd. 2921 (1966) and *Local Government Finance England and Wales*, Cmnd. 2923 (1966).

More will be said about local government management in Chapters 4 and 5, but two general works call for attention: J. H. Warren's *Municipal Administration* (Pitman, 1948) and B. J. Ripley's succinct and stimulating

Administration in Local Authorities (Butterworth, 1970), which provides an up-to-date survey and critical analysis of the internal working of local authorities. An important aspect of local administration is surveyed in P. G. Richards's *Delegation in Local Government* (Allen & Unwin, 1956). There are also numerous works on the organization and administration of individual services which the specialist will wish to consult: local government is better served in this respect than most sectors of public administration.

An informative article by J. Elliott on 'The Harris Experiment in Newcastle-upon-Tyne' in *Public Administration* Vol. 49, pp. 149–162 (RIPA 1971) throws a good deal of light on the widely discussed plan to combine the post of Principal Officer with that of Town Clerk.

CHAPTER THREE
Central–Local Relationships

The ideal of local government in a democratic society is that the people should enjoy maximum autonomy in the management of the community's affairs, but in fact local government can never be completely outside the concern of the central government. Its limitations will be determined by, and vary with, the conditions of the age. Before the emergence of the present local government system in Britain practical restrictions on mobility narrowed the scope of both local management and central control. Yet the system acquired a high measure of coherence through the paternalist approach of the landed gentry, in the interest of public duty and a genuine liking on the part of many of them for exercising administrative responsibilities. Co-operation with the centre was considerably facilitated by the fact that members of the same class occupied seats of power there.

With many of the community services now dependent upon financial and technical resources so large as to be beyond the scope of even the largest local authorities, a widespread interest and increasing involvement of the central government in local affairs appears to be unavoidable. Since it is generally held that it is desirable to keep down such central control and oversight to a minimum, it will often be necessary for the localities to decide whether or not at some points a degree of efficiency should be sacrificed in favour of increased autonomy.

Local government is of course a vital sector of a country's system of government. Its relationship with Parliament in Britain has already been made clear, though there is a modest variation in legal terms where the local authority has been set up under Royal Charter. With this not very important variation local authorities derive their powers solely from Act of Parliament public or private, and from orders under such Acts. As corporate bodies they are subject to the ordinary common and statute law, and may be called to account in the Courts not only for breaking the law but also for exceeding their powers under the Acts. The High Court may issue an Order of Mandamus to compel a local authority to carry out some duty cast upon it by law, but not if this is merely permissive or discretionary or the applicant has a substantial personal interest in the performance of the duty and there is an equally convenient remedy available.

The Central Government is much involved with local government bodies as part of the nation's administrative machinery. Its main means of influencing local government are: (1) through policy decisions in Cabinet and (2) by the use of the several Government Departments as channels of communication and control. In the policy-making sphere the existence of party representation on the local Councils is important. It is true that, whatever their predominant political attitudes, the local authorities are bound to implement the existing law, much of which will have been introduced under past administrations of differing political colours. Radically to reshape the administration the government has first to amend existing legislation, yet it is possible to exert certain pressures through the local administration, depending upon whether nationally prescribed services are administered as narrowly or as broadly as the statutes permit, for it is of the nature of such legislation that a reasonable degree of flexibility should be allowed in such matters. General exhortation is much more likely to have effect where the Government is addressing Councils with a majority in its favour. Such Councils will be less likely to drag their feet in implementing reforms, although even they will resent too much interference by the central administration.

Those Ministers who have special responsibility for local government matters (as mentioned in the next section) are available in Parliament to meet criticism of their stewardship in this field, but, as these responsibilities are only exceptionally involved in the local authorities' day-to-day administration, it follows that Parliament is not able in a general way to concern itself with such matters, or to use Question Time for this purpose beyond the extent to which a Minister's responsibilities are concerned. Nor is this in any sense a flaw, for in fact the real virtue of administration by an elected council is that the exercise of authority, through the agency of the councillors, is located on the spot, where it is subject to the electorate's direct representations and complaints. The handling of such approaches will be enhanced by the existence in the local authority's organization of an efficient public relations unit.

MINISTERIAL SUPERVISION

Responsibility for relations with the many local authorities rests with the functional Ministers in whose sphere the local authorities' specific operations are involved. By its nature the British system of distributing the work of the Central Administration among a group of departmental Ministers allocated according to function or service, precludes the placing of all central–local relationships in the hands of one minister. Proposals are often made for this to be done and there would no doubt be many advantages in such an arrangement. It would, however, need to be accompanied by radical changes in the machinery of government, such as, usually, such reformers do not intend; that is if they have thought about the subject so deeply! There is, however, a Minister who has general as well as specific responsibilities in this field, formerly the Minister of Housing and Local Government, whose functions were in October 1970 transferred to the new Department of the Environment. Apart from his responsibilities under statute for such matters as town and country planning and housing, the responsible Minister has general oversight of local government, including such residuary functions as are not specifically assigned to other Ministers. Similar responsibilities are exercised by the Secretaries of State for Scotland and for Wales, but the following ministers also have major responsibilities in this sphere: the Secretaries of State for the Home Department, for Education and Science, and for Health and Social Security. This does not complete the picture, since other Ministers may have responsibilities for important, though less extensive matters, such as the Youth Employment Service, provision of which is shared between the local authorities and the two central departments dealing with employment and education.

The Ministers' specific responsibilities vary widely from Department to Department, and even between services in the same Department. The differences are due to the varying technical and administrative requirements of the different services, but also to some extent to the varying views of Government and Parliament at the time the authorizing statutes are passed. Usually the responsibilities are specifically defined and limited, but in a few instances quite comprehensive powers have been conferred upon Ministers, notably in the principal Education Act of 1944, upon which the present educational system is based. Section 1 of this Act placed upon the Minister of Education (now the Secretary of State for Education and Science) the duty:

... to promote the education of the people of England and Wales and the progressive development of institutions devoted to that purpose, and to secure the effective execution by local authorities, under his control and direction, of the national policy for providing a varied and comprehensive educational service in every area.

Here, surely, the Minister is given very extensive powers to control the Local Education Authorities (mainly the Counties and County Boroughs) and to determine in detail what they should do, but in fact the actual administration of the Act has not concentrated upon the general powers. Difficulties between the local authorities and the Minister have related to specific powers, and it is the view of experts on the subject that the general powers of control and direction embodied in the clause quoted above are in fact determined by those set down in later sections of the Act. (See, for example, C. A. Cross, *Principles of Local Government Law* (Sweet & Maxwell, 1966 edn.) pp. 172–3.)

Under the various statutes Ministers are in a few cases empowered to issue directions, or to determine the way in which a service shall be carried out and the standards to be achieved by the issue of appropriate orders and regulations, some of which may be subject to Parliamentary oversight. It should be emphasized that, while the Minister initiates major action and is responsible for all action on the part of his Department, the vast majority of contacts between the centre and the localities takes place at administrative levels through the Departments' Civil Service staffs.

Normally such contacts are made between the Department and local authorities individually, but for their own protection and to formulate general or national policies, the several local Councils have formed associations, which to some extent take the place of the employers' associations of private industry. In local government these associations are of particular importance in providing channels of communication between bodies that take a natural pride in their autonomy. They are (1) the Association of Municipal Corporations (AMC), (2) the County Councils Association (CCA), (3) the Urban District Councils Association (UDCA), (4) the Rural District Councils Association (RDCA), and (5) the National Association of Parish Councils (NAPC). In addition the Local Education Committees (of the Local Education Authorities) have formed the Association of Local Education Authorities in England, Wales, Northern Ireland, the Isle of Man, and the Channel Islands (AEC) which, as an association concerned with a particular service, stands apart from the others.

The associations have been established to protect the interests of their member authorities, and their natural attitudes towards self-preservation have tended to support the maintenance of the *status quo*. This has not necessarily meant the same thing to each of them, and they have often been at loggerheads among themselves on proposed extensions and changes. Yet they have provided invaluable channels of communication not only between their own members but also with outside bodies and powers, and in particular with the Government, Ministers, and civil servants with whom they have business and who on their part welcome the facility they provide for discussion of policies and problems, and for the testing of new ideas with bodies able to represent such a large and diverse field. Latterly the associations have been instrumental in the establishment of common service bodies, of which local government has been developing a real need but whose natural development has often been retarded by the disintegrated nature of the field. These new sources include the Local Government Information Office, the Local Authorities Management Services and Computer Committee, the Local Government Training Board, and the Local Government Conditions of Service Advisory Board.

DEPARTMENTAL SUPERVISION

Contacts between the responsible Government Departments and the local authorities range from the mere transmission of information and informal conversations to the issue of definite orders under the Minister's authority. Yet it has always to be remembered that the local authorities are completely responsible under the statutes for their own management, and the Departments can only exceptionally interfere with the conduct of business inside the local authorities' offices and other establishments. This is very different from the Departments' relationships with their own regional and local offices operating in the same areas, sometimes side by side with those of the local authorities, but directly responsible through the Permanent Secretary to the Minister. Regarded as a whole, these central–local relationships are based upon influence other than power, which is as it should be if local government is to be responsible government.

In their contacts with the local authorities the several Central Departments employ their normal methods, both formal and informal, although these differ from department to department, mainly according to function but not unaffected by tradition. Thus general information, perhaps elucidating points in the statutes, is conveyed through the issue of printed circulars, advice is given in letters, often in reply to specific inquiries, and in some cases personal relations are developed, usually between senior officials of the local authorities and senior civil servants in Whitehall. These vary in effectiveness, as between larger and smaller authorities, as between those who are near the capital with reasonable access and those that are more distant, with the degree of compulsion or flexibility embodied in the Acts, with the traditional practices of the different Ministries, and with the personalities of the officials involved. Informal contacts are desirable and usually welcomed, but in practice the large number of authorities in the existing system render the maximum development of such relationships unattainable, especially with the staff resources available. In the main the pattern of these contacts is determined by the Ministers' broad responsibilities under the law, including questions of Government policy, but there are also, spread over the numerous local services in varying density and embodied in a long series of statutes, specific controls that the Departments have to implement and the local authorities are unable to avoid. These operate in a piecemeal way and do not conform to any specific or comprehensive code. The more important approaches are summarized in the following paragraphs.

Scheme-making

In order to give flexibility of application to the administration of new services, or reorganized services, by a variety of different authorities; to enable specific local needs and peculiarities to be taken into account; and to avoid cluttering up the statutes with unnecessary detail (which in many cases could not be foreseen in advance), Parliament has adopted the method of leaving it to the local authorities to plan and embody the detail of their administration in a 'scheme' (or 'proposal' or 'plan'), which must receive the approval of the responsible Minister before it can be put into operation. Such plans are usually called for by a certain date and Ministers, after due consideration of all the factors involved and discussion with the several interests concerned, usually draw up for general guidance a model plan embodying the factors to be covered by the scheme. The Minister has discretion to amend a scheme in any way, but as one of the great virtues of the method is that it enables specific local requirements to be met, within the terms of the statute and with the support of the local authority, any amendments will usually be made only after full discussion with the latter. The scheme once approved the local authority is expected to conform to it, and therefore such schemes have something of the nature of subordinate legislation in their effect. Apart from helping to mould the new administration to local needs, the process of scheme-making enables the Minister to ensure that a certain level of efficiency is achieved and that undue extravagance in operation is avoided. Schemes have been called for in the development of services in such areas as education, public health, social services, and town and country planning. Thus the Education Act, 1944 required local authorities to provide development plans covering their areas's needs in primary and secondary education, and also to propose schemes for divisional administration.

Inspection

One of the oldest controlling methods employed in government administration, inspection, is operated only in a few administrative spheres. There is no general local government inspectorate, if we exclude District Audit which, if transcending the functional divisions,

C

is confined to financial considerations (see below). No doubt the functional division of responsibilities at the centre has militated against such an institution developing, but it should be borne in mind that inspection interferes with the autonomy of the executive authority and should be employed by the Government only when it has special reasons for ensuring that specific standards are being achieved. The best known of these inspectorates are HM Inspectors of Schools and HM Inspectors of Constabulary (agents of the Secretary of State for Education and Science and the Home Secretary respectively). The members of these two inspectorates are appointed by the Crown, as are the Fire Service Inspectors, who are also responsible to the Home Secretary. It is the function of these inspectors to maintain regular contact with the operative branches of the respective services, with the dual object of informing the Department whether the required levels of efficiency and economy in running the services are being achieved and of providing the operating authorities with technical advice and making them aware of the Department's outlook. Transmission of information and experience based upon the working of the service in the several responsible authorities is in fact a vital contribution which the inspectors, from their daily wanderings among a variety of operating units, are in the best position to make, informally and without appearing to know best. This horizontal transmission of information has been of particular value in the education system, with its large number of individually managed schools, working under a profession that rightly enjoys a high degree of autonomy and considerable initiative in determining the content of the courses.

Inspecting officials sent out by central agencies to hold inquiries on the spot and to report back, for example on matters of planning and compulsory purchase of land and property, are not inspectors in the present sense. Also in a different category are the inspectors employed by the Local Authorities themselves to assist in the administration of certain services, e.g. public health, schools and weights and measures.

Adjudicatory and Appellate Functions

Under certain statutes facilities are provided for citizens to appeal to the responsible Minister against specified decisions of a local authority, for example under the Town and Country Planning Act, 1962 and the Highways Act, 1959. The Minister has similar appellate jurisdiction in certain cases of dispute between one authority and another, and between authorities and their employees. An instance of the former is afforded by the Children Act, 1948 as to which authority is financially responsible, and of the latter under the Local Government Superannuation Acts of 1937 and 1953, on certain pension matters. It should be noted that this is primarily a ministerial rather than a departmental matter.

Control of Personnel

While the individual local authorities are generally responsible for their own staffing and other personnel matters, certain conditions have been laid down in specific statutes, in a somewhat piecemeal manner, to impose safeguards and ensure the fulfilment of minimum standards. Although these rules do not amount to much in the aggregate, they certainly do diminish the local authorities' scope in an important managerial sphere.

Thus, as we have already seen, certain officials must be appointed, such as Clerks and Treasurers, Social Services and Education Officers, and so on. Some salaries are subject to approval, e.g. of County Clerks by the Secretary of State for the Environment. Dismissal may be subject to ministerial consent, as in the case of County Clerks and Medical Officers of Health. In a few cases specific professional qualifications are laid down. There are special rules for the appointment of certain officials. Thus both Chief Constables and Directors of Social Services have to be chosen from a short list of suitable candidates submitted for approval by the responsible Minister, who may call for the omission therefrom of a candidate he considers unsuitable. In the case of the Police Forces and Fire Services the Home Secretary has more extensive powers of regulation.

By-laws and Local Bills

Local authorities are empowered to make by-laws for various purposes: such as to ensure the 'good rule and government' of the

County or Borough, or for the 'prevention and suppression of nuisances therein'. This type of rule-making is closely regulated and subject to ministerial confirmation, so that the Committee on Ministers' Powers, 1932 classified it as subordinate legislation. The Ministers with general responsibilities for local government issue model by-laws for the general guidance of authorities, and these are usually adopted in shaping such rule making. Apart from the responsible Ministers, the Secretary of State and other Ministers may receive such powers of confirmation, depending upon the subject-matter.

Local authorities may acquire powers not covered by the ordinary statutes by promoting a Private Bill, which is subject to special parliamentary procedures designed to protect the interest of all who may be concerned. Interested Government Departments may report to the House of Commons on such bills, copies of which have to be sent to them. Officials of the responsible Departments are in frequent communication with the promoters of such Bills and in this way exercise considerable influence in ensuring the protection of Crown and public rights in the shaping of these measures. (See chart in Volume One, pages 226–8.)

AUDIT

Despite their considerable freedom with regard to the levying of rates, local authorities are subject to a number of controls in other directions, and these include the audit of their accounts which is prescribed by statute. This highly professional task is placed in the hands of District Auditors, who are civil servants now appointed and dismissible by the Secretary of State for the Environment. Although government officials, the District Auditors are not subject to the normal hierarchic instructions in performing their auditing duties but act professionally in accordance with a detailed code, with the object of bringing to light financial irregularities and not of implementing the Minister's specific policy instructions. The District Audit is imposed upon all local authorities except the Boroughs, whose accounts are statutorily subject to Borough Audit by three auditors, two elected by the electors and one appointed by the Mayor. However, Borough Councils may, by resolution, transfer the task either to professional auditors or to the District Audit. Moreover, the accounts of certain services are statutorily subject to District Audit and in these cases the Boroughs have no option but to fall in line. With the growing extent and complexity of local government financing more professional auditing procedures have gradually superseded former simpler methods.

The District Auditors' function is to assure themselves that proper and accurate accounting methods have been operated; to disallow any payments that 'are contrary to law'; to surcharge the person or persons responsible for such payments; and to certify the accounts, subject to any such disallowance or surcharge. Councillors or officials suffering such a serious sanction have the right of appeal to the High Court, except that, if the sum involved does not exceed £500, they have the alternative of appealing to the Minister, who may himself refer a question of law to the High Court. Both Minister and High Court have the power to cancel a surcharge where justification is found for the action that led to the surcharge.

The phrase 'contrary to law' has been broadly interpreted to cover unreasonable or excessive action on the part of the local authorities' servants. A case of historical interest, widely mentioned in the textbooks, is that of the Poplar Metropolitan Borough Council in 1925, whose decision to pay a minimum wage of £4 a week to its employees, a rate of pay that was above the minimum for such work at the time, was disallowed by the District Auditor and surcharged upon the Councillors, who preferred to go to prison rather than to pay. The auditor's decision was confirmed by the Divisional Court, reversed by the Court of Appeal and finally restored on appeal to the House of Lords, whose ruling was to form the basis of many future decisions.

VALUATION FOR RATING

Matters of rating are outside the province of the Central Departments, except for the influences exerted by the fact that the general grants are designed to make good rate deficiencies due to low rating capacity. It is true that the valuation, on which the rate is now based, is worked out by the Inland Revenue Department, but this is in the nature of an expert common service to the local authorities, replacing the earlier piecemeal method, which failed to do justice as between authority and authority.

GOVERNMENT GRANTS

The expansion of the system of Exchequer grants-in-aid to local authorities has undoubtedly increased the dependence of the authorities upon the Central Government. Such grants, related to approved expenditure, have to be accounted for in detail. Grants-in-aid for specific services are not payable unless the responsible Minister is satisfied with the way in which the service is administered and may be withheld if a minimum standard of efficiency is not achieved. As we have seen, where inspectorates have been introduced, e.g. in education and police, they are concerned in the assessment of such standards. In practice grants are rarely withheld, but it is the general influence, arising from the mere threat of such sanctions rather than from their specific application, that has the required effect. The threat of withholding the money is sufficient, since the possible alternative open to the Council, of carrying on without and making up the difference from the rate, is not likely to be acceptable to the electors, who will be highly critical of the Council's failure to achieve efficient administration. The effect of this sanction has certainly been weakened by the extension and scope of the general grant, to which the same rules apply but are not easily differentiated where a wide range of services is involved.

The most decisive effect of the grants-in-aid system is its general tendency to erode the Councils' sense of freedom and of compelling them to adopt a cap-in-hand approach to their paymasters. This is at the root of the movement to provide local authorities with more independent sources of income. Alternatively the Central Government could be given full financial responsibility for the services that are nationally based and administer them either (1) directly through the Central Departments, or (2) on any agency basis through the local authorities.

BORROWING

Local authorities need to borrow moneys, both to meet temporary shortages and to finance long-term capital projects, such as roads, schools, houses, and other constructional works. The degree of control has varied from time to time but today all borrowing by local authorities, except over short periods for purely revenue purposes, is subject to the consent of the responsible Department or the

Treasury. Exceptional arrangements for London entail agreement between the Greater London Council and the Treasury on the amount of capital expenditure and the sums to be borrowed, details of which have to be embodied in an annual Money Bill.

Local government funds may be raised in most of the normal ways, including the issue of stock, which is subject to the approval of the Department of the Environment and the Treasury. The Public Works Loan Board, a small Government Department under the control of twelve unpaid commissioners, who were first appointed in 1817 to make advances for public works, is also available to local authorities as a source of loans.

It is in the light of the considerable increase in the local authorities' needs and their effect upon the nation's financing as a whole, that the Government's interest in the extent of local authority borrowing and the degree of control to be exercised have latterly greatly increased. The Chancellor of the Exchequer has to take this factor into account when working out the annual Budget, and the Government's general financial policy in respect of the local government sectors is decided on the basis of these overall assessments. In her book, *The Ministry of Housing and Local Government* (1969), Dame Evelyn Sharp, a recent Permanent Secretary of that Ministry, expresses the view that 'the most powerful weapon in the Ministry's armoury of controls is, nowadays, the loan sanction' (op cit., p. 29).

DEFAULT POWERS

Central supervision and controls operate only through statutory powers justiciable by the Courts. Only in certain specific instances, where Parliament has included default powers in statutes dealing with local government matters, are Ministers able to take over the actual administration of local authority services, and such powers are only exercisable where the local authority has seriously failed to carry out its statutory duties. In such cases the Minister may appoint its own agents to carry on the administration, the costs incurred being charged upon the Council. These default powers are specific and not widely available, and are infrequently used. Otherwise the several controls mentioned operate upon and not within the local authority!

An example of the implementation of such default powers that stirred up a good deal of interest at the time, particularly enhanced by the strong views of the political groups on the subject, arose in 1954 when the Council of the City of Coventry refused to establish a Civil Defence Service as required by current legislation, on the grounds that, as no possible defence was available against atomic bombs, the whole effort would be a complete waste of resources. The Home Secretary, as the Minister responsible for Civil Defence and in execution of his default powers, appointed three independent Commissioners to organize and run the service in Coventry, the Council having to meet the expense. Subsequently, the Government came to very much the same conclusion about Civil Defence, though this does not mean that the local authority's way of challenging national policy was the right one.

THE GENERAL QUESTION OF CENTRAL CONTROL

While some of the Central Department's activities in relation to local government are of a constructive nature and others are of limited influence, the aggregate interference from the centre can be considerable and is bound to lessen the scope of local initiative. In the immediate post-war period so much dissatisfaction with central–local relationships had been manifested by local government spokesmen that the Government, activated by the Chancellor of the Exchequer's current concern with economy in manpower, decided to set up two Local Government Manpower Committees, for England and Wales, and for Scotland respectively, with the following terms of reference:

To review and co-ordinate the existing arrangements for ensuring economy in the use of manpower by local authorities and by those Government Departments which are concerned with local government matters; and to examine in particular the distribution of functions between central and local government and the possibility of relaxing departmental supervision of local authority activities and delegating more responsibility to local authorities.

The Committees, under chairmen representing the Treasury and the Scottish Office respectively, consisted of representatives of the several local authority associations and also of the Government Departments concerned with local government affairs. Certain broad principles were laid down and a large number of detailed activities were examined and discussed, but it cannot be said that radical solutions emerged. No doubt the discussions were useful in clearing away misconceptions on both sides and therefore contributed to achieving an improved understanding between the two governmental spheres. Each Committee produced two reports and the following quotation from the *Second Report* (Cmd. 8421) of December 1951 for England and Wales (see para. 9) puts the position in a nutshell:

. . . Here we are concerned only to re-emphasise the general principle already recognised in our First Report that the objective should be to leave as much as possible of the detailed management of a scheme or service to the local authority and to concentrate the Department's control at the key points where it can most effectively discharge its responsibilities for Government policy and financial administration. However much this principle is acknowledged, it tends not to be wholly carried out. It is understandable that anyone who is responsible for some activity should try to keep his finger on the detail of it; but this temptation should be resisted. Instances may occur where a close central control is necessary as a matter of deliberate policy; but, except in such special circumstances, we recommend that the general principle should be the one which we have adopted.

The attitudes of the Departments, with their individual traditions, functions and methods, are bound to vary. J. A. G. Griffiths in his valuable survey of these relationships suggests that the attitudes of the several Departments fall broadly into three categories, ranging from (1) complete *laissez-faire*, (2) through varying degrees of the regulatory, to (3) the basically promotional; and even differing, in some cases, as between the several services under the control of the same Department. These various departmental approaches are further differentiated according to specific methods and functional requirements, and by the degree of interest taken, ranging from comparative inactivity to high activity; departmental traditions, and the extent of public interest also playing their part. On the local authority side the attitudes also vary widely according to size— even within the same type of authority, e.g. between small and large County Boroughs—with the political complexion of the Council, and inversely to the distance of the locality from the Metropolis. There are also such technical matters as the frequency of impact of expenditure—high in the case of education and highways—and the ingrained attitudes of individual officials on both sides.

It is hardly surprising that, in such a diversely ramifying system, there should operate widely differing managerial approaches. Such even happens in large-scale organizations where, under a general policy-making authority, numerous executive units exercise a wide autonomy in operation, and different viewpoints develop at the different levels and in the several units on the same level. Only a generally accepted doctrine, or philosophy, of the proper basis of such relationships, coupled with highly professional competence manifesting itself in objective, sympathetic, and effective administering, would seem likely to reduce the problems of central–local relationships and achieve maximum co-operation between the two spheres. No doubt a reduction in the number of local government units, such as would be achieved by a radical structural reorganization and redistribution of functions, as is currently contemplated, would go a long way to facilitate such a solution.

LOCAL AUTHORITIES AS AGENTS OF THE CENTRAL GOVERNMENT

In some systems of government local authorities, apart from taking care of the administration of local services for which they have direct responsibility, act as agents of the central government in administering central services available in their own areas. As we have seen, in Britain the normal method of assigning services for which the Government retains major responsibilities is for the actual administration to be shared statutorily between the appropriate Central Department and the local authorities—as for example, in the cases of education and national health—with appropriate ministerial and administrative linkings, such as have been discussed in the present chapter. There are instances, however, where the element of agency is much greater, specific local officials or councils being made directly responsible to a central authority, as, for example, County and Town Clerks officiating as Registration Officers for the parliamentary constituencies, and Sheriffs and Mayors officiating as Returning Officers for the elections.

Civil Defence, the organization of which was so important during the Second World War and the early post-war period, was essentially a national service in which the major local authorities, in close co-operation with the police authorities, played a leading part and were directly responsible to the Secretary of State, who was empowered to determine their functions by regulations, with the safeguard that these had to be approved by affirmative resolution in both Houses of Parliament.

Under statute responsibility for the several types of highway is allocated to the Minister of Transport (now the Secretary of State for the Environment) and the various local authority Councils, as Highway Authorities. The Minister, who is responsible for the principal routes, may delegate his functions to the local authorities, who will be entitled to reimbursement for the expenses incurred (as distinct from any grants due from the Exchequer for services for which they are themselves responsible).

A much longer-standing government function, namely the Registration of Births, Deaths, and Marriages, is the responsibility of a special Crown appointee, the Registrar-General for England and Wales. (There are separate authorities for Scotland, Northern Ireland, the Channel Islands and the Isle of Man.) Originally, under the Poor Law Act, 1834, the responsibility of the Boards of Guardians, the task of registration in the localities was, under the Local Government Act, 1929, transferred, together with the major poor law responsibilities, to the County and County Borough Councils. In each of these local government areas there is one or more registration districts under Superintendent-Registrars, each district being further divided into sub-districts under a Registrar of Births and Deaths, who may or may not be responsible for the registration of marriages. These Superintendent-Registrars and Registrars are appointed by the local authority, but they hold office at the pleasure of the Registrar-General, to whom they are responsible for the administration of the service.

The major local authorities have had responsibilities for the registration and licensing of mechanically-propelled road vehicles and their drivers as far back as 1903, before the motor car had become a real problem. The system was more recently reconstituted under the Vehicles (Excise) Act, 1962, and is regulated by Order in Council. In discharging their functions the local authorities and their officers exercise the powers of Commissioners of Customs and Excise, as well as certain powers of HM Treasury in connection with the imposition and remission of penalties in relation to excise licences. Duties levied and fees received by the local authorities are paid into the Exchequer, out of which their expenses are met. The actual work is carried out in accordance with regulations made by the responsible Minister. As a consequence of the computerization of the system which has now been planned, the Vehicle and Driving Licences Act, 1969 has authorized the centralization of the system under the Minister of Transport (now Secretary of State for the Environment). This involves the taking over of the 189 Local Taxation Offices in England, Scotland, and Wales, hitherto run by the local authorities, and the assimilation of their staffs by the Civil Service. Under the new arrangement, with its computer centre at Swansea, the local network will be reduced to some eighty offices. The Minister is authorized to take over full responsibility from 1 April 1971, but the local authorities are expected to continue to participate on an agency basis up to such time as the new system is operational, which is expected to be between three and five years thereafter.

*   *   *

In conclusion, it is apparent that the relations between the local authorities and the central government are varied and somewhat incoherent; in the main annoying rather than oppressive to the former. There are in practice a range of intermediate stages between complete local authority autonomy and full agency. A case exists for a more clear-cut division between those services for which the localities are completely responsible and those in which they act, for administrative convenience, as agents of the centre; distinct financing arrangements being established for each category.

FURTHER READING

Introductory

This again is an important topic on which all the general works on local government will have something useful to say. Among the texts already mentioned C. A. Cross' *Principles of Local Government Law* (Sweet & Maxwell, 1966) contains valuable material on the subject. The problems are authoritatively discussed in Volume 1 of the Maud *Report on Management of Local Government* (HMSO, 1967). The main responsible Departments are dealt with in two volumes of the New Whitehall Series, namely *The Ministry of Housing and Local Government* by Dame Evelyn Sharp (Allen & Unwin, 1969) and *The Scottish Office*, by Sir David Milne (Allen & Unwin, 1957).

Historical and Advanced

The subject is comprehensively discussed in D. N. Chester's *Central and Local Government: Financial and Administrative Relations* (Macmillan, 1951), and in J. A. G. Griffith's more up-to-date *Central Departments and Local Authorities* (Allen & Unwin, 1966). Part 2 of the latter deals specifically with the following selected topics: Primary and Secondary School Building, Highways, Housing, Planning, Children's Services, and Health and Welfare Services. A good deal of information on the subject is to be gleaned from specialist works on the several services (in particular, education, health, planning, and police). The problems were examined from a regional viewpoint by a West Midland Group in *Local Government and Central Control* (Routledge, 1956).

The following official papers are still worth looking at: *First* and *Second Reports of the Local Government Manpower Committee*, Cmd. 7870 and Cmd. 8421 (1950/51), *First* and *Second Reports of the Scottish Local Government Manpower Committee*, Cmd. 7951 and Cmd. 8658 (1950/52) and *Local Government and Central Departments in Scotland*, Cmnd. 445 (1958), all published by HMSO.

CHAPTER FOUR

Local Government: The Changing Pattern

As we have seen, with the exception of London which was re-organized in 1963, there has been no major reconstruction of the local government of England and Wales since the present structure was completed with the legislation of 1888 and 1894. Scotland introduced a substantial change in 1920, when the Districts were constituted and the Parishes abolished. Functional readjustments to satisfy technological advances, demographic changes, and new government policies have nevertheless brought about abundant modifications in the existing structure and responsibilities, so that no one with any knowledge of the situation would confuse the system today with what it was at the beginning of the century. It is in fact remarkable that local government as constituted has been able to stand up so effectively to the strains—technological, social, and economic—that have borne upon it. The problem of evolving a local government system sufficiently flexible to cope with such strains and to accommodate the needs of different services subject to varying technical requirements was already receiving attention long before the present complex situation had emerged: note for example the Webbs' ingenious unit plan to which brief reference has been made.

As part of the normal working of the system changes in the status and area of existing local authorities have been provided for, but in no uniform way. Formerly a Borough of sufficient population (successively raised from a minimum of 50,000, to 75,000 and then to 100,000) could obtain County Borough status by private Act of Parliament, but, since such changes were bound to reduce the rate income of the County out of which the new County Borough was to be carved, such changes were invariably resisted vigorously by the Counties affected. Periodical reviews by the Counties of the several County Districts within their own boundaries were first authorized under the Local Government Act, 1929 and the Counties also have similar powers with respect to the Parishes. Rural and Urban District Councils could seek a charter of incorporation by petition to Her Majesty, a difficult and uncertain undertaking that had to surmount a series of legal and publicity hurdles, which had been created to ensure that the interested parties should have their say, and in fact strong opposition had to be met from many directions. However, the pattern has been changing all the time and different approaches have been adopted successively to cope with piecemeal modifications and more general reforms. The best way to see how the stage of acute crisis has been reached in the sixties will be briefly to look at these several approaches since the Second World War.

POST-WAR INVESTIGATIONS AND REVISIONS

Even before the war ended the Coalition Government had issued, in 1945, a White Paper on *Local Government in England and Wales during the Period of Reconstruction* (Cmd. 6579) in which many of the post-war problems were foreshadowed, including the trend towards wider areas of administration, transfer of certain major services away from local government, increasing financial burdens on ratepayers, methods of initiating area changes, and it was proposed to establish, on a more or less permanent basis, a Local Government Boundary Commission to undertake readjustments connected with County reviews and, where necessary, with existing Counties and County Boroughs. Such a Commission was set up by Act of Parliament before the end of the year.

The Local Government Boundary Commission were authorized to review the boundaries of local authorities in England and Wales, except London and Middlesex, but not to reallocate functions. They were empowered, after due investigation, to propose changes which, after proper advertisement and local inquiry, they could embody in an Order. In the case of Counties and County Boroughs such an Order was to be laid before Parliament. The Commission made extensive investigations and reported their findings in their three Annual Reports for 1946, 1947, and 1948. The *Report of the Local Government Boundary Commission for the Year 1947* (HMSO, 1948) is of particular interest. In it the Commission proposed an extensive revision of the existing system, embodying both single tier and two-tier arrangements. The existing Administrative Counties, with revised boundaries where necessary, were to continue as New Counties. The larger County Boroughs were to continue as 'all-purpose' authorities, but a category of New County Boroughs was to be introduced for County Boroughs with a population of between 60,000 and 200,000, which would be 'most purpose' authorities, leaving a few services in these areas to the New County authorities. Non-county Boroughs would continue as County Districts, but the distinction between the Urban and Rural Districts would be abolished. Some of these proposals fell within the terms of the existing legislation, but for others new powers and legislation would be needed. In any case the Commission had come to the conclusion that their powers were insufficient to achieve the objectives of the 1945 Act and they recommended that the position should be reviewed. The Government was not prepared to proceed on the lines suggested and in 1949 the Boundary Commission was wound up, leaving little but its interesting reports to show for its considerable efforts.

In the meantime two trends were significantly influencing the situation: (1) a reaction on the part of the local authority Councils against the introduction of larger regionally based areas that were being advocated in some quarters as a desirable local government development, a proposal that was prejudiced at the time by critical local impressions of the wartime Regional Commissioner system, designed for a quite different emergency purpose which fortunately had never developed, and (2) the development of the legislature's practice of switching certain functions away from second-tier authorities and concentrating them upon the Counties and County Boroughs: for example, in Education, Health, Police and Fire Services, and Town and Country Planning.

The need to remodel the local government system became more and more insistent as the pressures upon the authorities continued to mount and new problems to emerge, and the question of reform

could not be ignored for long, although it was clear that the pro-
tagonists of change were seriously divided on the solution to be
desired. The Government made new proposals for such reform in
White Papers issued in July 1956 (Cmd. 9831) and May 1957
(Cmnd. 161). In 1958 a new Local Government Act covered (1)
revision of the system of Exchequer grants, (2) introduction of
special machinery to review local government areas, and (3) extension
of the scope for delegation of functions by Counties to the County
Districts.

Under the new legislation separate Local Government Commissions were set up for England and for Wales. Their duties were
again restricted to the review of structure, except in certain Special
Review Areas, where the Commissions could also deal with functions. These Special Review Areas were the conurbations, a term
generally applied to widespreading congested urban areas, which
were designated for the purposes of the Act as Tyneside, West
Yorkshire, South-East Lancashire, Merseyside, and West Midlands,
but others could be added on representations by the Commission to
the Minister of Housing and Local Government. The areas mentioned were characterized by the variety of their local administration,
which had grown under the general rules and practices without
taking account of the conurbations' special needs, usually with
chaotic results.

To facilitate a solution to the local government problem the
Minister was empowered to give effect to the Local Government
Commissions' proposals, or in default of such could himself initiate
necessary changes. Regulations issued under the Act for the guidance
of the Commissions requested them, in their aim to establish
'effective and convenient local government', to pay attention to the
following matters: (a) community of interest; (b) development and
expected development; (c) economic and industrial characteristics;
(d) financial resources measured in relation to financial need; (e)
physical features, including suitable boundaries, means of communication and accessibility to administrative centres and centres of
business and social life; (f) population—size, distribution, and
characteristics; (g) record of administration of the local authorities
concerned; (h) size and shape of the areas of local government; and
(i) wishes of the inhabitants.

Provision was also made for the immediate review by the County
Councils of the boundaries of the County Districts within their areas

and for subsequent reviews to be made at ten-year intervals. New Boroughs were to continue to require the approval by the Privy Council of a petition to the Crown for incorporation, while County Boroughs were to need a population of at least a hundred thousand and to proceed by promotion of a Private Bill (but in view of the changes to be undertaken immediately by the Local Government Commissions this procedure was to be suspended for fifteen years from commencement of the Act).

London continued to receive separate attention. A Royal Commission under the chairmanship of Sir Edwin Savory Herbert thoroughly examined the position from 1957 to 1960. *The Report of the Royal Commission on Local Government in Greater London* (Cmnd. 1164) was presented to Parliament in October 1960 and, despite vigorous opposition in many quarters, its recommendations were substantially embodied in the London Government Act, 1963. The existing London area was to be extended to take in adjoining built-up areas of the Home Counties and on 1 April 1965 the new local government structure replaced the existing local authorities in the extended area (comprising the London County Council, the twenty-eight Metropolitan Boroughs, and other local authorities, including the entire County of Middlesex with the exception of three small areas protruding beyond the new London area, which went to Hertfordshire and Surrey). Only the City of London retained its existing structure and ancient privileges.

The new two-tier structure consists of (1) an elected Greater London Council, responsible for certain functions requiring a wide area of administration, notably town planning and traffic management, and interesting new responsibilities for co-ordination, research, and information, (2) thirty-two enlarged 'most purpose' elected London Boroughs, and the City of London, responsible for all other local government functions, except for (3) education, which in the case of the central area is now administered by a single Inner London Education Authority, managed by a Committee of the Greater London Council.

The new system designedly places the emphasis on the second-tier authorities, but the task of the Greater London Council, with something of the status of a regional authority, is greater than that of any other local authority in Britain, while its importance is enhanced by the fact of its overall responsibility for a national capital, bound to stand as an example to others both at home and abroad. During

1969 the Greater London Council took over responsibility for London Transport, working through the London Transport Executive.

In the meantime the two Local Government Commissions for England and for Wales had got down seriously to work, had covered many of the Special Review Areas, and produced a number of interesting reports and proposals. As was to be expected, their aims and definite proposals upset numerous interests vested and otherwise, and brought forth opposition from the existing local authorities. The procedures adopted to ensure proper advertisement and local inquiry, while intended to promote fairness to all concerned, had the inevitable result of slowing down implementation of the changes by the Minister. A strong case could always be made for the maintenance of the *status quo* and few chances were missed by those who felt themselves threatened, or in any way adversely affected, by the proposals as they emerged from the several inquiries. Thus when the English Commission decided that diminutive Rutland was too small to continue as a County, their first proposal that the County should be divided up among its neighbours met with such opposition that they modified their recommendation to the much more sensible solution of combining it as a whole with Leicestershire, but in the face of continued effective resistance from the local people the Minister decided that Rutland should continue as a separate County. In other words his decision was essentially political and not administrative. As the several informative reports appeared it became clear that, by the method of approach laid down for the Commissions, a general pattern of reconstruction was not likely to emerge. Treating the problems of each Special Review Area on its merits, different solutions commended themselves; for example, a two-tier system for the Tyneside Conurbation, whose problems had already been under close review way back in the thirties, and a series of contiguous County Boroughs for the West Midlands.

Proposals by the Welsh Commission, involving drastic revisions to the boundaries of the existing thirteen Counties of Wales and their reduction to seven, met with such opposition, mainly from the traditionalists, that in 1964 a fresh examination was ordered by the Minister. Revised proposals were put forward in a report on *Local Government in Wales*, Cmnd. 3340 presented by the Secretary of State for Wales in July 1967 but progress continued to be slow.

Scotland having decided not to establish a Local Boundary Commission, the Scottish Development Department undertook a survey, and issued in 1963 a White Paper on *The Modernisation of Local Government in Scotland* (Cmnd. 2067), putting forward for discussion proposals on structural reorganization and functional redistribution. But later, action on this was suspended pending further inquiry.

History was to repeat itself. In 1966, the Government-of-the-day, exasperated by the continuing opposition from many quarters to the Commissions' proposals and the failure of any coherent pattern to emerge from their endeavours, decided to replace the Local Government Commission for England with a full-scale Royal Commission, under the chairmanship of Lord Redcliffe-Maud, and also to establish a similar body for Scotland, under the chairmanship of Lord Wheatley.

The activities of the Local Government Commissions were thereby brought to an abrupt conclusion. Certainly some changes had been authorized but these were little enough to show for the Commission's seven years of research, argument, and striving, except perhaps for the large store of information that would be available to the Royal Commission.

An interesting outcome of the current County District reviews had been the introduction of a new type of local authority, through the demotion, under the terms of the Local Government Act, 1958, of certain non-County Boroughs, which were considered too small to carry out the normal duties of second-tier authorities. By assuming the status of Rural Borough, with the powers of a Parish, they were yet able to retain their older and often ancient dignities and to continue to appoint a Mayor and a Town Clerk.

Thus for two full decades after the Second World War, when the demand for radical change in local government was waxing strongly for most of the time, little was done to bring the system up to date. Even from the brief account given here it is clear that this was not for the lack of ideas. The main trouble was that the post-war governments were chary of antagonizing interests whose counteracting objections cancelled out any constructive solution and that such a solution was not easily definable in face of the rapidly changing environment which the new system would have to serve. The local authorities were as active as any in challenging most of the proposals, although in principle they recognized the real need for reform. On the latter point we need only note that the two inquiries, which we are about to summarize, were initiated by the local authorities themselves through their associations.

MALLABY ON STAFFING

The Committee on the Staffing of Local Government, together with the Committee on the Management of Local Government with which it shared a common secretariat, were appointed on 3 March 1964 by the Minister of Housing and Local Government, at the request of the four major Local Authority Associations. The terms of reference of the former were:

To consider the existing methods of recruiting local government officers and of using them; and what changes might help local authorities to get the best possible service and help their officers to give it.

The chairman of this committee was Sir George Mallaby.

The Committee's *Report*, published in December 1966, provided a detailed survey of the local authorities' staffing problems. The Committee were insistent upon the need for improved recruitment, career management, and training in local government. To facilitate the solution of difficulties, in handling such matters by a multiplicity of separate authorities with widely differing needs, it recommended that a Central Staffing Organization should be established to look after their collective interests in the personnel field. Certainly, local government had been backwards in organizing common service agencies, for which there was no doubt increasing scope.

While advocating the extended recruitment of university graduates in the administrative sectors, the Committee stressed the importance of maintaining openings for the ordinary school leaver, who, by means of training and the provision of facilities for professional study, should be enabled to play his full part in his chosen career. It was recommended that a Local Government Training Board should be set up, a proposal that was quickly adopted and, as we have already seen, the new body also assumed the work of the existing Local Government Examinations Board. Principal officers were to be given responsibility for selecting and appointing staff on behalf of the authority 'up to and including third-tier level in the departments concerned, making full use of the advice available in the Clerk's Department' (*Report*, p. 144). It should be noted that this is accepted management theory, but it is doubtful how far it can, or should, be applied in public services, at least without special safe-guards against favouritism or worse!

The Committee rightly insisted that steps should be taken to avoid the employment of highly qualified persons on work which less qualified or even unqualified persons could well perform, a very prevalent misuse of human resources both in administrative fields and in the professions. It was recommended that the Clerk should be recognized as head of the authority's paid staff and responsible for general management and execution, and that his post should be open not only to persons with a law qualification but also to mem-bers of other professions, including administrative staff. He was not, however, to be able to interfere (1) where principal officers were exercising responsibilities imposed upon them by statute, or (2) where their professional discretion and judgement were involved. The authorities were to be given powers to delegate the making of decisions to principal officers.

It was not within the province of the Mallaby Committee to pursue the question of more extensive changes in executive control, which was part of the task of the Maud Committee, to which we now turn.

MAUD ON MANAGEMENT

The Committee on the Management of Local Government, under the chairmanship of Sir John Maud (later Lord Redcliffe-Maud), appointed at the same time as the Mallaby Committee, was given the following terms of reference:

to consider in the light of modern conditions how local government might best continue to attract and retain people (both elected representatives and principle officers) of the calibre necessary to ensure its maximum effec-tiveness.

The Committee were highly critical on three weaknesses of the existing system:

(1) the survival, into a difficult technological age, of the com-mittee system moulded in the nineteenth-century tradition, involving (a) a lack of trust in allowing officials to get on with the job; (b) a normally high fragmentation of the work in numerous departments, which are seldom coherently organized by the Clerk, resulting in (c)

inefficient and undemocratic results, often involving members in spending too much of their time on matters of detail and impeding officers from exploiting their powers of initiative and expert skills;

(2) a loss of faith on the part of Parliament, Ministers, and Government Departments the responsibility of the locally elected bodies, and their capacity to attract the right sort of councillor and official, and

(3) the excessively wide gulf that too often exists between governors and governed.

It was recommended that a thorough reform of the local authorities' internal organization should be undertaken, aiming to ensure that council-members, while exercising sovereign powers and accepting responsibility for everything done in the Council's name, should delegate to officers the taking of all but the most important decisions. Committees of the Council should in future be essentially deliberative and only exceptionally exercise executive or administrative functions. Their number should be significantly reduced, even to as few as six, each dealing with a broad group of subjects. A major innovation should be the appointment, by all but the smallest authorities, of a management board of between five and nine council members, with a wide delegation of powers. The management board, as the sole channel through which business done in the committees reached the Council, would serve as the focal point for the management of the authority's affairs and supervise the work of the authority as a whole. Where the Council was organized on political lines provision should be made for minority representation on the board. Part-time salaries should be made to its members. Local authorities should also appoint a Clerk 'as undisputed head of the whole paid service of the Council' . . . not necessarily a qualified lawyer but chosen for qualities of leadership and managerial ability. He should officiate as chief official to the management board. Chief officers numbering not more than, say, six, should form a team under the Clerk's leadership, and report to the Council through him. Aldermen should cease to be appointed.

Relationships with central government should be loosened, and all matters of internal organization left to the local authority. To this end existing statutory conditions affecting internal administration should be reviewed, as well as ministerial responsibilities where such exist to intervene in the appointment or dismissal of principal officers. The authorities' dependence on central finance should be reduced, and, over and beyond their statutory responsibilities, they should be given 'general competence' to do what they think necessary for the good of the people they serve. A local government control office should be established 'to represent and promote the common interests of all types of local authority in relation both to central government and to the public, and also to serve as a centre of research and information for council-members, officers and the Press.' Closer relations between council and public should be sought, by all means available, to bridge the gulf between 'them' (the local governors) and 'us' (the public) and to increase the intelligibility of local government.

These far-reaching proposals are formulated in considerable detail and with abundant argument, based upon the voluminous evidence and research reports placed at the Committee's disposal, much of it included in the series of additional volumes of the Report (set out in the Further Reading list), which provide not only valuable information on the way the existing system works, but also interesting comparative studies of several systems abroad.

Before the Mallaby and Maud inquiries were complete a new Government had come into office and new steps had been decided upon. The two Royal Commissions, already referred to above, were surveying a much wider field.

ROYAL COMMISSION ON LOCAL GOVERNMENT IN SCOTLAND

Although publication of the *Report* of the English Royal Commission preceded that of the Scottish by some three months the latter's somewhat more straightforward task makes it more suitable for first consideration. Its main features are set out with exceptional clarity in *Scotland: Local Government Reform* (Cmnd. 4150–1, 1969) the *Short Version* of the Report of the Royal Commission on Local Government in Scotland, and this *Short Version* will therefore be summarized here. The terms of reference of the Royal Commission, under the chairmanship of Lord Wheatley, were:

to consider the structure of Local Government in Scotland in relation to its existing functions: and to make recommendations for authorities and boundaries and for functions and their division, having regard to the size and character of areas in which these can be most effectively exercised and the need to sustain a viable system of local democracy.

Setting out to discover 'the heart of the problem' the *Short Version* opens categorically:

Something is seriously wrong with local government in Scotland. It is not that local authorities have broken down, or that services have stopped functioning. The trouble is not so obvious as that. It is rather that the local government system as a whole is not working properly—it is not doing the job that it ought to be doing.

At the root of the trouble is the present structure of local government. It has remained basically the same for forty years, when everything around it has changed. The structure is no longer right, and it needs to be reformed.

There is ample evidence to show that local authorities on the whole are too small. The boundaries pay little need to present social and economic realities. Services are often being provided by the wrong sorts of authorities and over the wrong areas. The financial resources of authorities do not match their responsibilities.

Looked at as part of the machinery for running the country, local government is less significant than it ought to be. It lacks the ability to speak with a strong and united voice. Local authorities have come to accept, and even rely on, a large measure of direction and control from the Central Government. The electorate are aware of this. They are increasingly sceptical whether local government really means government. The question is being asked—and it is a serious question—whether, as an institution, local government is worthwhile maintaining at all.

At the outset the Commission recognized (*a*) that their approach would have to be thorough and radical, since defects in the current structure were too deep for mere patching; (*b*) that any replacing structure would have to be well-grounded and stable, and rest on a foundation of solid principle; (*c*) that the structure would need to function as a whole; and (*d*) that it should reach as far ahead as possible.

Weaknesses in the existing system that would have to be rectified included: excessive complexity of authorities; considerable variations in type and function; expensiveness; ineffective services (due to inappropriate areas, insufficient population, weaknesses in joint committee control where such is adopted and lack of control by rating authorities of moneys requisitioned by other authorities); lack of independence due to excessive central supervision; and lack of interest on the part of electors.

It was decided, therefore, that four main objectives should be kept in view:

(i) *Power*. 'Local government ought to play a more important part in the running of the country. It should be able to take on more responsibilities, and be less dependent on Central Government. This involves accepting a greater share of the financial burden (leaving less to be contributed by the taxpayer). It should be capable of pulling together as a whole.'

(ii) *Effectiveness*. 'Every local government service should operate on a scale which allows it to function properly, providing high standards of service, good value for money, flexibility to cope with future changes, and co-ordination of services that affect one another.'

(iii) *Local Democracy*. 'There should be an elected local council genuinely in charge of the local situation, and answerable to local people for its handling of it.'

(iv) *Local Involvement*. 'People ought to be brought as much as possible into the process of reaching decisions. There should always be means of expressing the local point of view. It is not good enough to rely on long range administration by officials at headquarters.'

In considering the three basic factors of (1) functions, (2) areas, and (3) authorities, the Royal Commission came to some vital conclusions.

(1) *Functions*. These they classified as Planning (strategic and local); Personal Social Services (education, social work, and health); Housing; Police and Fire (i.e. the Protective Services); Environmental Services (ranging extensively from street cleansing to food hygiene); and Amenity Services (such as museums, community centres, and parks). Certain of these services would have to be provided over much wider areas than had hitherto existed in Scotland, while others would have to be more locally administered.

(2) *Areas*. Local government services should be provided over areas that corresponded with genuine communities, natural groupings of population with interests and allegiances in common. Such communities could best be defined in terms of an area focusing on a town which forms its main centre, and to which the inhabitants of the area travel for business, shopping, and recreation. Thus the distinction between town and country could not be maintained. The

four levels of community existing in Scotland—parish, locality, shire, and region—were the most likely bases for creating local government and assigning functions.

(3) *Authorities.* 'A local authority is not just a body supplying services over a certain area. It is part of a system of local democracy.' This presumed three special features:

(*a*) *Independence,* involving direct election, self-financing, and the exercise of a suitable range of functions in its own right.

(*b*) *Viability,* to be strong enough, administratively and financially, to do the job well; to be able to attract good candidates, and to induce people to turn out to vote.

(*c*) *Community-based,* for 'unless its area corresponds with a genuine community, people will not think it is *their* authority.'

Having considered the three types of structure that might be suitable for the new system—namely, a system of 'all-purpose' authorities, a 'tier' system, or an all-Scotland authority—the Commission decided that, both on the score of flexibility and wide support, a 'tier' system (which they also favoured) was the most promising. It was therefore proposed that there should be an upper tier of seven Regional Authorities (Highlands, North-East, East, South-East, Central, West, and South-West) and a lower tier of thirty-seven 'shire' level District Authorities.

The Regional Authorities would deal with all large-scale services—comprising strategic planning, impersonal services and housing, and also social services—leaving to the second-tier District Authorities certain smaller scale services, such as local planning and redevelopment, housing improvement, libraries, environmental and amenity services, and the various regulative duties. The two sets of authorities would be independently elected and have their own means of raising finance, but, while they would carry out the designated functions in their own right, in a number of matters they would have to work closely together.

The new local authorities would consist of the elected councillors, working through a managerial group of their members, responsible for co-ordinating policy and its execution. There should also be effective co-ordination on the departmental side under a chief officer with real responsibility. The actual scheme for organizing the council business would be for each council to decide. Both elected members and officials should learn to delegate matters 'to the lowest and most local level consistent with the nature of the problem involved'.

Special attention should be given to development of effective communications with the community, and relations with the Central Government should be completely reviewed and radically loosened, responsibility for oversight of departmental arrangements affecting local government being concentrated in one branch of the Secretary of State for Scotland's Departments.

In addition, it was recommended that Community Councils should be established, at the option of the local communities. These would not be local authorities. Their main tasks would be to give expression to local opinion and to improve the amenity of their areas, but they would be competent to run certain services locally, by arrangement with the District and Regional Authorities, and to maintain traditional and ceremonial functions.

ROYAL COMMISSION ON LOCAL GOVERNMENT IN ENGLAND

The English Royal Commission, under the chairmanship of Lord Redcliffe-Maud, had a much more complicated task than that of its Scottish counterpart, but it was greatly assisted by the researches of the Mallaby and Maud Committees on Staffing and Management, whose reports have already been summarized. The Royal Commission's findings are embodied in a main *Report* of three volumes (Cmnd. 4040) and summarized in a '*Short Version*' (Cmnd. 4039). Its terms of reference were:

. . . to consider the structure of Local Government in England, outside Greater London, in relation to its existing functions; and to make recommendations for authorities and boundaries, and for functions and their division, having regard to the size and character of areas in which these can be most effectively exercised and the need to sustain a viable system of local democracy, and to report . . .

The Royal Commission recommended the replacement of the existing complexity of local authorities by a streamlined structure consisting (outside London) of sixty-one Areas each covering town and country, fifty-eight of which should have a single authority. responsible for all services, the remaining three—centred upon the conurbations around Birmingham, Liverpool, and Manchester—to have a two-tier system of authorities, consisting of a Metropolitan Authority, whose main functions should be concerned with planning, transportation, and major development, and an appropriate number of Metropolitan District Authorities, whose key-functions would be education, personal social services, health and housing. All these local authorities would be directly elected.

The sixty-one new local government areas, together with Greater London, should be grouped in eight provinces, each with its own Provincial Council, elected by the authorities for the unitary and the metropolitan areas (including, in the south-east, the Greater London authority). They would also be able to co-opt members.

Within the fifty-eight unitary areas and, wherever they were wanted, within the three metropolitan areas, local councils would also be elected to represent and communicate the wishes of the different localities in all matters concerning their inhabitants. At the outset these would normally succeed the existing County Borough, Borough, Urban District and Parish Councils. Such local councils would have the duty of representing local opinion, have the right to be consulted on matters of special interest to the inhabitants, and have the power to do for the local community a number of things best done locally. They 'would also have the opportunity to play a part in some of the main local government services, on a scale appropriate to its resources and subject to the agreement of the main authority'.

Thus in three metropolitan areas there will be two levels of authority as in London. But the rest of the country will be covered by unitary authorities. Their special feature is that they marry the planning and development of the area—where people will live and work and shop, how they will get about—with the education, welfare and personal services, so that *all* the main local government needs of *all* the people in the area can be considered from a single centre and provided for according to a single strategy. (*Short Version*, p. 9.)

With regard to internal organization and management a uniform system was not recommended. These were matters for the individual authorities, but it was proposed that two principles should be adopted, namely (1) integration and (2) delegation. (1) Integration, which means ensuring that all the different aspects of a council's work should be looked at as a whole, would call for a central committee to advise the council on its strategy and procedures, co-ordinate the work of the service committees, weigh the relative importance of the various measures each may wish to adopt and ensure that the best and most modern management methods are adopted. (2) Delegation involves a clearer definition of the respective roles of the elected member and the local government officer, the freeing of members from detailed matters, and the day-to-day running of the departments by the officers, who must be trusted to know where the boundary lies between key-questions and the rest.

It was claimed by the Royal Commissioners that their proposals would result in (1) greatly improved service to the public, (2) much more effective use of scarce resources of money and skilled man-power, (3) increased ability on the part of the local governors to meet the challenge of technological and social change, (4) more likelihood that people would recognize the relevance of local government to their own and their neighbour's well-being, and (5) the revitalizing of local self-government throughout the country, so that in England as a whole we would have more sense of taking an active part in our own government. There would be new opportunities for making local self-government a reality, involving a better balance between local and central government and more encouragement to take part.

All this was admirably conceived but, while improvements in the structure and working of local government are bound to bring dividends, it would be a mistake to underrate the importance of public attitudes to life in general and public service in particular in determining the effectiveness of institutions, both existing and projected.

The Royal Commission's Report was not unanimously supported. One member, Mr D. Senior, disagreed with the proposed pattern of all-purpose local authorities and with certain functional allocations, and propounded his own solution. This was considered important enough to have the substantial Volume 2 of the *Report* devoted to it, under the title *Memorandum of Dissent by Mr D. Senior* (Cmnd. 4040–1).

Mr Senior recommended the introduction of a predominantly two-tier system, consisting of 35 directly-elected Regional Authorities, responsible for planning, transportation, development functions (including water supply, sewerage, refuse disposal and other technical services), capital investment programming, police, fire and education; and 148 directly elected District Authorities responsible for the health service, the personal social services, housing management, consumer protection and all other functions involving personal contact with the citizen. There would, however, be four urban areas in which the same authority would exercise both regional and district responsibilities. The scheme would provide for the administration of certain regional functions at district level. Common Councils would be elected at grass-roots level, primarily to act as sounding boards for local opinion, but sharing with both District and Regional Councils a general power to provide non-statutory facilities and services for which the area's inhabitants were prepared to pay through a local precept on the rates. There would also be five Provincial Councils, predominantly nominated by the Regional Councils in the areas, which 'would be responsible for long-term strategic planning and for bringing the needs and aspirations of each province as a whole to bear on the discharge by central government of its responsibility for the healthy growth of the national economy'.

REFORM OF LOCAL GOVERNMENT IN WALES

Taking into account the special problems of local government in Wales—in particular, communications difficulties between north and south and the small size of many of the existing authorities, due to the sparseness of population in the mountain areas—the Local Government Commission for Wales, in their Reports of 1961 and 1963, had put forward proposals for the replacement of the existing 13 Counties by 5 (later revised to 7) new Counties, and recommended the retention, with certain readjustments, of the County Boroughs of Cardiff, Newport, and Swansea. The County Borough of Merthyr Tydfil was to be reduced to non-county status. Not surprisingly these proposals met with a good deal of opposition, and action was suspended.

Following the abandonment of the two Local Government Commissions for England and for Wales, the question of Welsh reform was in 1965 handed over by the Secretary of State for Wales to an Inter-Departmental Working Party (consisting mainly of senior officials of the interested Government Departments). Because of the special nature of Wales' problems their consideration was excluded from the purview of the two major Royal Commissions appointed in 1966 for England and for Scotland. The Working Party's proposals were published in the Secretary of State's White Paper, *Local Government in Wales* (Cmnd. 3340, inappropriately issued in a blue cover) which was presented to Parliament in July 1967.

The White Paper repeated the Local Government Commission's

proposals for the County Boroughs and returned to the original plan for five Counties, made up as follows: *Gwynedd* (Anglesey, Caernarvonshire, Denbighshire, Flintshire, and Merioneth); *Powys* (Montgomeryshire, Radnorshire, and Breconshire); *Dyfed* (Cardiganshire, Carmarthenshire, and Pembrokeshire); *Glamorgan* (as at present, but including Merthyr Tydfil and excluding the Rhymney Valley); and *Gwent* (Monmouthshire, with the Rhymney Valley). The new Counties would be divided into a reduced number of Districts (36 in place of the existing 164), which were no longer to be classified into distinct urban and rural categories. An interesting proposal was that a Welsh Staff Commission should be introduced 'to consider and keep under review arrangements for the recruitment and transfer of all local government employees' and other staff problems arising from the reorganization.

The Working Party were also concerned with the provision of means for dealing with broad problems at an all-Wales level. An advisory Council for Wales, to express Welsh opinion, had been appointed in 1949 and subsequently replaced by the Welsh Economic Council, introduced in 1965 as part of the new economic planning machinery. These arrangements, however, had left a gap, particularly with regard to cultural matters. It was therefore proposed to crown the new structure with an all-Wales advisory and promotional body, to be known as the Welsh Council, replacing the Welsh Economic Council but with wider functions, including power to co-ordinate the activities of existing authorities in Wales, such as the Development Corporation for Wales, the Wales Tourist Board, and the Welsh Arts Council. It was to be appointed by the Secretary of State, after appropriate consultations, and to be assisted by the secondment of Civil servants, and perhaps of local government officials. These proposals were also met with a good deal of opposition.

To deal with certain objections with regard to South Wales the Government published a further White Paper on *Local Government Reorganization in Glamorgan and Monmouthshire* (Cmnd. 4310, 1969). This proposed replacement of the existing Counties of Glamorgan and Monmouthshire, together with the associated County Boroughs, by three unitary authorities on the pattern recommended by the Radcliffe-Maud Commission for England, covering Cardiff and East Glamorgan; Swansea and West Glamorgan; and Newport and Monmouthshire, respectively.

[The complexities of local government reform in Wales are

instructively summarized and discussed in an article by J. E. Trice on 'Welsh Local Government Reform—An Assessment of *ad hoc* Administrative Reform', in *Public Law*, 1970, pp. 277–97.]

SEEBOHM ON THE SOCIAL SERVICES

In the meantime in 1965 a committee, under the chairmanship of Mr Frederic Seebohm, had been appointed 'to review the organization and responsibilities of the local authority personal social services in England and Wales, and to consider what changes are desirable to secure an effective family service'. The *Report of the Committee on Local Authority and Allied Personal Social Services* (Cmnd. 3703) published in 1968, had an important bearing on the current movement for local government reform.

The Committee's inquiry covered important social services as well as those included in the National Health Service—i.e. children, education, housing, and welfare—and their problem therefore transcended the scope of the Local Health Authorities' part in the NHS. Their main conclusion was that the several services, then distributed among several departments of the local authorities (Counties and County Boroughs), served by different groups of officials and experts, were ill-co-ordinated and needed to be brought together in each authority under a new Social Service Department equipped to provide a comprehensive service. The adoption of such a plan, for which the Seebohm Committee made a good case, would certainly affect any proposed reorganization of the NHS. Another of the Committee's proposals—namely, that there should be one central Government Department responsible for relationships between the central government and the new local social service departments, as well as for providing the overall national planning of these social services, social intelligence and research—would not be compatible with the system of control needed for an integrated National Health Service. The members of the Seebohm Committee, dedicated enthusiasts for their field of social activities and convinced of the need for much better co-ordination in this field, fell into the common error of imagining that what seemed best on the ground would be equally applicable at the centre, where, to satisfy all the numerous proposals of this sort, depending very much upon the particular viewpoints of their advocates would indeed, if acted upon,

D

lead to a chaotic patterning of the Central Administration, reminiscent of the lilliputian outcome instanced in the Haldane Report.

The Seebohm Committee's proposals, so far as they affected the local authorities, have been substantially introduced under the Local Authority Social Services Act, 1970, which laid upon the responsible authorities (Councils of Counties, County Boroughs, and London Boroughs, and the Common Council of the City of London) the duty of establishing a social services committee, with a majority of Council members, but with power to co-opt suitable outsiders. The Councils were to appoint a Director of Social Services, with qualifications as prescribed by the Secretary of State for Social Services and an adequate staff, to co-ordinate the wide range of social services (as listed in the Act) which had already been assigned to the local authorities under numerous Acts of Parliament. In exercising these functions the Councils were to be subject to the Secretary of State's guidance. It will be observed that this legislation runs against the Maud Committee's proposal that local authorities should be relieved of detailed statutory prescription affecting internal management and the appointment of staff.

PROGRESS ON GENERAL REORGANIZATION

Following the publication of the English Royal Commission's proposals, the Government announced its acceptance of the three main principles, namely:

... that a major rationalization of local government was called for, that a marked reduction in the number of units with executive responsibility was needed, and that the anachronistic division between two and country should be ended.

This was followed up by the publication, in February 1970, of a White Paper setting out in detail the Government's proposals for *Reform of Local Government in England* (Cmnd. 4276). These followed substantially the Royal Commission's plan for a single-tier system, with certain modifications and amplifications. It was intended to put in hand preparation of the necessary legislation without delay, but expected that it would take three or four years to complete the reform. A statement for Scotland was promised, and the existing proposals for Wales were currently under review.

It should be emphasized that, while the urgency of reform was generally accepted and the Government's endorsement of the Royal Commission's plan was widely supported, there were many who would have preferred the two-tier alternative and no doubt the White Paper proposals would have come under heavy criticism in the consultative stage.

However, the calling of a general election in June 1970 and the consequent change of Government put the problem back into the melting-pot. It could at least be said that the new Government had abundant information on which to shape its own proposals.

Only in Northern Ireland, under the urgent spur of political and social unrest, had a more advanced stage in local government reform been reached before the end of 1970. During December the Prime Minister of Northern Ireland announced his Government's acceptance of proposals[1] to replace the existing system of Counties and Districts by a new structure of five Areas (comprising the existing Belfast area and four other Areas each with a population of about 250,000) divided into 26 Districts. Each Area would be under a Board, directly responsible to Ministers for the major functions: each District under an elected Council responsible for such matters as civic improvement, entertainment, environmental health, cleansing and sanitation, gas undertakings, cemeteries and crematoria, enforcement of building by-laws, licensing of dance halls, markets and abattoirs, as well as ceremonial.

In February 1971, the Conservative Government published three White Papers, presenting their plans for local government reform in the several parts of Great Britain. The most radical modification of the preceding Government's plan was embodied in *Local Government in England: Government Proposals for Reorganization* (Cmnd. 4584, 1971), which opted for the two-tier structure and in this respect England, Scotland, and Wales would fall into line should the changes be made as now proposed. A statement of policy in this White Paper (p. 7) is of general interest:

In the Government's view, there will always be conflicts between those who argue for large scale organization on grounds of efficiency and those, on

Report of the Review Body on Local Government in Northern Ireland, 1970. Cmd. 546.

the other hand, who argue for control by a body close to the people for whom the service is designed. The Government obviously must seek efficiency, but where the arguments are evenly balanced their judgment will be given in favour of responsibility being exercised at the more local level.

The new system in England (excluding Greater London) would consist of forty-four new Counties, bringing together all urban and rural areas within their boundaries, and each divided into Districts which would absorb the existing borough, urban district and rural district areas and normally have populations of 40,000 or more. Six of these Counties, covering the main conurbations (Merseyside, South-East Lancashire and North-East Cheshire, West Midlands, West Yorkshire, South Yorkshire, and the Tyne and Wear Area) would be known as Metropolitan Counties and be divided into Metropolitan Districts with a different allocation of functions from the rest. Thus the generally successful County Boroughs would be superseded as all-purpose authorities, and it is on this point that considerable resistance to the proposals seems likely.

As far as possible, existing boundaries would be followed and ways would be sought to retain existing attributes and dignities of the boroughs. Parish Councils would continue in the rural areas and possibly an equivalent arrangement would be available for small towns included in the new Districts.

Functions would be allocated to the Counties and Districts on a standard pattern, as set out in the White Paper. The County Councils would be responsible for the services requiring a wide basis of administration, while the District Councils would deal with the remainder, although on the same principle some matters, such as planning and housing, would be divided between the two levels. Education, personal social services and libraries would be among those services allocated to the County Councils, except in the Metropolitan Counties where they would be assigned to the Metropolitan District Councils. The drawing up of district boundaries outside the Metropolitan Counties would be open to consultation with the localities, and a Local Government Boundary Commission would be established to make recommendations regarding the final pattern of the new Districts, and would subsequently form part of the permanent machinery for keeping local government areas and electoral divisions up to date. Certain administrative details concerning such matters as the term of office of councillors, their allowances, the timing of elections, and the retention or not of aldermen, would be subject to consultation.

The White Paper *Reform of Local Government in Scotland* (Cmnd. 4583, 1971) generally endorses the Wheatley Commission's proposals for a two-tier structure of Regional and District Authorities, except that there would be eight Regions instead of seven, and 49 Districts instead of 37. Interested parties would be consulted on the Royal Commission's proposal that the new authorities should be elected as a whole every four years, the district elections falling midway between the regional elections.

The Welsh Office's paper *The Reform of Local Government in Wales: Consultative Document* (HMSO, 1971) also endorses the two-tier pattern of seven large Counties, each with three to eight Districts (numbering 36 in all). Thus the previous Government's proposal to retain single-tier arrangements for Swansea, Cardiff, and Newport is also superseded. They would form Districts respectively in the new Counties of West Glamorgan, East Glamorgan, and Gwent.

Generally, a number of important matters remain to be settled, in particular finance, about which a Green Paper was issued in July 1971 (see below). Other such subjects include the appropriate structure for a system of local government ombudsmen, the transfer of local authority personal health services to the reorganized National Health Service which is projected, and the effect of the forthcoming findings of the Crowther Commission on the Constitution on the development of regional administration.

The White Papers propose a time-table for the changes: legislation covering the English reforms to be introduced during the 1971–2 session, the new areas to be designated by the end of 1972, the elections to be held towards the end of 1973, and the new authorities to take over on 1 April 1974. In Scotland the respective dates would be a year later.

The Green Paper on *The Future Shape of Local Government Finance* Cmnd. 4741 (HMSO, 1971)—offered 'as a basis for consultation' and 'public discussion of the possibilities set out in it' (para. 50, p. 8),—was presented to Parliament jointly by the Secretaries of State for Scotland, for the Environment, and for Wales, and the Chief Secretary, Treasury. It examines the existing rating and grants-in-aid systems, as well as other favoured additional sources of revenue, most of which have been adopted in one country or another, but are often expensive to collect or the collection of which has to be closely associated with the central tax system. The Green Paper does not of course come to any conclusion—that is not the purpose of a Green Paper—but the argument points towards the improvement and supplementation of the rating and grants methods rather than to any revolutionary innovation.

After such a long search for an improved system of local government in these islands, which was virtually launched by the War-time Coalition Government's *White Paper* (Cmd. 6579) in January 1945, few would deny that a speedy conclusion to the controversy was long overdue. However, in light of recent history, the insistent clash of interests, and the vicissitudes of politics which no government can foresee, it would perhaps still be wise not to expect too much!

FURTHER READING

As the present chapter is largely a progress report on the proposals for local government reform that are already under consideration (1971), and the relevant official papers have been mentioned in the text, it is not proposed to provide an additional list at this stage.

PART TWO

Other British Public Administration

CHAPTER FIVE

Nationalization and the Public Corporation

As explained in Volume I, nationalization in its modern, pre-Second World War phase, had chosen the public corporation as the appropriate means, largely under the dynamic influence of Herbert (later Lord) Morrison, and that socialists in general had come to prefer this means to the former accepted methods of direct management by municipalities or government departments. The post-war trend, as manifested in the Labour Government's general socialization policies, led to the loss by local government, to the new corporate bodies, of certain transport undertakings, electricity supply, gas manufacture and supply, hospitals and new town development.

BANK OF ENGLAND

The first step in this new phase was taken when the privately organized, but largely Government controlled, Bank of England was nationalized in 1946. This was to a large extent a curtain-raiser to the new developments, undertaken specifically to satisfy a party political demand for a move against the powerful City interests, rather than an essential administrative development. It was certainly a portent of what was to follow.

Founded as long ago as 1694 as a private banking corporation to raise money in support of the war against France, the Bank of

England—already the Government's banker—with the passing of the Charter Act in 1844 had become the country's central bank. Thenceforth it was to be steadily built up as the instrument through which the Treasury, as controlling institution in the Government's financial system, would be able to influence the national, and indeed during the immediate pre-1914 era, the world, economy. The new 1946 legislation did little more than formalize a relationship that had developed steadily to meet the nation's changing and expanding needs. Henceforth the Bank's Court of Governors were to be appointed by the Crown, the Chancellor of the Exchequer exercising a general supervision and the Bank in its turn gaining increased powers of direction over the commercial banks, which however were not nationalized. The Bank's assets were transferred to the Treasury, but the Bank retained a good deal of autonomy with which the Government did not normally interfere, though the latter was well placed to ensure that the Governor was fully aware of its financial policies, and that it expected the Bank to use its expertise and special knowledge to ensure that these were fulfilled.

COAL

The coal-mining industry had for long been at the centre of controversy, and even before 1939 statutory attempts had been made to encourage the industry to concentrate and put its house in order. In 1930 a Coal Mines Reorganization Commission had been given the duty of encouraging the formation of larger and more efficient coal-mining units, but the results had been disappointing, for the Commission had been clothed with insufficient power to achieve the objectives expected of it. The Commission's hands were strengthened in 1938, when ownership of the coal seams was transferred to the State, but the Second World War had put an end to further progress. The war's disturbing impact was in effect to prove the last straw and at its termination in 1945 the industry's condition was parlous. Coal supply was bound to occupy a key position in any general scheme of industrial planning, and it is not surprising that the post-war Government should give nationalization of the industry priority in its programme of reform. Its hands in this were certainly strengthened by the report of an inquiry, already put in hand in 1944 under the chairmanship of Mr (later Sir) Charles Reid (Cmd. 6610, 1945), which urgently endorsed the need for a radical reorganization of the industry.

Under the Coal Industry Nationalization Act, 1946, the National Coal Board (NCB) was established, as a public corporation, to take over the coal-mines and subsidiary undertakings and to run the industry as a single enterprise. The NCB consisted of a chairman and eight other members, to be appointed by the Minister of Fuel and Power (subsequently renamed Minister 'of Power' and in 1970 assigned to Secretary of State for Trade and Industry), who was empowered to give the Board directions of a general nature on the exercise and performance of their functions in relation to matters seeming to the Minister to affect the national interest. A minimum of interference in day-to-day management was clearly intended. Compensation to the coal-owners, calculated on a 'net maintainable income' basis, was paid by means of Government stock, but financing was to be made by advances by the Treasury through the Minister. An interesting provision covered the appointment by the Minister of separate Industrial and Domestic Coal Consumers Councils, to consider and report upon matters represented to them by consumers or put forward by the Minister himself.

This Act is of special interest for its influence upon the pattern of subsequent nationalization measures. As is so frequently the case with the development of political institutions, and despite a large amount of general theorizing and philosophizing, the actual changes were highly empirical, certain to come up against unexpected difficulties in practice and to call for radical recasting. The original size of NCB was increased to twelve and provision for part-time membership was introduced by the Coal Industry Act, 1949.

The Acts did not attempt in this case to define the internal organization of the vast consolidated industry which was to emerge. This was left to the Board, which initially reshaped the industry in nine geographically based Divisions (coinciding more or less with the existing coalfields). These Divisions, except for the small South-Eastern Division which was too compact to need further division, were divided into Areas under managers, to whom the necessary powers were delegated. The basic unit was the individual colliery under its own manager. Later, Group Managers were introduced to co-ordinate groups of collieries.

Serious management and organization difficulties led to the appointment by NCB of a committee under Dr A. Fleck to examine the situation. The consequent *Report of the Advisory Committee on Organization,* published in 1955, which led to a good deal of discussion, accepted the industry's general organization but criticized the managerial principles that were being followed. It made a valuable contribution to the discussion of such principles and deserves to be consulted from this wider viewpoint. The NCB subsequently introduced changes on the lines recommended, touching upon such matters as the achievement of a high degree of decentralization (such as already existed) with a proper measure of control from the top through modern management methods (which did not). The duties of the members of the Board were reallocated, so that the chairman and deputy chairman were freed of routine duties, while the six full-time members were to have their individual functional responsibilities, though not full departmental executive responsibility as had previously been adopted and discarded in 1951. The actual membership of NCB from 1955 consisted of the Chairman, Deputy Chairman, six full-time and four part-time members.

With the closing down of less productive collieries and the concentration of production in the more efficient and up-to-date collieries, the five-stage structure which had originally emerged—Board, Divisions, Areas, Groups, Collieries—had become too complicated, the chain of command much too long, and it was decided, as from 1st April 1967, to abolish the divisional coal boards and the groups, leaving a three-layer management structure of Board, Area General Managers, and Colliery Managers.

CIVIL AVIATION

Also in 1946 reorganization under public control of the rapidly expanding air transport industry was undertaken by confirming the existence of the British Overseas Airways Corporation (BOAC), already established in 1939 but immediately taken over for war purposes, and adding two similar organizations—British European Airways (BEA) and British South American Airways (BSAA)—with responsibility for routes in the European and South American zones respectively. BSAA soon failed to fulfil its expectations, and under the Air Corporations Act, 1949 it was merged with BOAC, leaving the latter to share the field with BEA. Unlike most of these post-war schemes of nationalization the air lines were not regarded as a complete monopoly and, with the continuing expansion of this type of travel and the advent of a Conservative Government much less wedded to the policy of State management, private airlines were given increasing scope, and a degree of competition was maintained in this important sphere. The need for concluding reciprocal arrangements with foreign airlines bringing passengers and freight into the country and competing on all oversea routes would have restricted monopoly trends in any case. It should also be noted that in this field, as with the railways, questions of safety militate against full competition, and air services are subject to approval of the Air Transport Licensing Board, a regulatory authority now appointed by the Secretary of State for Trade and Industry, to grant licences to operate regular air services and to control charges on internal routes.

BOAC and BEA are public corporations of the normal pattern, with an organization centrally directed but executively patterned according to the particular airway networks which the corporations control, requiring offices and agencies in many places at home and abroad and close intercommunication, increasingly computerized, with other airway undertakings and forming a closely interrelated worldwide system. Each corporation originally had a Chairman, a Deputy and from five to eleven members, appointed by the responsible Minister (now the Secretary of State for Trade and Industry). Subsequent changes added a part-time Deputy Chairman to BOAC and reduced the total membership of BEA by two to between three and nine and its Deputy Chairman to part-time status. Co-ordination between the two Boards was improved in 1963 by arranging that the Chairman of each should be a member of the other.

The state of the industry was examined by a special Committee of Inquiry into Civil Air Transport, appointed in 1967 under the chairmanship of Sir Ronald Edwards, which reported in May 1969 (Cmnd. 4018). Later in the year the Government followed up with a White Paper on *Civil Aviation Policy* (Cmnd. 4213), accepting generally the Committee's findings and making definite proposals for the improved integration and working of the airlines, but action on the lines proposed in the White Paper was suspended by the change of Government in June 1970.

However, the new Conservative Government is following a similar policy and, under new legislation (1971) it is proposed to introduce a Civil Aviation Authority with general responsibility for the industry and a British Airways Board to exercise strategic control of the public sector authorities, BEA and BOAC.

The several airlines use airports provided by other authorities, privately or publicly managed. In Britain many of these airports have been developed by the neighbouring local authorities, an interesting late development of municipal enterprise to meet an expanding need of considerable importance to the local community. The main airports on the other hand have been nationally developed and up to 1965 were managed by the responsible Government Department on Civil Service lines. Under the Airports Authority Act, 1965, the British Airports Authority (BAA) was constituted to take over and manage the four major airports of Heathrow, Gatwick, Prestwick, and Stansted. The corporation pattern here is similar to the others discussed, the Board consisting of a part-time Chairman, a part-time Deputy and four to eight members, part or full time, now appointed by the Secretary of State for Trade and Industry. Under the present arrangement two of the six members are full time and fill the posts of Chief Executive and Financial Controller respectively. Provision is made on the Executive for the participation of the General Managers of the four airports. Obviously, co-ordination of the ground services for air transport is an important public responsibility, whose inevitable growth is likely in future to greatly extend the scope of the central authority.

INLAND TRANSPORT

In planning to bring rail, road, and inland waterways transport into one national scheme, the post-war Government were attempting a much more complicated task than that presented by the other industries chosen for nationalization. It is true that a sort of sample experiment on the proposed lines had already been successfully undertaken with the establishment of the London Passenger Transport Board in 1933, and the main line railways, still in the hands of four major companies, had already been subjected to central control during two world wars. The task of bringing in the multifarious road services, mostly locally based and shared between the public and private sectors, and to consolidate the different types of inland transport into an effective national network was to prove too great, particularly at a time when the nation's resources were being stretched to the limit and the task of deciding priorities was becoming both more necessary and more difficult.

Under the Transport Act, 1947, the British Transport Commission

(BTC), with a membership of Chairman and from four to eight others appointed by the Minister of Transport (now the Secretary of State for the Environment), was introduced to take over the various transport undertakings and to co-ordinate and develop the new transport system. The Minister was empowered to establish separate Executives, in the form of boards, to act as agents of the Commission in the several functional spheres. At the outset five such Executives were appointed to deal respectively with Railways, Docks and Inland Waterways, Road Transport, London Transport, and Hotels. The new London Transport Executive was the existing London Passenger Transport Board in a new guise, and no doubt its mere existence had had an important influence in shaping the general structure then being established. In 1949 the Road Transport Executive was divided and reorganized as a Road Haulage Executive and a Road Passenger Transport Executive. These Executives, which were to run the several services for the British Transport Commission, enjoyed wide executive responsibility for their services. The Commission was mainly concerned with the shaping of national policy, general co-ordination of the whole field, and the provision of certain common services.

Alone among the nationalized industries transport was to have a tribunal—i.e. the Transport Tribunal—for the independent determination of charges, but this was really the continuance of a system already functioning for the railways, since the Transport Tribunal took over the duties of the old Railway Rates Tribunal, as well as the surviving duties of the Railway and Canal Commission and the Road and Rail Tribunal.

Consolidation of inland transport was still in progress when in 1951, with the advent of a Conservative Government, further action was suspended, and the whole policy of nationalization urgently reconsidered. Under the Transport Act, 1953, responsibility for the various services, other than London Transport, was invested in the British Transport Commission and, with the exception of the London Transport Executive, the system of executives was abandoned. Now directly responsible for running the several services, the Commission set up a series of Area Railway Boards for the management of the railway system, and introduced separate boards of management for Docks, Inland Waterways, and Road Passenger undertakings. Pending disposal of the Road Haulage undertakings, which were to be denationalized, these were regrouped in a number of limited companies. The failure of this policy was to be admitted in 1956, when Road Haulage was reorganized as British Road Services, subsidiary to the British Transport Commission. The new Area Railway Boards consisted of a Chairman and from two to six members, each Board working through a Chief Regional Manager responsible for day-to-day management.

Despite these drastic changes the railways, out-of-date systems that had been further overstrained under the impact of war, still failed to pay their way. In fact, the great revolution in road transport which was now under way had an impact upon the situation such as only a highly efficient and economical rail system could have hoped to master. As part of their drive to cope with the problem, BTC in 1955 put forward a detailed British Railways Modernization Plan, involving heavy investment in modern track, substitution of diesel and electrical propulsion for steam, and widespread re-equipment in other directions. Heavy government financing continued to be necessary and a policy of closing unremunerative lines was introduced in 1961, when an industrialist from outside the industry, Dr (later Lord) Beeching, was made chairman of BTC at a salary twice the normal rate for the post.

A further complete reorganization had already been officially sponsored in a White Paper on *Reorganisation of the Nationalised Transport Undertakings* (Cmnd. 1248, 1960), and it could well be asked whether any sphere of activity could have survived so many structural upheavals in such a short time, without becoming a chronic organizational invalid. Under this drastic revision, authorized by the Transport Act, 1962, the British Transport Commission received its *coup de grâce* and any pretensions of moulding inland transport into a comprehensive national service went by the board. The several services came under individual boards, appointed by and directly responsible to the Minister of Transport, who was to be advised by a Nationalized Transport Advisory Council. The new authorities, independent of each other, were the British Railways Board (with Dr Beeching as Chairman), the London Transport Board still maintaining its pre-war identity, the British Transport Docks Board, and the Inland Waterways Authority, all organized as public corporations. The Transport Holding Company, was also established, to group and hold the shares of the road passenger and haulage undertakings and certain other activities (including British Road Services, Tilling (Buses) Group, Scottish Omnibus Group,

Road Freight Shipping Services, and Thomas Cook and Son Ltd.) which continued to operate under the Companies Acts through their own boards. The new Railways Board was authorized to establish and work through six Regional Railway Boards (shortly reduced to five), to whom specific functions were to be delegated. The railway catering services were reorganized as British Transport Hotels Ltd, a subsidiary of the British Railways Board. The Transport Tribunal survived, but with diminished responsibilities.

Co-ordination of the transport industry had now been brought back to Government policy-making level, and any idea that the whole industry could operate as one abandoned. Nationalization, although substantially maintained, despite the Conservative Government's normal views, was henceforth to be much less intensive and a considerable dispersion of responsibility was prescribed. While the railways continued to be in trouble, the other branches undoubtedly gained from their release from the overriding control of a British Transport Commission which had been forced to give constant attention and priority to railway problems.

However, the advent of a Labour Government in 1964 foreshadowed a further review of the transport situation and, following the issue in 1967 of a series of Official Statements on *Railway Policy* (Cmnd. 3439), *Transport of Freight* (Cmnd. 3470), *Public Transport and Traffic* (Cmnd. 3481), and *British Waterways: Recreation and Amenities* (Cmnd. 3401), a revising statute was passed.

The Transport Act 1968 authorized the establishment of a National Freight Corporation with the task of providing, or securing the provision of, a properly integrated service for the carriage of goods by road and rail within Great Britain. The new Corporation was to take over the responsibilities of the road haulage subsidiaries of the Transport Holding Company and the sundries and freight liner activities of the Railways Board. A Freight Integration Council was also introduced to consider matters arising in the provision and operation of the integrated freight transport service, whether referred to them by the responsible Ministers or initiated by the Council itself. The passenger transport subsidiaries of the Transport Holding Company were transferred to two new public authorities, called the National Bus Company and the Scottish Transport Group.

To facilitate the planning of local transport services on a larger scale the Ministers were empowered to designate Passenger Transport Areas, within which there were to be established new Passenger

Transport Authorities operating through Passenger Transport Executives. The new authorities were to be appointed mainly by the local authorities in the designated area, but the Minister was authorized to appoint up to one-seventh of the total membership. Four of these authorities were introduced during 1969 for the conurbations of Manchester, Merseyside, Tyneside, and West Midlands.

The Transport Act, 1968, also made further provision for the existing transport boards—namely the Railways Board, the London Passenger Transport Board, the Docks Board, and the British Waterways Board—and laid upon the Railways Board and the National Freight Corporation the duty of reviewing, and reporting to the Minister on, the organization and efficiency of their activities within twelve months of the coming into operation of the provisions of the Act, and from time to time thereafter as they or the Minister might deem necessary. The Minister may then give direction to secure the efficient organization and conduct of the activities of the Board or Corporation, and to approve any subsequent reorganization.

Under the Transport (London) Act, 1969, authorizing changes in the organization and management of transport in London, general responsibility for the services of the London Passenger Transport Board was transferred from the Minister to the Greater London Council (GLC), as the statutory transport planning authority for London. The GLC were empowered to appoint a new London Transport Executive, to which initially the members of the existing Board (except the Chairman) were transferred, and to take responsibility for the control of policy, finance, and broad operation.

The time was also considered ripe to take a more concentrated look at the ports, including those already nationalized under the existing British Transport Docks Board. A substantial further step towards consolidation was foreshadowed in the White Paper, *The Reorganisation of the Ports* (Cmnd. 3903), published in January 1969, but action on these proposals was halted with the change of Government in June 1970.

ELECTRICITY SUPPLY

The nationalization of the electricity supply industry embodied in the Electricity Act, 1947, had the advantage of following upon important steps along the road to State ownership already taken before the

Second World War. Furthermore the industry was not hampered by an excessive burden of out-of-date plant like coal and railways, or of serving a comparatively static market like the railways and gas at the time.

Apart from the establishment of (1) the Electricity Commissioners in 1919, as a general policy-making and supervisory body, staffed on a quasi-Civil Service basis, and (2) the Central Electricity Board in 1926, a public corporation empowered to undertake bulk generation of electricity and the construction of a national grid, there had been a further development during the war, under the Hydro-Electric Development (Scotland) Act (1943) which established, as a public corporation, the North of Scotland Hydro-Electric Board, to develop the hydro-electric capacities of the Highlands. At the time of nationalization some two-thirds of the supply side of the industry was already controlled by numerous local authorities as part of their municipal trading programme.

In 1947 electricity generation and supply in Great Britain, outside the North of Scotland area, were taken over from the existing public and private bodies and placed under the general supervision of the British Electricity Authority, consisting of a Chairman and four to six other members, appointed by the Minister (originally 'Fuel and Power' but later 'Power'), and four Area Board Chairmen, chosen in rotation. The Authority was to have direct responsibility for generation, replacing the Central Electricity Board. Distribution was placed in the hands of fourteen Area Electricity Boards in the main regions, each consisting of a Chairman and five to seven members appointed by the Minister after consultation with the central authority. In order to carry out their responsibilities for the generation of electricity the British Electricity Authority established their own executive plants in each region, operating in parallel with the Area Boards, who took over the existing supply undertakings, both public and private, already operating in their area. Consumers Councils were set up in each Area, selected by the Minister from certain groups concerned with the industry, with a Chairman, who became *ad hoc* member of the Area Board.

In 1953 it was decided to separate the Scottish sectors of the industry and to place them under the supervision of the Secretary of State for Scotland. This involved the detachment of the two Area Boards operating in the south of Scotland and their amalgamation into a new South of Scotland Electricity Board, linked up with the existing North of Scotland Hydro-Electric Board, thus consolidating the division of this nationalized industry on a national basis, an arrangement not so far adopted for other nationalization schemes. The British Electricity Authority was re-titled the Central Electricity Authority.

Following the early experience of nationalization and the specific findings of the Herbert Committee of Inquiry into the Electricity Supply Industry, which reported in January 1956 (Cmd. 9672) a substantial reorganization was introduced by the Electricity Supply Act, 1957, which largely restored the pre-war pattern, while retaining full nationalization.

The Central Electricity Authority was abolished and its general controlling and management functions, including finance, were divided among (1) the twelve existing Area Electricity Boards and (2) a new Central Electricity Generating Board, dealing with the generation of electricity on similar lines to the pre-war Central Electricity Board, superseded under the 1947 legislation. A new Electricity Council was established as a general co-ordinating body advisory to the Minister (similar in function to the original Electricity Commission). Its membership, appointed by the Minister, consisted of a Chairman, two Deputy Chairmen (one full-time and one part-time), three members (one part-time), three members from the Central Electricity Generating Board, and the twelve Chairmen of the Area Boards. Consumers Councils were set up in each Area, selected by the Minister from certain groups connected with the industry, with a Chairman who became *ad hoc* member of the Area Board.

The retreat towards the pre-war pattern could have represented a judgment on the precipitancy of the nationalizers, who had too eagerly discarded a system merely because they needed to do something different, or it could have reflected the reactions of the governing Conservative party which preferred its former solution. The new Electricity Council both in its function and membership clearly demonstrated the influence of gas industry experience, referred to in the next section. Structuring the electricity supply industry has been made abnormally difficult by the complexity of changes in supply and demand of electricity, e.g. an increasing demand for more power and need for expansive capitalization, offset by changing power availability in other fields—gas, oil, and nuclear energy—in unexpectedly differing proportions.

More recently the Electricity Council has had its powers extended to include the taking of central policy-making decisions for the industry, including responsibility for the capital investment programme and covering also the programmes of the individual boards. It is also expected in future to keep under review both the organizational structure of the industry and the performance of the individual parts and to make recommendations for the improvement of a Board's performance, without, however, divesting the individual Boards of their statutory responsibility for the finance and efficiency of the undertaking.

GAS

In the original post-war drive to nationalize basic industries the gas industry was not rated very high in the scheme of things. Gas had come to be considered one of the less effective of the fuel and power means whose use was not likely to expand very much. The import of natural gas from overseas and the discovery of gas not far from our own shores were still in the future, although there were new processes available for the production of gas that had good prospects. In this case the interests pressing for the continuance of the *status quo* were much more powerful than in the other nationalized industries.

The Gas Act, 1948, provided for the appointment by the Minister of Fuel and Power (now the Secretary of State for Trade and Industry) of a Gas Council and twelve Area Gas Boards for the whole of Great Britain. The former was to consist of a Chairman, a Deputy Chairman, the twelve Area Board Chairmen, and five to seven other members. Thus, like the electricity supply industry the gas industry was placed under a constellation of public corporations, except that, unlike the original Electricity Commission, the Gas Council was a general policy-making and co-ordinating body with certain common service responsibilities, leaving the executive powers of running the industry firmly in the hands of the Area Boards, whose Chairman constituted the majority of the Council. In 1964, the electricity supply industry approached nearer to this distribution of powers, but opinion has moved towards the position that the gas industry, whose importance has been greatly increased by technological advances and expanding use, now needs stronger direction from the top. The industry's system of Consumers Councils, with their Chairmen as *ad hoc* members of the Area Gas Boards, is similar to that of the electricity supply industry.

In 1965, under a new Gas Act, the Gas Council was given increased powers to co-ordinate the development of the industry on a national basis and empowered to manufacture or acquire gas in bulk for sale to the Area Boards, or in special circumstances to consumers. To cope with these additional powers the administrative sectors of the Gas Council have had to be extended.

IRON AND STEEL

There has been more controversy about the need to nationalize the iron and steel industry than about any other. It was included in the list for nationalization by the first post-war Labour Government, but here, apart from real technical difficulties, there was much less unanimity in the Government party and the conversion was not given first urgency.

Before the war a measure of reorganization of the iron and steel industry had been brought about at the instance of the Import Duties Advisory Committee, established in 1932 to assist the implementation of general tariff policy. During the war the industry had been controlled by the Government, through the supervision of the Minister of Supply, while in 1946 an Iron and Steel Board had been established to maintain a measure of public control. The Iron and Steel Act, 1949, replaced the Board by an Iron and Steel Corporation with authority to take over the securities of certain firms in the industry. Thus nationalization in this instance was to be achieved through a holding corporation, and although concentration of production would eventually have been achieved through amalgamations, the Corporation were directed to secure the largest degree of decentralization consistent with the proper discharge of their duties. The numerous smaller firms, characteristic of the industry, were to be left in private ownership, subject, however, to a system of licensing.

The Iron and Steel Corporation of Great Britain was to consist of a Chairman and six to ten other members, appointed by the Minister of Supply. Following the example of other nationalization schemes the statute provided for the establishment of a consumer council and, to deal with appeals on questions of compensation for the former shareholders, a Iron and Steel Arbitration Tribunal. The Corporation (whose appointment was delayed till 2 October 1950) on 15 February following took over the securities of 298 of the more important companies. However, a change of government brought about a radical change in policy before the system had had time to get under way, and denationalization was authorized in the Iron and Steel Act, 1953. The Iron and Steel Corporation ceased to function on 13 July of the same year. Under the new Act an Iron and Steel Holding and Realization Agency, consisting of three to six members appointed by the Treasury, was set up to perform the task of disposing of the securities which had been taken over by the Iron and Steel Corporation. At the same time a new Iron and Steel Board was established to exercise a comprehensive public supervision of the industry.

There is a good deal to be said for this sort of State supervision of industries which are held to be of special importance to the nation, without going to the extreme of ownership, which seems to add to its responsibilities without substantially increasing its powers. However, with the advent of the new Labour Government in 1964, the situation had again to be reviewed and the looser form of central supervision was again rejected. A new plan for a radical reorganization of the industry was outlined in the White Paper on *Steel Nationalisation* (Cmnd. 2651) which was presented to Parliament in April 1965. The new solution was understandably modified by the changed conditions that had come about since the previous brief period of nationalization. Despite the continued efforts of the Iron and Steel Holding and Realization Agency to dispose of the previously nationalized companies to private owners, one major concern (Richard Thomas and Baldwin Ltd.) and a number of smaller enterprises remained in its hands.

Under the Iron and Steel Act, 1967, the new Iron and Steel Corporation was to be appointed by the Minister of Power (now Secretary of State for Trade and Industry) and to consist of a Chairman and from seven to twenty members, of which ten were actually appointed, made up of three full-time Deputy Chairmen, three other full-time members (later increased to four), and three part-time members. They took over the major firm from the Iron and Steel Holding and Realization Agency and thirteen other large companies from private ownership. The Iron and Steel Board was dissolved.

The management structure of the new Corporation was discussed in their *Report on Organisation 1967* (Cmnd. 3362) issued after the promulgation of the Iron and Steel Act. Members of the Board had been given functional responsibilities, the three Deputy Chairmen dealing individually with Operations, Administration, and Technical Matters. The main structure had been reorganized by arranging the fourteen major firms in four geographical Production Groups (Midland, Northern and Tubes, Scottish and North-West, and South Wales), each with its own Group Board. Subsequently the Groups were each divided into working Divisions.

But this was only an interim step towards a more rational system. In their *Second Report on Organisation* (H.C. 163, 1969) the British Steel Corporation stated:

52. As a result of its experience in operating the present system of multi-product Groups it has become clear to the Corporation that this system by its nature impedes rationalisation and the optimum utilisation of the Corporation's assets. Accordingly the Corporation has decided that the present system cannot continue if the Corporation is to realise in the long run its basic objective set out at the beginning of this report and to discharge its statutory responsibility for seeing that the direction of its activities is organised in the most efficient manner.

53. The Corporation has therefore concluded that a new system of organisation should be established and that, as soon as it is possible to implement the new arrangements, the present type of multi-product Group organisation should cease to exist.

It was proposed that, while certain matters should continue to be dealt with centrally, e.g. capital expenditure, finance, prices and commercial policy, personnel and social policy, development planning, and many overseas activities, the new system should be based on a small number of product divisions.

The outcome of the Corporation's further considerations was the reconstitution, from 29 March 1970 of the industry (on lines similar to the existing non-nationalized Imperial Chemicals Industries Ltd.), into Product Divisions in the place of the Regional Groups, the original firms losing their identity. The new structure comprised a General Steels Division, a Special Steels Division, a Strip Mills Division, a Tubes Division, and two specialist sections covering Constructional Engineering and Chemicals respectively.

A management feature, whose development will be watched with interest, is the experiment in worker participation whereby a number of paid part-time employee directors have been added to the Boards.

These Directors, selected from inside the industry, serve in their personal capacity and not as representatives. They continue with their normal duties, but are required to relinquish any trade union offices during their directorships. The appointments are made by the Chairman of the Corporation, in consultation with the TUC.

Under the new Government (1970) further changes are expected.

POST OFFICE

With the conversion on 1 October 1969 of the long-established Post Office from Government Department to Public Corporation status, the latter sphere of public activity gained a massive extension and the Civil Service lost nearly half its personnel. The change had been under serious consideration for some time, a loosening up of the Post Office's links with the State having been recommended in the White Paper, *The Status of the Post Office* (Cmnd. 989) published in 1960. The White Paper recommended (1) the separation of Post Office finances from the Exchequer, (2) the abolition of the annual Parliamentary Estimate procedure and the Treasury control that goes with it, (3) its replacement by effective, but nevertheless flexible, Parliamentary control, and (4) that the staff should remain part of the Civil Service. These proposals were embodied in the Post Office Act, 1961, and the new system worked smoothly.

As a consequence (during the session 1965–6) of bringing the Post Office within the purview of the Select Committee on Nationalized Industries, that Committee undertook a thorough review of the Department, so far as it fell within the Committee's terms of reference. The *Report and Proceedings of the Committee*, issued on 24 February 1967, supported the proposal that the Post Office should become a public corporation and made proposals with regard to the structure and management of the new authority, and its relations with the Minister. The Government followed up immediately with its White Paper on *Reorganisation of the Post Office* (Cmnd. 3233, 1967), two paragraphs of which set out succinctly the special obligations of the new Corporation and its relationships with Parliament:

11. The essential purpose of the change will fail unless the Corporation has effective freedom of a kind appropriate to a nationalised authority.

Yet the special role of the Corporation's services in the social fabric of Britain, and its monopoly of providing many of them, must carry special obligations. The Government intend that these requirements should be reflected, both in the legislation and in the relationships of the Corporation with its users, with Parliament and with the Minister.

17. The constitution and responsibilities of the Corporation will be embodied in legislation. Its accountability to Parliament will be different from that at present. There will no longer be a Minister answerable to Parliament for its day-to-day activities. But both Houses will have the opportunity to consider the Report and Accounts of the Corporation when these are laid before Parliament every year. The work of the Corporation will be subject to scrutiny by Committees of the House of Commons. Increases in the total amount it may borrow will need to be approved by the House of Commons.

Preliminary steps to the introduction of the new system were taken by an internal reorganization of the existing Department into virtually two separate, largely independent, 'businesses' for Posts and for Telecommunications respectively, each under its own Managing Director, continuing for the time being under the general direction of the Postmaster-General.

The Post Office Act, 1969, abolished the historic Office of Master of the Post Office and redistributed the business of his office among:

(1) a Minister of Posts and Telecommunications with powers of general ministerial control and supervision of the Post Office and certain powers of direction;

(2) the Post Office, reconstituted as a public authority, with corporate status, consisting of a Chairman and six to twelve part-time or full-time members, appointed by the Minister, after consultation with the Chairman, with power to provide (*a*) postal services and telecommunications services, (*b*) banking service by Giro, (*c*) data-processing services, and (*d*) services for HM Government, etc. and local government and national health authorities; and

(3) a Director of Savings, appointed by HM Treasury, to take over from the former Post Office functions connected with National Savings, including the Post Office Savings Bank, renamed the National Savings Bank. The Director of Savings acts as chairman of a Board controlling the new Department for National Savings, which also absorbed the two National Savings Committees (for England and Wales, and Scotland) dating back to the First World War, and is empowered to contract with the Post Office for savings business to be

undertaken as in the past at post office counters throughout the land.

The new Act also provides for the establishment of a Post Office Users National Council for the British Isles, with separate Users Councils for Scotland, Wales, and Monmouth, and Northern Ireland (whose chairmen would serve on the National Council) with power to consider matters referred by the Minister, representations by or on behalf of users, and matters which appear to the Council to be ones to which consideration should be given, and to report to the Minister.

Although the operation of postal services by authorities outside the Central Government is not unique—for example, there were the private postal monopolies of the German princely house of Thurn and Taxis which operated in the Habsburg Empire from 1501 to 1866, and the postal services of Kenya, Uganda, and Tanzania today operated as a public corporation by the East African Community, which developed out of the former East African Common Services Organization in 1967—the normal practice is for the State to maintain close control of such services. The new development in Britain is bound to evoke a good deal of interest both at home and abroad, and may possibly mark a new trend. Whether, however, the basic reasons for the change, namely to get rid of the traditional Civil Service strait-jacket and to introduce the drive of the competitive industry, will be achieved by the new arrangements remains to be seen.

It may well be that the gap between the two forms of management have in this case tended, owing partly at least to prejudice and ignorance, to be somewhat exaggerated. In the first place there has always been a considerable difference between the Civil Service attitudes of the Post Office and those of the rest of Whitehall: in the second place it is by no means clear that the Public Corporation, as it has developed since 1945, has actually developed, or indeed been able to develop, the cost-conscious and profit-seeking attitudes of private industry, where in any case the standard of accomplishment varies widely. There was certainly the advantage offered of cutting down the size of an inflated Civil Service, though not without loss of the energies formerly engendered by the steady flow of Post Office civil servants to other Government Departments, and the loosening up of the Civil Service could have been achieved in other ways; e.g. by dividing it into a series of specialist or functional Civil Services, on the lines of HM Diplomatic Service.

SOME GENERAL CHARACTERISTICS

A common factor in the nationalization activities summarized in the present chapter is the management of the industries by public corporations, an instrument now more popular for this purpose than control by central department or municipality formerly were, although these are not completely superseded. Except for the Bank of England and the steel industry, it will be noted that the several nationalizations referred to have to do with power and communications, a situation that has been considerably reinforced by the transfer in 1969 of the Post Office (postal and telecommunications services) to similar status. In fact the provision of power and communications (in the form of transport and message transmission) constitute such a vital and basic sector of the nation's infrastructure that a high degree of public control is today essential to the efficiency of any advanced society. These power and communications institutions are the equivalent in the social sphere of the nerve and artery networks of the human body. The public corporation, as a managing institution is not of course confined to the nationalized industries, but is widely adopted for the management of other types of public business, as will be seen in the next chapter. This is not the place to go deeply into the actual working of these bodies or to attempt a comparative study of the several industries, fields in which there is much scope for further research and development, but four topics at least deserve preliminary attention, namely Appointment, Management, Personnel and Labour Relations, and Consumer Consultation.

Appointment

The public corporation is a legal entity with corporate rights and responsibilities. Its authority usually derives from statute although in a few cases it has been established by Royal Charter. Its controlling body is a board which, unlike that of the local authority, is not elected but appointed. The appointments are normally made by the designated Minister, or Ministers, though in some instances the Crown, which in practice amounts to much the same thing, except that in the latter case the Prime Minister and Government will take a greater interest in the actual appointments. Alternative methods of appointment have been proposed; for example, through a system of workers' representation but this has not been popularly supported. The Port of London Authority, set up under statute in 1908 and sometimes cited as the first to the modern corporations, has a majority of elected members, but this provides commercial as well as public services and is a special case. In order to introduce a degree of objectivity in its appointment the original London Passenger Transport Board, introduced in 1933, was nominated by a group of six Appointing Trustees, who were holders of specific positions at the time (namely the Chairman of the London County Council, a representative of the London and Home Counties Traffic Advisory Committee, the Chairman of the Committee of London Clearing Bankers, the President of the Law Society, the President of the Institute of Chartered Accountants in England and Wales, and, to fill vacancies after the first establishment of the Board, the Board's own Chairman) but this seems merely to have diffused responsibility without ensuring a special suitability of choice, and was not continued or subsequently copied. Thus we are left with ministerial selection, which is a form of political patronage, but as the Minister concerned can be questioned in Parliament on his actions such choices have usually been made responsibly, although the system could work very differently if an extremist party came into power!

Broad categories of persons from whom selections should be made may be laid down in statute. For example, in the case of the National Coal Board the Minister is to select 'persons appearing to him to be qualified as having had experience of, and having shown capacity in, industrial, commercial and financial matters, applied science, administration or the organization of workers' a wide enough net almost bound to apply in one way or another to any suitable person. The Minister will certainly take soundings in well-informed quarters before making appointments, but the choice is his alone and those chosen do not act in a representative capacity. The appointments are short-term, usually five years, and board members are subject to dismissal for good cause. Many come from outside the particular industry. As was to be expected numbers of experienced businessmen have been selected (though the field here has been restricted by the fact that the public corporations do not pay such high salaries for their top people as are paid in industry) as well as trade unionists, professional men, and civil servants. For example, it was shown in 1956 (Tivey, op. cit., p. 93) that, out of 272 board members, as many as 106 were also directors of private firms. A good case can be made, both on the basis of competence and equity, that more appointments should go to insiders, but this would call for radical modifications in the present approach, as is in fact being tried in the case of steel. Many of the Boards have part-time members who can bring independent views to bear but naturally they are less influential than their full-time colleagues.

Management

Unlike the local authorities, which are generally multi-purpose, the public corporations are specialist bodies concerned with specific functions, techniques, and areas of activity, although these can be broad enough in special cases like the Commonwealth Development Corporation. The boards have both policy-making and managerial, or executive, functions in varying degrees. In the electricity and gas industries, where control is shared among a constellation of corporations, policy-making and execution have to some extent been assigned to different types of authority. The Electricity Council today and the Gas Council, at least up to 1965, when its powers were extended, have been mainly concerned with general policy, co-ordination and certain common service matters, such as information, research, and training. The members of some boards are given direct managerial responsibility for specific internal activities. Both types of board, often known as policy boards and functional boards, have their own advocates. Thus the Herbert Committee on the electricity supply industry were in favour of the former, while the Fleck Committee on the coal industry were in favour of the latter. Usually there is a mixture of the two approaches, and in any case the solution actually adopted will depend upon the basic circumstances and structure of the industry, varying with geography, technology, type of service provided, and even history. For this reason the study of actual organization structures is important and can be extremely illuminating. Co-ordination of a board's business will depend much upon the chairman, who occupies a key-position and has the advantage of seeing the picture continuously and as a whole. Strong chairmen are favoured, and the natural disadvantages of the plural executive are widely minimized by practical leadership. If well chosen the chairman is something more than *primus inter pares*.

The public corporation form aims at combining public ownership with management on commercial principles, and the industries so controlled are expected to pay their way, as the official phraseology states 'taking one year with another'. In the experimental period between the wars this principle was generally advanced for preferring the public corporation to the governmental type of organization, and subject to the industries paying their way it was understood that parliamentary and governmental supervision would be kept to a minimum. Since 1945 much more central control has been introduced and, apart from varying political approaches, it seems that there has been a natural trend for this to increase rather than to diminish. The corporations are expected to charge prices for their services that are sufficient to meet both capital and running costs and also to pay off debts accumulated through the payment of compensation to former owners. In some cases loans have had to be provided by the Exchequer to meet continuing deficits—the railways being the saddest example of this need. However, it is not only the burden of the past that has had to be paid for, but the current cost of providing services that are of a social rather than a commercial nature, and the view is now accepted that for the running of such services the public corporations should receive adequate subsidies from the State. A prominent example of this sort of service is instanced, also by the railways, in the provision of services on lines which provide valuable transport facilities in particular areas that are not remunerative and for which suitable alternative means are not readily available. The Post Office has had to face up to similar problems from the very beginning, when providing certain postal deliveries, or telephone lines, say to farms and small hamlets in thinly populated hill country which obviously cost much more per unit than the general run of services and which therefore, judged purely on a commercial basis, it would pay the authority not to provide.

Personnel and Labour Relations

The boards of the nationalized industries appoint and dismiss their own managerial and operative staffs, who acquire no special status. They are not Crown servants, nor do they enjoy the advantages or suffer the restrictions of civil servants. They occupy the same legal position as workers in the private sector and enjoy the advantages normally available to workers in large-scale organizations, some of which in fact, in such matters as training and joint consultation, are safeguarded in the authorizing statutes. In contrast to the Government Departments their task is not primarily administrative, but the production and supply of goods and services, and they require to employ large professional and industrial staffs, many of whom are members of trade unions operating in both the public and private fields. The boards determine the terms of contract and conditions of service offered to their employees, but these naturally are subject to the normal pressures of the labour market. The staffs of the public corporations do not form a co-ordinated service in any way. Such cross links as exist are mainly professional or occupational.

Consumer Consultation

In order both to weaken the objection that the public corporation is an unrepresentative form of public institution, and to provide some measure of participation to the consumers of the nationalized industries' products and services—which in most instances practically coincide with the community as a whole—Government and Parliament have been concerned to devise means to involve the public in the public corporations' activities. The pattern was set by the Coal Industry Nationalisation Act, 1946, which provided for the appointment by the Minister of an Industrial Coal Consumers' Council and a Domestic Coal Consumers' Council, to represent both the National Coal Board and the consumers of the several types of fuel.

The responsible Minister decides the size of the consumer or consultative councils—normally about twenty—and in making his selections is expected to have regard to representations made by organizations of interests involved. The two councils, in their respective fields, are empowered to consider matters concerning the sale and supply of the various fuels, either on their own initiative or following representations by consumers; to report to the Minister where action appears to be necessary; and to deal similarly with any matter which the Minister himself proposes.

In the case of electricity and gas there are similar arrangements, but in these industries consultative councils are regionally based in parallel with the Area Boards, whose chairmen sit on them as *ad hoc* members. The Area Boards are required to keep the consultative councils informed on their plans and arrangements for carrying out their statutory functions, and the councils may make representations thereon to the Boards. To bring them into close contact with consumers the consumers' councils are required to appoint committees or individuals as local representatives, and to refer to them matters arising in their own areas. If the consumer councils are not satisfied with the Area Boards' handling of their representations they have access both to the Electricity or Gas Councils and to the Minister, either of whom has power to issue directions to the Area Boards. These consumer councils appoint their own staff, but accommodation is provided and costs are borne by the Area Boards. Other nationalized industries have arrangements suited to their particular needs, but the principles are the same.

It would be wrong on the evidence available to write off these consumers' councils as a complete failure, but they certainly have not lived up to the hopes that their introducers entertained and the consensus is one of disappointment. They have had their successes of course, notably in the case of railway closures which raise a good deal of opposition in the areas affected, in which case the consultative bodies have been able to make vigorous representations on the users' behalf. In general, however, there has been a lack of interest and support on the part of consumers for these bodies. This is perhaps not surprising when one considers the similar lack of interest in our local government institutions which, after all, impinge much more obviously and continuously, upon citizens' interests. Lack of information about the consultative councils, of their functions or mere existence, and poor publicity have been singled out as important weaknesses, as undoubtedly they are, but the modern democratic society's lack of civic interest and involvement seem to be at the root of the trouble, and here the educationalists must take a share of the blame. The dual function of these councils to act as both adviser and investigator, has been criticized as importing an incompatible element into their working, especially where their chairmen sit as members of the Boards. Yet it may well be that the mere existence of the councils, even with but lukewarm consumer support, renders the Boards more careful of consumer interests than they would otherwise be, so that the councils act as watchdogs in the public interest almost by default. This is a negative factor that cannot be assessed.

E

There is also the fact that the public corporations are to the public somewhat shadowy institutions which appear to differ little, if at all, from any other large-scale non-governmental bodies, and, as consumers, members of the public are inclined to react to them very much as they react to such privately organized enterprises. Their image is similar, depending individually upon the degree of consumer satisfaction that their management and staffs are able to stimulate. In other words the idea of the socialist philosophers that nationalization would, through a sense of public ownership, induce a new kind of relationship between the new public institutions and the citizen, has failed to materialize. It is true that the several industries discussed here (other than the Bank of England) have competent and forthcoming internal public relations branches which, unlike most governmental agencies (with notable exceptions like the Public Trustee Office, the Savings Department, and the former Post Office), do not find a lot of use for ordinary advertising. The nationalized industries have certainly been effective enough in this, indeed in some directions have led the field, but commercial advertising however well handled is not by its very nature concerned with inculcating a public service approach.

The autonomy of the public corporations has been subject to certain checks, and increasingly as the test of profitability has tended to weaken. A degree of accountability and control has been developed, and this important topic, which bridges the gap between the Government and this branch of the public sector, will be considered in Chapter Seven, after a more extended survey of the public corporation and other autonomous agencies has been made.

FURTHER READING

Introductory

Constant changes make this part of the subject even more difficult than others to keep in focus. Among the general surveys J. F. Sleeman's *British Public Utilities* (Pitman, 1953) is informative and comprehensive. Two recent works that can be strongly recommended are Leonard Tivey's *Nationalisation in British Industry* (Cape, 1966) and W. Thornhill's *The Nationalized Industries: An Introduction* (Nelson, 1968). R. Kelf-Cohen, in his *Nationalisation in Britain: The End of a Dogma* (Macmillan, 1958) takes a refreshingly controversial viewpoint, while a critical survey sponsored by the Fabian Society is to be found in *The Lessons of Public Enterprise* (Cape, 1963), containing contributions by a number of experts, under the editorship of Michael Shanks.

Among the numerous pamphlets on various aspects of the subject issued by the Acton Society Trust, one that provides an interesting introduction to a burning topic, is Lord Simon's *The Boards of Nationalized Industries* (Longmans, 1957). Up-to-date information on the activities of the several corporations is to be obtained from their *Annual Reports*, which are officially published.

Historical and Advanced

For a broader survey of public corporations in the inter-war period T. H. O'Brien's *British Experiments in Public Ownership and Control* (Allen & Unwin, 1937) and L. Gordon's *The Public Corporation in Great Britain* (Oxford, 1938) will still repay study. Also of considerable historical interest is Herbert (later Lord) Morrison's *Socialization and Transport* (Constable, 1933) which deals with the original establishment of the London Passenger Transport Board.

The earlier history of the Bank of England is admirably recounted in Sir John Clapham's *The Bank of England*, in two volumes (Cambridge, 1944), which covers the period from its founding up to 1914. The Bank's present functions and organization are authoritatively surveyed in the *First Report from the Select Committee on Nationalized Industries (Session 1969–70): Bank of England* (HMSO, 1970).

From a comparative viewpoint the establishment of the Tennessee Valley Authority in the United States is of considerable historical interest. C. H. Pritchett's *Tennessee Valley Authority* (Chapel Hill, US, 1943) provides an authoritative account, while D. E. Lilienthal's *TVA: Democracy on the March* (Pen, 1944) contains a philosophic explanation of the project by the Authority's first Chairman.

The most comprehensive and reliable of current general texts on the whole subject is W. A. Robson's *Nationalized Industry and Public Ownership* (Allen & Unwin, 2nd edn. 1962). This may be supplemented by A. H. Hanson's compilation of authoritative texts from various sources *Nationalization: A Book of Readings* (Allen & Unwin, 1963).

On the individual industries student's will wish to consult the specific White Papers and other official reports referred to in the text, and also the detailed reports of the Select Committee on Nationalized Industries, which are mentioned in the Further Reading list at the end of Chapter 7 of this Volume. But there are also certain special Reports on the individual industries which have an important bearing on general principles and policies: notably the Fleck *Report of the Advisory Committee on Reorganization of the National Coal Board* (National Coal Board, 1955), the Herbert *Report of the Committee of Inquiry into the Electricity Supply Industry* (Cmd. 9672, 1956), and the Edwards *Report of the Committee of Inquiry into Civil Air Transport* (Cmnd. 4018, 1969). Two other reports of particular interest are: the British Railways Board's *The Reshaping of British Railways: Report and Maps* (HMSO, 1963) and the British Waterways Board's *Interim Report on the Future of the Waterways* (HMSO, 1964).

CHAPTER SIX

Miscellaneous Corporations and Other Autonomous Agencies

A characteristic of modern public administration is the large number of pluralist bodies in the form of corporations, boards, commissions, committees and similar authorities that flourish on the fringes of the major government institutions, from which they differ generally in being nominated—a product of patronage—rather than elected. Their functions range widely over the production of goods and services, as characterized by the instances discussed in the preceding chapter, through a variety of executive, regulatory, investigatory, informational, and advisory services in almost every field of activity. This is not a new form of public institution. Commissions of various sorts have been set up from early times, rising to a flood during the nineteenth century: some have continued from that period, including the Public Works Loan Board, the Charity Commission and that strange survival, the Royal Commission for the Exhibition of 1851.

Today the number of such bodies is increasing, not only to deal with public activities that are apparently not thought to be suitable for existing governmental bodies, but also to meet a constant call from the public and specific interests for the establishment of new supervisory institutions. For, despite the widespread condemnation by one section of the public of government action in general, usually from an 'anti-bureaucratic' standpoint, requests are being urged almost daily by others for the government to provide aid in and

supervision of new spheres of activity. Thus, for example, governments have come to take a special interest in cultural and sporting
matters formerly held to be solely the concern of the private sector
and individuals.

It would require a separate volume to do justice to this branch of
public administration and only a few examples have been selected for
mention under several broad headings. Most of these bodies fall
under the general supervision of one of the Ministers or Government
Departments, but the degree of the latters' interest varies considerably.

OTHER NATIONALIZATION

It is well to bear in mind that the public corporation, as an instrument
of management, is not confined to the sphere of nationalization,
while nationalization has operated under different forms which,
despite current trends, cannot be ruled out as suitable alternatives in
the future.

Perhaps the most interesting survival of nationalization by
Government Department is the liquor production and supply
activities of the State Management Districts—confined to the
Carlisle, Gretna Green, and Cromarty Firth areas—responsibility
for which is placed, in the first area, with the Home Secretary and in
the others with the Secretary of State for Scotland. In these areas the
public-houses, as well as a State brewery, are managed by civil
servants, under the general supervision of an Advisory Council, with
a membership consisting of selected officials, participants in the
brewing trade, and other experienced persons, appointed jointly by
the two Ministers. This is the legacy of a First World War scheme
to reduce drunkenness among war workers in these areas, where
important munitions works were concentrated, and it is a tribute to
the planners of that time that State Management has been successfully maintained ever since, despite the varying philosophies of
subsequent governments. This long-standing experiment in public
management is now (1971) to be terminated.

The future of atomic power was already being visualized during
the Second World War, when the release of atomic energy was a
priority scientific problem of the military authorities. At first a
responsibility of the Department of Scientific and Industrial Research (subsequently merged into the Ministry of Technology)

it went over to the Ministry of Supply after the war where it remained until 1954, when the growing industrial possibilities of the new power rendered its transfer to an autonomous body, of the public corporation type, desirable. The United Kingdom Atomic Energy Authority was therefore established, ministerial responsibility being passed over to the Lord President of the Council, who at the time had a general interest in science. The Authority was to consist of a Chairman and seven to ten members, but subsequent legislation increased its size to fifteen members plus the Chairman, all appointed by the responsible Minister.

As successor to the branches of the Ministry of Supply responsible for atomic energy development, the UK Atomic Energy Authority took over many of the existing staff and at the outset maintained the Civil Service staffing pattern, although now of course there was ample scope to modify it to meet the special needs of the work. The Minister had the normal relationship of ministers responsible to Parliament for general supervision of public corporations, except that to deal with special considerations arising from the secrecy and danger elements in the Authority's operation, his powers of direction were somewhat wider. The financial arrangements were modified too by the need to retain Exchequer financing through funds voted by Parliament, subject to the annual estimating system, under the supervision of HM Treasury and accountable to the Comptroller and Auditor-General. Thus the UK Atomic Energy Authority remained a sort of hybrid, spanning the departmental and public corporation fields.

OTHER INDUSTRIAL BODIES

There are numerous other public and quasi-public bodies in the industrial field. Of particular interest are the Herring Industry Board, introduced under the Herring Industry Act, 1935, and the White Fish Authority, introduced under the Sea Fish Industry Act, 1951, both established to reorganize, develop, and regulate these two branches of the fishing industry. Their membership is small, three and five respectively, and is appointed from outside the industry by the Minister of Agriculture, Fisheries, and Food, the Home Secretary and the Secretary of State for Scotland, acting jointly. The two Boards submit informative annual reports to the Ministers, who lay them before Parliament.

An interesting regulatory body is the National Research Development Corporation, introduced in 1949 under the Development of Inventions Act of the previous year. It has the important duty of developing and exploiting inventions resulting from public research. Usually the actual exploitation is entrusted to industry, but the Corporation may carry out the work themselves. Advances are made out of the Exchequer, but the Corporation is expected in the long run to be self-supporting. Its membership consists of a Chairman and Managing Director and four to ten other members, now appointed by the Secretary of State for Trade and Industry.

In order to provide for an increase in assistance in areas where unemployment continued to persist, the Board of Trade were authorized under the Local Employment Act, 1960, to designate Development Districts and to provide suitable industrial and commercial premises, loans, and other types of assistance to suitable enterprises. Management of the estates and individual factories, thus financed by the Board of Trade, was to be undertaken by three Industrial Estates Corporations for England, Scotland, and Wales, appointed by the President of the Board of Trade and financed entirely through the normal departmental estimates and under the Board's general directions. These corporations took over the properties and responsibilities previously assigned to five Industrial Estate Companies, which were superseded under the new legislation. General responsibility for these operations, once under the Minister of Technology, has returned to the Secretary of State for Trade and Industry.

Two authorities concerned with employment ought to be mentioned here: namely, the National Dock Labour Corporation and Remploy Ltd., both of which are now appointed by the Secretary of State for Employment.

In 1946 the Dock Workers (Regulation of Employment) Act was passed with the object of continuing the system of decasualization of labour in the ports which had been introduced during the Second World War. The object of the legislation was the establishment of a permanent scheme to ensure greater regularity of employment for dockworkers and to secure that an adequate body of workers should be available in each port for the efficient working of the docks. As the employers' and workers' representatives had been unable to agree on a suitable plan the Minister of Labour and National Service had been compelled, under his statutory responsibilities, to have a scheme prepared. The National Dock Labour Board was established to carry it out. Its membership usually consisted of Chairman, a Vice-Chairman, four members representing dock employers, and four members representing dockworkers. The Board delegated day-to-day administration to a series of local boards, consisting of an equal number of employer and employee representatives, for each port or group of ports. The Board was responsible for the general policy and administration of the scheme and an important duty was deciding the number of dockworkers to be included in the registers of available labour. The employers were also registered. The scheme provided for a guaranteed payment to registered dockworkers not fully employed. The cost of the scheme was met by contributions from the employers, and it was therefore self-supporting. Following the *Final Report of the Committee of Inquiry into certain matters concerning the Port Transport Industry* (Cmnd. 2734, 1967) known as the Devlin Report, the original arrangements were modified to provide for the placing of each registered dockworker in permanent employment with a licensed employer, and thus complete de-casualization of the industry was achieved.

Remploy Ltd. is a non-profit-making company established under the terms of the Disabled Persons Act, 1944, to provide training facilities and employment for registered disabled persons who are unlikely to obtain work under normal conditions. Its directors are chosen from among businessmen, trade union officials, and people with a particular interest and experience in this field. Remploy is, in fact, a productive organization empowered to equip and run workshops, provide hostel accommodation and facilities for home workers. It receives loans and grants from the Exchequer through the vote of the Department of Employment, and its products are sold in the usual way in the open market.

Administrative and judicial arrangements of special interest have been devised to deal with problems of monopoly and restrictive practices. Under the Monopolies and Mergers Act, 1948, the Monopolies Commission was constituted to investigate and report on monopolies referred to them by the Board of Trade, who, in co-operation with other interested Departments and subject to Parliamentary approval, were authorized to take appropriate action on such reports. The scope of the Monopolies Commission was strengthened and extended by new legislation in 1965. In the meantime the Restrictive Trade Practices Act, 1956, had provided for the appointment of a Registrar to keep a Register of Restrictive Trading

Agreements and to bring such agreements before the Restrictive Practices Court, which was also provided for under the Act. The Court may find such restrictive practices contrary to the public interest, in which case the agreement will be void, and the Court can make orders preventing the parties from operating their agreement. However, the rules are modified in respect of agreements of national importance, or relating exclusively to exports. The responsible authority is now the Secretary of State for Trade and Industry.

Under the Industrial Relations Act, 1971, (1) the Industrial Court has been renamed the Industrial Arbitration Board, (2) a National Industrial Relations Board has been set up, (3) the Commission on Industrial Relations, originally a Royal Commission, is reconstituted a statutory body, and (4) the new Office of the Chief Registrar of Trade Unions and Employers' Associations is established to deal with registrations under the Act.

In addition to the foregoing examples in the industrial sphere there are a number of bodies organized as private companies in which the Government has a controlling interest. Examples of such arrangements, existing in 1968, are the British Petroleum Ltd. (through two directors nominated by the Treasury, with certain veto rights); the British Sugar Corporation Ltd. (through three directors appointed by the Minister of Agriculture, Fisheries and Food and the Secretary of State for Scotland, directions in certain circumstances issued by the two Ministers, and moneys provided by the Sugar Board); Short Bros and Harland Ltd., manufacturers of aircraft and components (through appointment of eight out of the twelve directors by the Secretary of State for Trade and Industry, and the ownership of a majority of shares); the Upper Clyde Shipbuilding Group, a holding company operating four shipyards (through appointment of Board, in proportion to Government's holding of shares); and the Cowal Ari Sawmilling Co. Ltd. (through appointment of two Directors, and participation in the appointment of a third Director, by the Forestry Commissioners as debenture owners).

COUNTRYSIDE

Foremost in time as well as in importance, among those public bodies operating in the countryside, is the Forestry Commission, which was often considered by early students of the public corporation as a representative example of that genre. It was set up in 1919, largely to repair the ravages of the nation's natural timber reserves caused by the war effort. The members of the board were appointed by the Crown and some of them had to have specialized knowledge and experience of forestry, but the Commission was subject to directions from the Treasury, who had to find the necessary moneys, and its administration was organized on the lines of an ordinary government department on a civil service staffing basis. Since its job was very much a long-term operation, from which immediate financial returns could not be expected, and which was intimately bound up with considerations of national defence and economic policy, it was essentially a public service with long-term objectives. The Forestry Commission has since the Second World War been placed under the general supervision of the Minister of Agriculture, Fisheries and Food and the Secretary of State for Scotland. It is an autonomous public department covering the whole of Great Britain, whose permanent head, with the title of Director-General, is responsible to the Commissioners, appointed by the Crown, which, like the similarly constituted Boards of Inland Revenue and of Customs and Excise, have become assimilated to the Civil Service, except that in the case of the Forestry Commission an expert element is retained through the appointment of a number of unpaid part-time Commissioners from outside.

In Scotland a Crofters Commission, of up to six members, was introduced under the Crofters (Scotland) Act, 1955, to undertake the task of reorganizing, developing, and regulating crofting in the seven crofting counties in the north of Scotland, of promoting the interests of crofters there and of keeping under review matters relating to crofting. The Commission is subject to such directions of a general nature as the Secretary of State for Scotland may give. This regulatory body had a predecessor in 1886, but that had ceased to exist in 1911, when its functions had been absorbed by the Land Court, which is a special feature of Scottish administration. Crofting is small-scale hill farming which, under modern conditions, depends largely upon the existence of wider services and amenities for its success. It is an important duty of the Crofters Commission to collaborate with other bodies in providing such auxiliary economic and social supporting services. Appointed and organized on similar lines, there is also the Red Deer Commission which is concerned with the conservation and control of that species of deer.

An administrative development of a quite different kind in the same field was the series of Marketing Boards established under the various Agricultural Marketing Acts, going back to 1931. These Marketing Boards, which have been introduced for various commodities (e.g. eggs, hops, milk, wool, and potatoes), are producers' organizations with statutory powers to regulate the marketing of the designated product. The specific scheme has to be approved by Parliament and by a majority of the producers concerned. Such a Marketing Board will have a membership of between eight and twenty-four members elected by the producers, apart from a minority, of at least two and up to one fifth, appointed by the responsible Minister. The object of setting up these Boards is to improve marketing arrangements and to raise the quality of the product, but consumers often object that they create monopoly conditions and enable high prices to be maintained, while those producers who do not support the scheme naturally object to being subjected to regulations imposed by the majority of the industry, though not necessarily the most efficient. This is an example of public administration carried out by members of the community, whose interests are taken to coincide with the general interest, which may sometimes be taking a good deal for granted!

The arrangements for the sugar-beet industry are of special interest. Production and control are looked after by a privately organized company, the British Sugar Corporation Ltd., and a supervisory Sugar Board, in accordance with the terms of the Sugar Act, 1956. The Corporation is concerned with the manufacture of refined sugar from home-grown sugar beet. It is the sole buyer of sugar beet, but, as refiner, competes with others. Three of the firm's fourteen Directors are appointed by the Minister of Agriculture, Fisheries, and Food, and the Secretary of State for Scotland with Treasury approval, one of the three then being chosen as Chairman by the two Ministers, who, in defined circumstances, may give directions to the Corporation, which otherwise acts commercially and not necessarily according to official policy. The Sugar Board, appointed by the Minister of Agriculture, Fisheries, and Food, with Treasury approval, is empowered to raise a surcharge on all sugar in order to finance the Government's commitments to buy Commonwealth sugar and home produced sugar beet, and to buy and sell Commonwealth sugar, in fulfilment of these commitments. Out of the surcharge the British Sugar Corporation receives from the Sugar Board payments representing the difference between the guaranteed price for sugar beet and the commercial price which the Corporation could pay in a free market. The Sugar Board operates according to the Statute, but the Minister has powers of direction in certain minor matters and may, with Treasury approval, make orders varying the surcharge rate, on the advice of the Board. The Treasury and the Sugar Board have minority holdings in the Corporation's ordinary shares.

RECREATIONAL AND CULTURAL

First to be considered under this heading are certain bodies concerned with the countryside whose functions therefore qualify them for consideration under the foregoing heading: in particular the Countryside Commissions and the Nature Conservancy.

A National Parks Commission for England and Wales was established under the National Parks and Access to Countryside Act, 1949, with responsibilities for the preservation and enhancement of natural beauty and for encouraging provision or improvement of facilities for enjoyment. Its members, all of whom, except the Chairman and his Deputy, were unpaid, were appointed by the Minister (latterly of 'Housing and Local Government'). The Commission's expenses were paid out of Parliamentary moneys and its staff were civil servants. One of its duties was to designate areas suitable for National Parks, the actual authority for their creation being given by Order in Council, approval by the Minister. The individual parks were administered locally, in accordance with schemes variously shaped to meet local conditions. Since such National Parks usually extended over more than one county, management was normally placed in the hands of a joint planning board, representative of the several local authorities whose territories fall within the boundaries of the park. A park falling entirely within the area of a single county was normally made the responsibility of a special Park Committee of the County Council.

Good work was done by the National Parks Commission but, owing partly to lack of local initiative often due to shortage of money, the new bodies failed to achieve as much as their original sponsors had hoped for. The Countryside Act, 1968 set out to remedy this situation. The older Commission was replaced by a more powerful Countryside Commission, with functions relating to the countryside over and beyond the areas of the National Parks. Its members are appointed by the Minister, after consultation with local authority associations and other bodies concerned with the countryside. The Countryside Commission is required to appoint a Committee for Wales, partly from its own members and up to four from outside, to whom they may delegate, with the Welsh Secretary of State's concurrence, such functions of the Commission as relate to Wales and Monmouthshire. In addition local authorities were now empowered to provide County Parks, for the financing of which Exchequer Grants were made available. Up to 1969, twenty-five National Parks had been designated in England and Wales.

Scotland had been content to achieve the same aims as the National Parks legislation through existing legislation, but under the Countryside (Scotland) Act, 1967 it established its own Countryside Commission with powers of the type covered by both the earlier and the forthcoming England and Wales legislation. The new Commission was to consist of up to fourteen members, appointed after suitable consultations, by the Secretary of State for Scotland.

Another important body in this field is the Nature Conservancy, which covers the whole of Great Britain. It was established under Royal Charter in 1949 'to provide scientific advice on the conservation and control of natural flora and fauna of Great Britain; to establish, maintain and manage Nature Reserves in Great Britain, including the maintenance of physical features of scientific interest; and to organize and develop the research and scientific services relative thereto'. The Nature Conservancy now forms part of the structure of the Natural Environment Research Council (NERC), established by Royal Charter in 1965, which is responsible to the Secretary of State for Education and Science, whose broader responsibilities cover a varied group of scientific projects and other activities.

Co-operation in this sphere is also provided by the voluntary Council of Nature, established in 1858 to co-ordinate the activities of some 450 natural history and conservation societies whose objects are to avert threats to wild life in Britain. It receives grants through the Department of Education and Science, as well as other bodies.

An important public institution deserving to be mentioned in the present connection is the Royal Botanic Garden at Kew, founded as a royal collection as far back as 1760, which was taken over by the State, came under the control of the Colonial Office in 1841 and is now the responsibility of the Ministry of Agriculture, Fisheries, and Food. Popularly known as Kew Gardens, it comprises an outstanding plant collection and research centre which is famed throughout the world.

A public service that falls completely in the private enterprise sector is provided by the National Trusts. The first was the National Trust for Preservation of Places of Historic Interest and Natural Beauty in England, Wales, and Northern Ireland, founded under the inspiration of Octavia Hill, Robert Hunter, and Canon Rawnsley in 1895, and incorporated under the National Trust Act, 1907. Its widespread activities, clearly indicated in the extended title, are paid for by private subscription, donations, legacies, and rents from properties. The National Trust for Scotland was established on similar lines in 1935. These Trusts purchase land and buildings worthy of permanent preservation, in order to preserve beautiful surroundings and to give access of the public to buildings and sites of artistic and historical importance. The properties are, where appropriate, let out for farming and residence. The National Trusts, solely on the basis of voluntary effort and support, supplement, in the preservation of the national heritage, the services of such public bodies as the Department of the Environment, the Forestry Commission, and the Countryside Commissions.

In the field of culture the broadcasting institutions have important and characteristically modern contributions to make. The British Broadcasting Corporation (BBC) early among the public corporations to emerge in 1926, continued to build up its services as a leading world agency in the development and expansion of communications by means to wireless telegraphic processes. Apart from its national function of providing a general news, information, educational, and recreational service, it developed, especially during the Second World War, a world-wide news service in many languages paid for, not out of the normal licence revenues, but as a public service supported by Exchequer grants. After the war its great achievement was the development and expansion of a comprehensive television service. The BBC continues to operate under Royal Charter, which is renewed from time to time after the current situation has been thoroughly reviewed. Its finances continue to be raised through licences, originally issued by the Postmaster General now by the Minister of Posts and Telecommunications, and its organization has been extended and modified empirically to accommodate technical developments which often have widespread repercussions.

The chief innovation in the field of broadcasting in the organizational sense arose as a result of the introduction of competition in the television service. Following a good deal of agitation against the monopoly of the BBC, that had gained support in the post-war period, especially in connection with the development of television, which held out the prospect of bright new advertising profits to industrialist and entrepreneur, the Independent Television Authority (ITA) was added to the list of public corporations by the Television Act, 1954. The ITA, which was also appointed by the Postmaster General is controlled by a board consisting of the Chairman, Deputy Chairman and from five to eight other members. Since the main object of this innovation was to commercialize a part of the national television service and to introduce a substantial element of competition within this sector of the broadcasting system, the new development represented a measure of denationalization, even though oversight of the new service was to be maintained within the public sphere through the new Authority.

In their first Annual Report (published in 1955) the ITA stated that their aim was to create a system of free television to put beside a free press. Although the Authority itself may in certain circumstances provide programmes, the intention of the new legislation was that the programmes should be provided by contractors, who would pay for the service and repay themselves by renting advertisement time. For this purpose a number of private companies have been established, among whom the available transmitting time is apportioned on a contractual basis. There is keen competition for these contracts, which are redistributed periodically. The Act lays down the general rules within which the ITA has to ensure that the programme companies work and the Authority itself has issued agreed 'Principles for Television Advertising' which are to be followed. The basic engineering services are provided on an agency basis by the Post Office.

Today there can be no doubt about the commercial success of this system. Advertising certainly pays the ITA and the associated companies. Yet there are widely differing views as to the desirability of this development, both from the viewers, who have to put up with constant interruptions while advertisements are being interpolated in the programmes, and by those who doubt whether competition is a proper means for developing the nation's cultural and educational assets, or the most economical way of distributing resources of this type (see page 130).

To cope with the special conditions of wartime a Council for the Encouragement of Music and the Arts was founded in Britain by the Pilgrim Trust in 1940, to encourage and aid the public performance of music and drama at a time of chronic disorganization when the need for cultural recreation was at its highest. Out of this admirable initiative emerged the Arts Council of Great Britain, as an independent public body, established under Royal Charter of 9 August 1946. It exists 'for the purpose of developing greater knowledge, understanding and practice of the fine arts exclusively, and in particular to increase the accessibility of the fine arts to the public; . . . to improve the standard of execution of the fine arts and to advise and co-operate with Government Departments, Local Authorities and other bodies on matters concerned directly or indirectly with those objects . . .' Its achievements in this field have been considerable and are of continuing importance. Although it is appointed by the Secretary of State for Education and Science, in conjunction with the Secretaries of State for Scotland and for Wales and is financed by Exchequer grant, the Arts Council is an independent body staffed on non-civil service lines. It works through an Executive Committee, selected from among its own membership and through separate Scottish and Welsh Committees, and is advised by specialist Panels on Art, Drama, Music, and Poetry. There is a separate Arts Council for Northern Ireland, similarly motivated and organized, and financed by the Northern Ireland Government. A similar body for operation abroad exists in the British Council, which will be described in Chapter Nine.

Continuing in the sphere of culture reference must be made to the museums, art galleries, and similar institutions in which the nation is rich. These may be publicly or privately owned and organized, responsibility for the public institutions being shared mainly by Central Departments and Local Authorities. In some cases national museums and galleries are directly administered by the responsible Department (usually the Department of Education and Science or the Scottish Office) but others are the responsibility of Standing Committees of Trustees, usually chosen from among people noted for their understanding and interest in the subject-matter of the collections, working through a civil service Director and supporting staff. An important instance is the British Museum, which has a highly qualified staff and, as its three Principal Trustees, the Lord Chancellor, the Lord Archbishop of Canterbury, and the Speaker of the House of Commons. Financing through the Exchequer is supplemented by personal gifts. The Trustees of the Imperial War Museum include, appropriately, representatives of Commonwealth Governments. For the co-ordination of the several institutions of this type, and *inter alia* the stimulation of donations for their upkeep, HM Treasury established in 1931 the Standing Commission on Museums and Galleries, having a person of note as Chairman and assisted by a paid Secretary. Similar bodies with the main object of making surveys of ancient buildings have been established in the form of standing Royal Commissions 'on Historical Monuments' for England, 'on Ancient and Historical Buildings' for Scotland, and 'on Ancient and Historical Monuments' for Wales respectively.

A comparative newcomer to the recreational sphere, with important trading and cultural objectives, is the British Tourist Authority, established by the Board of Trade (now Department of Trade and Industry) under the Development of Tourism Act, 1969, to take over and extend the functions of the former British Travel Association. It is supported by three separately organized English, Scottish, and Welsh Tourist Boards, each consisting of a Chairman and up to six other members, appointed respectively by the President of the Board of Trade,[1] and the Secretaries of State for Scotland and for Wales. The British Tourist Authority itself consists of a Chairman and up to five members, as well as the Chairmen of the three Tourist Boards. Each of these bodies appoints its own staff, who are not servants or agents of the Crown, but the Ministers exercise control of staff numbers and salaries. Annual reports and accounts are required by the Ministers, the latter for audit by the Comptroller and Auditor-General.

The functions of the British Tourist Authority are (*a*) to encourage people to visit Great Britain and people in Great Britain to take holidays there, (*b*) to encourage the provision and improvement of tourist amenities and facilities in Great Britain, and to take the necessary action. The national Tourist Boards are empowered to promote tourist publicity and to encourage the improvement of tourist amenities. They will be able, under the authority of an Order in Council, to register and grade tourist accommodation, and also to give financial assistance to suitable tourist projects in their areas.

[1] Now associated with the Secretaryship of Trade and Industry.

The Minister, after consultation with a Tourist Board, is empowered to give it directions of a general character, or specific directions with regard to loans and grants.

THE NATIONAL HEALTH SERVICE

This Service, as it emerged under the National Health Service Act, 1946, is an interesting example of a composite organization to which the three main sectors of public administration—central government, local authority, and public corporation—each makes its own contribution. Hospitals had existed in medieval times, largely under ecclesiastical provenance, and the modern system of health and practitioner services goes back to the reforms of 1834 when the responsibilities of the Poor Law system were extended to take care of the health of the indigent poor. A central authority for public health developed by way of the Poor Law Commissioners, the Board of Health (1848–58), the Local Government Board (from 1871), culminating in the establishment of the Ministry of Health in 1919, which, apart from health, was concerned with general local government matters, including town and country planning. Certain health matters had been acquired in the meantime by the four National Health Insurance Commissions (for England, Ireland, Scotland, and Wales) and the Ministry of Pensions, all of which were to be absorbed, the former immediately by the new Ministry of Health, the latter much later as part of the combined Ministry of Pensions and National Insurance. During the nineteenth century successive statutes had entrusted new public health functions to the existing local authorities. Private hospitals had developed piecemeal, largely under the impulse of private charity, and with the abolition of the old system of poor relief, under the Local Government Act, 1929, the poor law infirmaries were taken over for general purposes by the local authorities. Over the same development period and, as a consequence of important discoveries in medical science, new professions for medical practitioners, dentists, pharmacists, midwives, and nurses had developed under the general supervision of statutory registration bodies.

By the time a consolidated National Health Service was introduced in 1948 (under the National Health Act, 1946), the Ministry of Health, which was to be responsible for the new service in England

and Wales, had lost its town and country planning responsibilities to a new Ministry of Town and Country Planning in 1943, and its national insurance responsibilities to a new Ministry of National Insurance in 1945. Three years later, in 1951, its general local government responsibilities went to a new Ministry of Local Government and Planning (almost immediately retitled 'of Housing and Local Government') which also absorbed the Ministry of Town and Country Planning. The aim of the 1946 legislation was to bring under the Minister of Health's administrative umbrella (1) the existing personal health services located mainly with the local authorities at various levels, (2) the hospital services shared between the local authorities and voluntary organizations, and (3) the medical practitioners serving the new service, who understandably resent any idea that they should become state servants. Hitherto some doctors had been involved in the limited panel service associated with the existing National Health Insurance (which was being absorbed into the Beveridge scheme of National Insurance assigned to the new Ministry of National Insurance). In 1968 the Secretary of State for Social Services assumed responsibility for the National Health Service in England and Wales.

In Scotland responsibility for the National Health Service, suitably moulded to the needs of that country, was assigned to the Secretary of State for Scotland, and, on 1 April 1969, the National Health Service in Wales (organized on similar lines to the English) became the responsibility of the Secretary of State for Wales, in a new Health Department of the Welsh Office (replacing the former Welsh Board of Health). It should be emphasized that, despite the division of responsibility at Ministerial level and consequent organization differences, the National Health Service in Great Britain is a single system open to all residents in the three communities and dispensing similar benefits. It is, with minor exceptions (covering certain charges for prescriptions, dentures, and spectacles), substantially a free service (available even to visitors from abroad) and is mainly financed out of the Exchequer, although certain financial support is provided through the National Insurance contributions (a development since the scheme was introduced that has tended to confuse the differing principles on which the health and insurance schemes were respectively based).

In order to make full use of existing institutions and also to satisfy the professional interests whose co-operation was essential, it was decided to organize the new National Health Service under the general direction of the Minister on a tripartite pattern in which (1) the hospitals, (2) the personal health services, and (3) the practitioner services were differently organized.

(1) The Hospitals, grouped on a regional basis broadly similar to the normal regional pattern applied to the central Departments, but modified geographically to accommodate the teaching hospitals (attached to the various universities), were brought together under the general control of the Minister, subject to normal Exchequer financing through the departmental votes, but not under direct Civil Service management.

In each region a Regional Hospital Board was appointed by the Minister as a corporate body, after consultation with the associated university, organizations, and representatives of the medical professions, the Local Health Authorities in the area (see (2) below), and any other bodies which appeared to the Minister to be concerned. The membership, which varied between twenty-two and thirty-two, acted not as representatives of the several interests but in their personal capacity, and were unpaid. They appointed their own staffs of full time paid officials who were neither civil servants nor local government officials.

The Regional Hospital Boards were responsible, under the Minister, for administering the hospitals in their region, but they delegated the day-to-day management of the hospitals, grouped in convenient areas, under Hospital Management Committees, also unpaid, which the Board themselves appointed, after consultation with the Local Health Authorities, the Executive Councils (see (3) below) and representatives of the hospital staffs and other interested bodies. In England and Wales the teaching hospitals were independently organized under their own Boards of Governors, appointed directly by, and responsible to, the Minister. The associated schools for training doctors remained the responsibility of the individual university. In Scotland the teaching hospitals were brought into the main regional structure.

(2) Personal health services in the hands of the local authorities were regrouped under the County and County Borough Councils, operating as Local Health Authorities (LHAs). Some of the second-tier authorities thus lost their former functions in this field. The newly co-ordinated services included arrangements for the care of expectant mothers and children under five not attending school,

provision of midwives, health visitors, home nursing and ambulance services, and for vaccination and immunization arrangements. It was originally planned that the LHAs should provide Health Centres in which groups of doctors and other medical staff could pool and provide their services in close co-operation, but, except in a few areas, this development was slow in getting off the ground, due mainly to the lack of professional enthusiasm and financial resources.[1] Grants-in-aid from the Exchequer are made to the local authorities to assist these services.

(3) For the co-ordination of the several autonomous professions concerned in the National Health Service special Executive Councils were set up in each of the LHA areas, or in combinations thereof. Each Executive Council had a membership of twenty-five. This included the Chairman, appointed by the Minister, the remaining twenty-four members being divided equally between lay and professional appointees. Eight of the lay members were appointed by the LHA and the remaining four by the Minister. The twelve professional members—seven medical, three dental, and two pharmaceutical representatives—were appointed by the three professional committees set up under statute in each area to represent the members of the several professions actually practising in the area, known respectively as the Local Medical Committee, the Local Dental Committee, and the Local Pharmaceutical Committee. In 1968 membership of the Executive Councils was increased by four, two to represent the General Ophthalmic Services and two appointed by the Minister. The Executive Councils were executive, co-ordinative, and adjudicatory bodies. Their functions included registration of all persons electing to use the National Health Service and to whom registration cards had to be issued, the maintaining of lists of, and contracts with, practitioners participating in the Service, the assessment of payments due for services rendered, and dealing with complaints of, and disagreements between, citizens and practitioners. They also appointed their own staffs and were financed by the Exchequer.

Under the earlier system medical practices were treated as private property which was transferable by sale in the ordinary way. Under the new NHS practices were allocated by a Central Medical Practices

[1] At the end of 1969, in England and Wales, there were 131 Health Centres in operation. See *Annual Report of the Department of Health and Social Security* for 1969.

Committee, set up by the Minister, with a membership mainly of doctors. There was also a central Dental Estimates Board to examine certain estimates for dental treatment and appliances.

To mould and extend existing institutions to form a consolidated health service, such as was designed by the National Health Act, 1946, was bound to encounter difficulties. To equip the new service with the right type of personnel, to provide it with adequate finances, and, above all, to consolidate effectively the several and, in many ways, very divergent sectors was not likely to be achieved without much effort and attendant heartburnings. Yet, despite the unavoidable teething-troubles, the great improvement that the new system offered over the former services, with their many gaps and inadequacies, was very quickly evident and, despite a good deal of criticism, there can be little doubt that to the people at large the new Service, proved to be a considerable boon.

There is not space here to summarize the criticisms and proposed changes to the NHS that have been offered from time to time, but an inquiry that certainly deserves to be mentioned is that made by a small committee under the chairmanship of Mr C. W. Guillebaud and explained in the *Report of the Committee of Enquiry into the Cost of the National Health Service*, published in January 1956. There had been a good deal of criticism of the increasing cost of the service, a quite normal reaction by a powerful minority of the public to publicly administered services, especially those with a rising budget, but as was pointed out by the Committee and others, when the fall in the value of money was taken into account—and those who play about with figures too often fail to do this—the increase in actual cost in relation to national resources had not been unreasonable. The Committee examined certain proposals put forward with the aim of improving the integration of the NHS, covering such ideas as the transfer of responsibility for the hospitals to the Local Health Authorities, the integration of the Executive Councils with either the LHAs or the Regional Hospital Boards, the transfer of the entire service to a specially appointed national board or public corporation, and so on. The Committee saw drawbacks in all these 'cures' and felt that in any case—wisely it would appear—sufficient time had not then elapsed for the existing tripartite system to prove itself.

By the end of the sixties, however, the time was ripe for a reconsideration of the entire position and three official reports are of particular interest. The first is the *Report of the Committee on Local*

Authority and Allied Personal Social Services, the Seebohm Report, dealing with a wide range of services, including some that are associated with the National Health Service. This has already been outlined in Chapter Four of this volume.

Two Green Papers, also published in 1968, on *The Administrative Structure of the Medical and Related Services in England and Wales* and *Administrative Reorganisation of the Scottish Health Services*, put forward for discussion proposals for the reorganization of the National Health Service north and south of the border respectively. Both Reports favoured concentrating the several branches of the Service under Area Boards, numbering some forty to fifty in England and Wales and between ten and fifteen in Scotland. Each Board would have a Chairman and about fifteen members responsible for managing the combined service with a local organization shaped to the needs of the particular area. The responsible ministers would continue to exercise a general oversight, with a relationship to the new Area Boards similar to their present relationship with the Regional Hospital Boards. Both Reports favoured the inclusion of an adequate complaints procedure and the appointment, on the analogy of the Parliamentary Commissioner for Administration, of a Health Commissioner.

As was to be expected these Green Papers led to a good deal of discussion and the proposals were criticized on a number of grounds. In consequence, the Government reconsidered the position and, early in 1970, issued a further Green Paper on *The Future Structure of the National Health Service* with amended proposals. This initiation of further discussion affords an excellent example of the democratic approach to administrative reform.

The new Green Paper reiterated the case for the unification of the NHS and, in view of the fact that the bulk of its finance must come from central sources, for the retention of full responsibility for administration in the hands of the Minister. It was agreed that the new Area Health Authorities, which were to have the main responsibility for administration of the NHS in the localities, should operate in parallel with Local Authorities, in the areas proposed for the new local government structure (see Chapter Four of this volume), with special arrangements for London.

In drawing the lines between the services, appropriate respectively for the NHS and for the Local Authorities, it was proposed 'that the services should be organized according to the main skills required to provide them rather than by categorization of primary user'. This would mean that the Area Health Authorities would administer all those services provided by the several medical professions, which would comprise (1) the existing hospital and specialist services, (2) the existing family practitioner services, (3) those services at present provided by Local Health Authorities which conform to the new definition, and (4) the school health service. The new Local Authorities would be left with a wide range of social and public health services for which numerous other specialists are responsible. This somewhat unusual form of categorization, receiving its inspiration from the peculiar requirements of health administration, seems bound to give rise to a good deal of controversy.

The proposed new Area Health Authorities, with a possible membership of between twenty and twenty-five, would be appointed on the basis of one third by the Local Authorities, one third by the health professions, and one third and the chairman by the Minister. They would be directly responsible to the Minister. It was proposed that their internal organization should be unified and based upon the several functions, and not follow the tripartite division or be based upon the separate professions within the service. Although the Area Authorities would not be hierarchically linked with the Ministry there would need to be several Regional Health Councils, in larger areas similar to those of the existing Regional Hospital Boards, to deal with a number of important matters requiring large areas of administration: such as, certain rarer specialisms, postgraduate medical and dental education, staff training, blood transfusion services, and the planning of ambulance services. The Central Department itself would require to be reorganized with the object of strengthening the unity of the NHS, and in this capacity would perform some functions at present carried out by the Regional Hospital Boards.

The new Government's consultative document (1971), proposing to reorganize the NHS on a two tier basis of regional and area authorities, supported by local community councils, is now under consideration.

VOLUNTARY 'PUBLIC' ADMINISTRATION

As the social historian well knows, many of the social services in Britain owe their origins to non-governmental or voluntary institutions. Thus, in medieval times the Church provided alms and social services on a considerable scale to the poor and needy, while, with the rise of industrial society, voluntary agencies of many types grew up to provide, on a self-help basis, the means for grappling with the evils engendered by the new capitalism.

The growth of the Welfare State inevitably eroded the voluntary service sector. Thus, when the present National Insurance scheme was introduced in 1948 the new Ministry of National Insurance absorbed the voluntarily organized Approved Societies, which had participated in administering the earlier scheme of National Health Insurance under the statute of 1911. Yet voluntary organizations have continued to find many tasks to hand, and their activities have been restricted more by the availability of funds than by the limits of need for their services.

The field of voluntary service is still much too wide to receive adequate justice here. It must suffice the reader to be aware of its existence and to realize that here, in the fringes of public administration as it were, is an important range of institutions capable of extending the scope of public administration deeply into the private, non-business, field. Some of these bodies have a variety of purposes, some merely personal or concerned with the furtherance of group interests and designed to exert pressures on public opinion and to obtain public support (see, for example, reference to 'interest groups' in Chapter Ten of this volume) and only incidentally providing services that might well become the concern of government; while at the other extreme there are a few whose activities are completely public, perhaps shared with other public authorities.

Among the voluntary, privately financed bodies that perform invaluable public service are the National Trusts, already mentioned. Another body performing a public service of outstanding importance is the Royal National Lifeboat Institution, which maintains lifeboats and fast inshore rescue boats at strategic points around the coasts of the United Kingdom. It is financed by voluntary donations and subscriptions and largely operated, in particular by the lifeboat crews, on a voluntary basis. The services provided by the Institution are an exceptional example of non-official public effort, quite remarkable for its efficiency in an age when the rescue service calls more and more for the deployment of advanced technical equipment.

A definite adjunct to the public services was introduced at the outbreak of the Second World War in 1939 when Citizens Advice

Bureaux were set up in the localities to provide advice on difficulties arising as a result of population dislocation, explaining to the citizens the official arrangements for dispersal and, in particular, advising them on the authorities to be approached for further information. After the war the local authorities were enabled to make grants in aid for the continuance of such Bureaux, and many have done so. With the increasing complexity of the public sector and its activities such advice is needed even more today than it was during the war emergency, when officialdom was necessarily on its toes. There is in fact room for a network of such offices to aid citizens in obtaining effective contact with and understanding of the official machinery. A major difficulty for these CABs has been in ensuring that their staffs, as part-time volunteers, keep themselves up-to-date on the ever-changing administrative situation. Experience shows that emphasis should always be placed on directing the inquirer to the right quarter for enlightenment and leaving the provision of detailed information to the responsible authorities. With so much administrative complexity, much of it unavoidable, it is very easy for even the best informed outsider to be a bit off target with his advice. Nevertheless, the CABs and their voluntary workers perform an essential task and the question can well be put whether the time has not come for the establishment of a series of information clearing houses at strategic points to keep the local network informed on the changing situation, or perhaps a computer should form the core of this necessary service.

There are a multitude of voluntary institutions which provide, sometimes as their major object, sometimes incidental to their main function, invaluable public services. At a risk of appearing invidious when there are so many admirable bodies doing this sort of work, one or two should be mentioned to indicate the type of activity that one has in mind. Thus there is the Royal National Institute for the Blind and the National Library for the Blind, which supply Braille publications; the British Legion, among a number of bodies caring for disabled ex-service people among others, and the several Discharged Prisoners' Aid Societies which are associated with the local prisons and, now co-ordinated under the National Association of Discharged Prisoners' Aid Societies, provide a variety of services for persons who have served prison sentences, mainly to enable them to settle down and to obtain regular employment.

Some of the bodies under this heading have been so successful as to be widely copied abroad and thus to extend their influence into the international sphere. Notable among these is the Salvation Army, a religious and social reform movement, started in London by William Booth (1829–1912) in the 1860s and given its present name in 1878. Organized, somewhat incongruously in the light of its Christian mission, on a military basis with army rankings, it campaigns against the evils of society, notably in its early days against drunkenness, when it drew upon itself the bitter opposition of the beer shops faced with bankruptcy by its successes. Apart from caring for the poor and providing social service for the down-and-outs at home, the Salvation Army undertakes missionary work overseas. Its present world-wide organization began to develop in 1880, when it sent out a commissioner to organize a Salvationist settlement in Philadelphia, USA.

The Boy Scout movement for the development of citizenship among boys was launched as 'Scouting for Boys' in 1907 by General Sir Robert (later Lord) Baden Powell (1857–1941) of Mafeking fame. As the Boy Scouts Association, it was incorporated by Royal Charter in 1912. The movement soon spread overseas and became a world-wide youth movement. A parallel Girl Guides Association was founded in 1919. As a matter of fact the Boy Scouts were not the first in this particular field, since a movement, combining characteristics of both the Salvation Army and the Boy Scouts, was founded in the shape of the Boys' Brigade as early as 1883. Based upon church membership the organization is still active.

These few examples of voluntary public administration having been quoted to demonstrate the interest and variety of the particular field, the reader who is sufficiently interested must be left to follow his own track into the territories of self-help. These institutions have made a splendid contribution in the past and there is no reason to believe that the need for such unselfish service will be superseded by the extension of the Welfare State. In fact some would argue, with a good deal of reason, that the boundaries of that state, as it now exists, could well recede in some spheres in favour of voluntary service. Certainly the increase of leisure in the New Society should broaden the scope for such participation.

An Independent Broadcasting Authority, on lines similar to ITA, is to be set up to introduce a commercial local radio service, financed from advertising.

AUTONOMOUS BODIES, closely associated with the Central Administration as at 1 January 1971.

N.B. The Autonomous Bodies listed below are classified according to the revised Haldane headings—I to X—as defined in Vol. I, p. 80, and arranged within each heading according to the date of their establishment in their present form,

I Public Works Loan Board (1817)
  Exchequer and Audit Department (1867)
  Development Commission (1910)
  University Grants Committee (1919)
  Bank of England (1694/1946)
  National Economic Development Council (1962)
  National Board for Prices and Incomes (1965) *disbanded 31.3.71*
  Office of the Parliamentary Commissioner for Administration
    (1967)
  Decimal Currency Board (1967)
  Commission of the Constitution (1969)

II Corporation of Trinity House (1514)
  Commission of Northern Lighthouses (1786)
  Forestry Commission (1919)
  Monopolies Commission (1948)
  UK Atomic Energy Authority (1946/1954)
  Crofters Commission (1955)
  Air Transport Licensing Board (1960)
  Industrial Estates Management Corporations, for England,
    Scotland, and Wales (1960)
  Highlands and Islands Development Board (1965)

III Industrial Court (1919) *but see p. 112*
  Civil Service Arbitration Tribunal (1924/1936)
  Remploy Ltd. (1945)
  Commission on Industrial Relations (1969) *but see p. 112*

IV Royal Hospital, Chelsea (1691)
  Industrial Injuries Advisory Council (1946)
  National Insurance Advisory Committee (1946)
  Regional Hospital Boards (1948)

  V HM College of Arms (1483)
     British Museum (1797)
     Medical Research Council (1913/1920)
     Imperial War Museum (1920)
     National Library of Scotland (1925)
     British Broadcasting Corporation (1922/1926)
     Agricultural Research Council (1931)
     Standing Commission on Museums and Galleries (1931)
     British Council (1934)
     Arts Council of Great Britain (1940)
     National Research Development Corporation (1948)
     Church Commissioners for England (1704, 1836/1948)
     Nature Conservancy (1949)
     Independent Television Authority (1964)
     Science Research Council (1965)
     Natural Environment Research Council (1965)
     Social Science Research Council (1965)

  VI Commission of the New Towns (1961)
     Water Resources Board (1965)
     Race Relations Board (1966)
     Countryside Commission for Scotland (1967)
     Countryside Commission [for England and Wales] (1950/1968)
     Community Relations Commission (1968)
     Royal Commission on Environmental Pollution (1970)

  VII Charity Commission (1853)
     Law Societies (Legal Aid) (1950)
     Council on Tribunals (1959)
     Law Commission (for England and Wales) (1965)
     Scottish Law Commission (1965)

  IX Crown Agents for Oversea Governments and Administrations
      (eighteenth century/1833)
     Commonwealth Institute (1902)
     Commonwealth War Graves Commission (1917)

  X Civil Service Pay Research Unit (1956)

The five Research Councils, listed under V above, are of particular interest as public bodies established to look after the Government's responsibilities for research in the fields of medicine, agriculture, science, the environment and social sciences respectively. While their structure and staffing are similar to those of Government Departments, these bodies are immediately responsible to expert Councils instead of a Minister and their research duties are largely carried out by numerous autonomous institutes and survey units.

The Research Councils have an interesting history. Set up originally as Committees of the Privy Council under the general responsibility of the Lord President, they were so organized as to be freed from immediate political direction. The same principle was applied to the Department of Scientific and Industrial Research (DSIR) when it was introduced during the First World War, also as a Committee of the Privy Council. With the assignment of responsibility for civil science to the Secretary of State for Education and Science in 1964, the latter replaced the Lord President as general sponsor of the Research Councils. Certain of the institutes and laboratories concerned with practical research were attached to the relevant Department, like the Board of Trade or Ministry of Agriculture, Fisheries and Food. Similarly much of the work of DSIR was absorbed in 1964 by the new Ministry of Technology (now part of the Department of Trade and Industry) and DSIR was abolished. The status and organization of these Councils are at present under consideration.

FURTHER READING

Introductory

A general picture of this miscellaneous public sphere is not easily obtained. There is a good deal of information about a number of the many institutions in the current issue of *Britain: An Official Handbook* (HMSO) and also in E. N. Gladden's *British Public Service Administration* (Staples Press, 1961). Most readers will wish to follow up a particular line of interest, and a good deal of information will be obtainable from the *Annual Reports*, which most public authorities publish.

Historical and Advanced

Of the many works on the General Post Office, Howard Robinson's

Britain's Post Office (Oxford, 1953) is highly recommended. Recent changes were foreshadowed in the White Papers on *The Status of the Post Office* (Cmnd. 989, 1960); *Reorganization of the Post Office* (Cmnd. 3233, 1967); and also the *First Report from the Select Committee on Nationalised Industries*, Session 1966–7, *The Post Office* (HMSO, 1967).

The documentation of the broadcasting services is voluminous. The development of the services and of ideas about them can be followed up in the official reports of successive inquiries: namely, the Ullswater *Report of the Broadcasting Committee, 1935* (Cmd. 5091, 1935), the Beveridge *Report of the Broadcasting Committee, 1949* (Cmd. 8116, 1951), and The Pilkington *Report of the Committee on Broadcasting, 1960* (Cmnd. 1753, 1962). Among the many excellent individual studies R. H. Coase's *British Broadcasting: A Study in Monopoly* (Longmans, Green, 1950) is highly recommended. Both the BBC and the ITA publish informative annual Handbooks.

The National Health Service and its forerunners are well covered in numerous historical and analytical texts. An excellent and reasonably detailed account is provided by J. S. Ross in his *The National Health Service in Great Britain* (Oxford, 1952) while a comprehensive survey from the American viewpoint is provided by A. Lindsey in *Socialized Medicine in England and Wales* (Univ. of N. Carolina, 1962). Among the official publications to be studied are *The General Practitioner and the Hospital Service*, by the Scottish Health Services Council (HMSO, 1952); *Report of the Committee on the Internal Administration of Hospitals*, by the Central Health Services Council (HMSO, 1954); the Guillebaud *Report of the Committee of Enquiry into the Cost of the National Health Service* (Cmd. 9663, 1956); the Hall *Report on the Grading Structure of Administrative Staff in the Hospital Service* (HMSO, 1957), and the *Green Papers* on reorganization (HMSO, 1968 and 1970) mentioned in the text.

Individual studies are admirably represented by *Trinity House* (Sampson Low, 1947) by H. P. Mead; *The Royal Hospital, Chelsea* (Hutchinson, 1950) by C. G. T. Dean; and *London's Water Supply 1903–1953* (Staples Press, 1953), a review of the work of the Metropolitan Water Board, issued by the Board.

Two basic texts on voluntary services are A. F. C. Bourdillon's *Voluntary Social Services* (Methuen, 1945) and Lord Beveridge's *Voluntary Action* (Allen & Unwin, 1948). These can now be brought up to date by Mary Morris's wide-ranging *Voluntary Work in the Welfare State* (Routledge, 1969). Also recommended is Margaret E. Brasnett's short introduction, *The Story of the Citizens' Advice Bureaux* (published on their behalf by the National Council of Social Service, 1964).

CHAPTER SEVEN

Public Corporations: Accountability

One of the main claims made in favour of the public corporation, in preference to a central department or a local authority, for the management of public enterprises and services, is its capacity to operate independently on industrial or commercial lines without the normal brakes of responsibility to Parliament and the restrictive rules of public finance that have to be applied to the ordinary governmental institutions. Yet once it was decided that Ministers, vested with oversight of specific sectors of the nation's activities, would have broad statutory responsibility for the public corporations whose operations fell within their functional spheres, it followed that only a very strict self-denying ordinance would restrain Parliament from exerting pressures along those channels through which ministerial responsibility of one form or another operated, and there has in practice been plenty of scope for the development of widely varying attitudes as to the degree of oversight to be exercised.

Radical changes in the scope of the public corporations require the introduction of new or amending legislation, and a Minister's responsibility to Parliament under existing legislation is strictly limited to specific activities, but in developing national policies the public corporations form an increasingly important sector which the government can influence in numerous informal non-statutory ways. More directly, through the manipulations of finance, the Chancellor of the Exchequer has to ensure that the public corporations, by

F

acting out of step with the other sectors of the economy—for example, by adopting an unacceptable pricing policy—do not draw excessively upon the nation's funds for capital investment. In view of the importance of this factor it is proposed to look at the financial aspect before discussing the specific ministerial responsibilities.

FINANCIAL POLICY

The Government has adopted the method of communicating their policy with regard to the nationalized industries by means of White Papers issued through the Chancellor of the Exchequer. The White Paper, entitled *The Financial and Economic Obligations of the Nationalised Industries* (Cmnd. 1337), of 1961 reiterated the already established policy that the several undertakings should pay their way taking one year with another, and went on to consider the corporations' financial objectives in relation to revenue account, capital account, and prices and costs.

The White Paper explains the Government's aim to do what a number of earlier inquiries into individual industries had not been able to do; namely, to provide

a general review of the manner in which the general principles—and, in particular, the economic and financial principles—which were established in the nationalising statutes have been applied in practice.

It goes on to state (para. 2):

In the course of this review the Government have consulted the boards of nationalised industries about the statutory obligations as they stand and their applicability for the future. The review has been conducted against the background of the Government's general policy in relation to nationalised industries. The relevant aspects of this are as follows. First, the task of government is to ensure that the industries are organised and administered efficiently and economically to carry out their responsibilities, and that they are thus enabled to make the maximum contribution towards the economic well-being of the community as a whole. Second, although the industries have obligations of a national and non-commercial kind, they are not, and ought not to be regarded as social services absolved from economic and commercial justification.

Apart from its detailed explanation of the Government's financial policy this statement indicated a broader interest in the organization and working of the nationalized industries that was bound to transcend the normal limits of official interference such as the advocates of the public corporation as an autonomous instrument of public activity normally accepted.

Six years later, on 7 September 1967, a Government of a different political outlook announced that price increases in the nationalized industries would in future be referred to the National Board for Prices and Incomes (see Vol. I, p. 290), and followed up with a new White Paper on the nationalized industries under the title *A Review of Economic and Financial Obligations* (Cmnd. 3437), which aimed at bringing up-to-date the statement of 1961, in the light of technological and other changes that had taken place in the meantime and in relation to industry as a whole.

The new White Paper discussed the role of the nationalized industries in relation to investment, prices, costs, financial objectives, and so on, emphasizing again the high degree of collaboration expected between Government Departments and the industries. An important point was made to the effect that

where there are significant social and wider economic costs and benefits which ought to be taken into account in their investment and pricing these will be reflected in the Government's policy for the industry: and if this means that the industry has to act against its own commercial interests, the Government will accept responsibility. (para. 37.)

Instances of this type of unremunerative but highly desirable service that come readily to mind as affecting most citizens at one time or another are those postal deliveries to distant farms and other country places, and highly convenient but under-used and unremunerative railway services on lines that would be closed down, if profit were the only test. A much clearer instance is provided by the BBC's oversea broadcasts, already mentioned, which should not be financed out of the licence fees paid by home listeners and in fact are financed out of Exchequer funds.

The last three paragraphs of the White Paper provide an illuminating summary of the role of the Government in this connection, and deserve quoting:

38. Though the responsible Ministers and their Departments are in frequent contact with the nationalised Boards about matters affecting Government policy, it is not the Government's intention to interfere in the day-to-day management of the industries. Nevertheless the Government

must accept a large measure of responsibility for the general lines of economic development which are followed in this vital sector of the economy, and in its relations with the nationalised industries will have in mind the considerations outlined in this White Paper, and in particular that increases in costs should whenever possible be absorbed by greater efficiency rather than be passed on to the consumer, and that price increases should be capable of being publicly justified.

39. The annual Investment Review provides a regular occasion for reviewing the state of each industry. Then the Government normally gives firm approval for the agreed level of capital expenditure for the forthcoming financial year and provisional approval (subject to some limitation on the extent to which funds are to be committed) for the following year: and also gives its views on the outline of investment proposed for subsequent years. The programmes for most industries extend five years ahead, and with industries in which investment take a long time to mature, this longer-term look is of key importance. The implications of the investment programmes for the Exchequer—and hence for the short and long-term balance of the economy—must always be considered, though it is not intended to express financial objectives in terms of self-financing ratios. It is also during the Investment Review discussions that the Government is able to take account of the general balance of investment between individual nationalised industries, and between them collectively and the rest of the economy, in order to ensure co-ordinated development in the context of planned growth of the economy.

40. This White Paper is intended to show how investment, pricing and efficiency policies will be taken into account in setting financial objectives, rather than to make any change in the basic relationship between the Government and the nationalised industries. It reviews the features and principles which are common to all nationalised industries and which underlie their relationship to the Government. The circumstances of the industries are however very diverse and will be taken into account in formulating detailed policies for the sectors concerned.

MINISTERIAL RESPONSIBILITIES

Despite constant reiteration of the principle that public corporations are not answerable for their day-to-day management, and the consequence that the responsible Minister is not answerable for the day-to-day conduct of business by the corporation, the responsibilities actually laid upon Ministers by Parliament are sufficiently extensive to raise doubts as to the room for manoeuvre actually left to the Boards as managers. A full-scale examination of the problem was made during the 1967-8 session by the Select Committee on Nationalized Industries (see below) and communicated to Parliament in their comprehensive three volume Report on *Ministerial Control of the Nationalised Industries* (HC 371, 1968). The Select Committee define and discuss ten guiding principles, which deserve to be listed (see *Report*, Vol. I, pp. 34-9):

I. Ministers should be concerned with securing that the industries operate in the public interest.

II. Ministers should seek to ensure the efficiency of the industries by exercising a broad oversight of them, but should not become involved in management.

III. The industries should otherwise be left as free as possible to carry out the policies required of them as efficiently as possible.

IV. There should be clear demarcation of responsibilities, both between Government Departments and between Ministers and Boards.

V. The methods of Ministerial control should be mainly strategic rather than tactical.

VI. The nature of Ministerial control need not be wholly formal.

VII. The Ministers and the industries should be publicly accountable.

VIII. The measure of management should not be purely commercial success or social achievement but should be the efficiency with which the industries carry out the joint commercial/social duties given to them.

IX. The ultimate sanction for bad management may be dismissal or non-reappointment in post, but improvement of management should be the first objective.

X. Proper and fruitful exercise of Ministerial control depends on the attitudes and ability of both Ministers and Members of Boards.

The several and quite numerous Ministerial responsibilities may be grouped under five headings (as, for example, in the Administrative Staff College's publication *Accountability*).

1. *Appointment of Boards*. The Minister's responsibility for selecting and dismissing the boards of the corporations clearly constitutes his most effective means of influencing the activities of these bodies. Not only does the Minister decide what sort of person shall be appointed and take into consideration the kind of views he holds, but the fact that he has the power of dismissal is bound to have a pervasive influence upon the appointee, rendering him more amenable to the Minister's advice than might normally be the case. Of course the shortness of the term of appointment, commonly for five years, may mitigate such influences, but there is always the

possibility, and indeed the desirability of reappointment, as well as the probability that persons who are *persona grata* will be eminently eligible for similar positions in other corporations. The extent of the patronage thus exercised by Ministers and by, or on behalf of, the Government is considerable and tends to increase; and, while there is little evidence to suggest that the appointees' political allegiance is given excessive weight, there is sufficient evidence that competence for the particular post is not given the high priority that it should receive. In a number of cases the Acts themselves lay down conditions as to the types of experience to be sought in making such appointments, but the conditions are too general to place any real curb upon the Minister's choice, nor indeed is this their intention. There are instances where the Government has clearly gone out of its way to appoint a person of generally accepted competence to take over a responsible post at a particular juncture, as, for example when, in 1961, Dr R. (later· Lord) Beeching (from Imperial Chemical Industries) was appointed to the chairmanship of the British Transport Commission to deal with the difficult problems of railway reorganization.

2. *Issue of Directions.* Under the several statutes the responsible Ministers are usually given authority to issue directions to the public corporations on matters of policy, and are required to authorize specific actions on their part. Such powers, if widely used, could substantially diminish the public corporations' autonomy. The Coal Act, 1946, set the general pattern by empowering the Minister, after consultation with the National Coal Board, to give them directions of a general character as to the exercise and performance of their functions relating to matters which appear to him to affect the national interest, and placed upon the board the duty of giving effect to such directions. In practice there has been little occasion to use such powers, which have been regarded as being of an emergency nature, though it could have been otherwise. There are a number of specific instances where ministerial authority is required before a public board can take action, on matters such as the compulsory acquisition of land and the promotion of Bills in Parliament, in the case of the Electricity and Gas Councils to define and vary the extent of the Area Boards.

3. *Control of Financial Policy.* Under the Statutes Ministers have a number of responsibilities in connection with such matters as borrowing and the issue of stock (since 1961 subject to the Government's

arrangements), the establishment of reserve funds, the application of surplus revenues, and the authorization of certain grants; and there have been a number of interventions on prices.

4. *Submission of Reports and Accounts.* The statutes require the public corporations to prepare annual reports for submission to the responsible Minister, for laying before Parliament, an essential means for making available information about the activities of these bodies which might otherwise be shrouded in mystery. They must also submit annual accounts to the Minister, and with certain exceptions mainly among the earlier corporations, these also have to be laid before Parliament. The wide availability of the sort of information contained in these documents is essential if real accountability of the corporations to Parliament and people is to be secured, though of course the mere publication, especially at a time when we are literally overwhelmed with such information, does not in itself ensure its effectiveness in achieving accountability. There must be sufficient public interest and the means for effective scrutiny. For achieving the latter purpose the Select Committee on the Nationalized Industries has been set up by the House of Commons, a matter to receive attention in the following section.

5. *Advisory Committees, Consumer Councils, and Consultative Councils.* As we have already seen the several responsible Ministers are involved in the appointment and use of these consultative bodies as sounding boards of public opinion and sources of informed advice on public views, reactions, and complaints on the activities of the public corporations. Introduced by Governments with the best intentions, to help to mitigate basic non-democratic elements in this particular sector of public administration, the use of these bodies has been restricted by the failure of the public, no doubt for a variety of reasons, from making full use of their services.

Ministerial authority under these several headings amount to a comprehensive ability to oversee, and, if necessary, to participate in (some might say 'interfere with') the activities of the numerous public corporations and similar bodies. But it does not end there. It is obvious that, to carry out so many statutory duties, a Minister must set up within his Department branches suitably organized and staffed to maintain the administrative links needed to ensure that the corporations' responsibilities are properly understood and met. Such administrative units have to work in close communication with their opposite numbers in the corporations and the tendency is for them to take a much more continuous and detailed interest in the corporations' activities than is laid down or was intended by Parliament when the statutes were approved. This has been brought to light and commented upon by the Select Committee already mentioned.

Among a number of proposals for improvement made by the Select Committee on Nationalized Industries in their Report on Ministerial Control, and probably the most interesting to which discussion is bound to return, was that a new Ministry of Nationalized Industries should be established to take over from existing Ministers 'those responsibilities . . . that are chiefly directed at overseeing and seeking to ensure the efficiency of any of the nationalized industries' (*Report*, Vol. I, p. 193, para. 892).

The twelve principal responsibilities thus to be transferred were listed as follows, providing a useful reference list of ministerial controls, apart from the responsibilities for the wider public interest, which it was recommended should remain with the several functional Ministers at present exercising both controls:

   (i) The appointment (and dismissal) of the members of all the Boards.

  (ii) Laying down the adopted pricing and investment policies for the industry.

 (iii) Agreeing the financial objective that follows from (ii) above.

 (iv) Reviewing investment programmes and approving investment projects.

  (v) Approving capital structures and borrowing.

 (vi) Furthering co-ordination and co-operation between industries in the interests of their commercial efficiency.

 (vii) General oversight of the structure and organization of the industries with regard to their efficiency.

(viii) Undertaking or making arrangements for efficiency studies.

 (ix) Approving research programmes, training and education programmes, etc.

  (x) Approving the forms of the Accounts.

 (xi) Laying Annual Reports and Accounts before Parliament.

(xii) Accounting to Parliament for all their own activities and answering on the adjournment debates, etc., on the activities of the industries as commercial bodies. (*Report*, para. 893, pp. 193–4, condensed.)

Such an across-the-board allocation of ministerial responsibilities at operating levels would cut deeply into the general principle of allocating such responsibilities on a functional or service basis and would add an element of confusion to the existing ministerial structure. It is not surprising therefore that the proposal was rejected by the Government in their White Paper on *Ministerial Control of the Nationalised Industries*, Cmnd. 4027 (1969), replying to the Select Committee.

The Government accepted the Select Committee's point, that there were two ministerial responsibilities which could be conceptually distinguished: namely (i) for the efficiency, in the economic and financial sense, of the industries themselves, and (ii) for the wider public interest. While it was recognized that the proposed arrangement had certain advantages, the Government, after careful consideration, 'concluded that the disadvantages of a major change in the machinery of government on these lines would substantially outweigh the advantages'. In support of their conclusions the Government argued (1) that under the proposed arrangement policy decisions now involving one Minister would commonly involve two; (2) that the proposal rested upon too ready an assumption about the ease with which the sector responsibility (ii), and the efficiency responsibility (i), could in practice be separated into self-contained compartments; (3) that the sub-division of responsibilities in relation to each nationalized industry and the creation of the new Ministry at arms length from the sector responsibilities would mean more work and more staff in Government and in the nationalized industries, which would each be concerned with the two Government Departments; and (4) that the establishment of the proposed Ministry would not reduce intervention in the management of the industries, as the Select Committee hoped and expected.

PARLIAMENTARY RELATIONSHIPS

The assignment of specific functions and duties to individual Ministers for the nationalized industries has meant that these Ministers are continuously responsible to Parliament, and particularly to the House of Commons, on these specific matters, and since there were strongly contrasting attitudes in Parliament as to the degree of control that was desirable, it was certain that there would be similarly contrasting attitudes as to the intensity of the supervision ranging from almost complete autonomy to almost complete control, that Parliament should exercise. Generally it can be said that Parliament, having chosen this method of public control for the high degree of managerial freedom that the public corporation was capable of exercising with a minimum of government interference, inconsistently seeks to improve the means at its disposal to strengthen its own control. Understandably, the Ministers in their governmental capacity are not inclined to encourage parliamentary inquiry, since this may increase their own burdens and broaden the scope of the inquest into their administrative activities.

There are several occasions when the policies being pursued in connection with the nationalized industries (public corporations) can be brought under review in Parliament, but in the main these are occasional, since such matters have to compete with others of particular current interest. These occur, for example, on substantive motions or by other means on Supply days, on the reports and accounts of the industries and of the Select Committee on Nationalized Industries, and on short adjournment debates at the end of a day's business. There are also the probings at Question Time, which offer a more regular means for raising points touching upon Ministers' responsibilities, although these do not provide occasions for debate.

The provision of information on the structure and working of the several nationalized industries for the information of the Government and Parliament—and of course the public—other than those required annually under the statutes has been dealt with in different ways. Where a special need has arisen reviews of this sort have been sought through specially appointed Committees or Royal Commissions, and some outstanding instances have been mentioned: for example, the Fleck Committee on Coalmining which reported in 1955, the Herbert Committee on Electricity Supply which reported in 1956, and the Guillebaud Report on the National Health Service which also reported in 1956. There is also the established practice of appointing a Royal Commission or Committee to look at the BBC when the periodical renewal of its charter is under consideration.

The problem of such Parliamentary supervision was investigated by a Select Committee on Nationalized Industries appointed for the purpose in 1952. The Select Committee considered the scope for parliamentary questions, which some members wanted to extend into

the realms of daily management, but it concluded that such questions were only admissible upon matters for which Ministers were
statutorily responsible and that detailed questions on the management of the nationalized industries were inadmissible. On the matter
of inquiries consideration was given to the idea that such inquiries
should be of an *ad hoc* nature and held at not too frequent intervals
so as to avoid the impression within the industries that someone was
constantly prying into their affairs and thus restricting their autonomy. This method was considered suitable enough where special
circumstances called for such inquiries, as in the instances already
mentioned, but a more regular review was held to be desirable and,
against considerable opposition, it was agreed that a Select Committee should be appointed regularly to keep Parliament informed
on the activities of the several public corporations responsible for the
nationalized industries. The proposed committee was to inform
Parliament 'about the aims, activities and problems of the Corporations and not of controlling their work'. It was also recommended
that the new committee should be provided with expert staff which
would include 'an officer of the status of Comptroller and Auditor-
General who should be an officer of the House of Commons, with
high administrative experience . . .'

Acting upon these recommendations, a new Select Committee on
Nationalized Industries was appointed by the House of Commons
on 7 July 1955, but—characteristically—without the special official
and staff. Its terms of reference were found in practice to be so
restricting that by the 14 November of the same year the Select
Committee had decided to give up in despair, reporting to Parliament
that '. . . the Order of Reference as at present drafted leaves insufficient scope to make enquiries or to obtain any real information
regarding the Nationalized Industries which would be of any real
use to the House'.

Opposition to the introduction of such a system of inquiry continued in many quarters, but the case to do something about it
proved so insistent that the following year a Select Committee (of
eleven members) with rather less restrictive terms of reference was
appointed specifically 'to examine the Reports and Accounts
of the Nationalized Industries established by statute whose controlling Boards are appointed by Ministers of the Crown and whose
annual receipts are not wholly or mainly derived by moneys provided
by Parliament or advanced from the Exchequer'. Its first report,

which dealt briefly with the South of Scotland Electricity Board and mainly with the North of Scotland Hydro-Electric Board appeared in October 1957, and set the pattern for the Select Committees on the Nationalized Industries (Reports and Accounts) which have since been appointed sessionally. Its final paragraph deserves quoting as a fair indication of the sort of leads that such inquiries, even at their more modest levels, can offer:

The Board is however still subject to a lot of criticism, some of which is unfair, and most of which is readily answered. Your Committee regret that not one of the Board's Annual Reports has been the subject of substantive debate in the House of Commons. They hope that this Report and the debate which they hope it may provoke in the House will help the Board. (*Report*, p. 16.)

The Select Committees adopted the practice of examining one industry at a time, with the consequence that the several nationalized industries would be investigated only once in a period of years. The Select Committee reports, which have appeared annually often in two or three substantial volumes, have made available a good deal of information about the working of the industries, and the activities and views of the Departments responsible for their oversight, including oral evidence and printed statements of considerable interest.

It soon became evident from these proceedings that much of the agitation against the appointment by Parliament of such a committee had been misconceived. At least the Committee was making available to MPs information that would not otherwise have been readily accessible, in addition of course to the reports and accounts which would have been available in any case. The prejudice against the existence of such a committee, which had been widespread, gradually dissolved, so that today it is not easy to see what the fuss was all about. Now the wheel has turned the other way, and a just criticism would be against the House of Commons itself for not making as much of the information at its disposal as it could and indeed should do. There have been occasions when the debate on such a report laid before Parliament has been confined mainly to those MPs who have actually served on the Select Committee.

After dealing with the Scottish Electricity Boards in 1957, subsequent Committees dealt with the National Coal Board in 1958, the two Air Corporations in 1959, British Railways in 1960, the Gas

Industry in 1961, the Electricity Supply Industry in 1963, and London Transport in 1964. In the meantime they had issued a report in 1962 reviewing what had been done by the industries covered by the first three reports to meet points of criticism raised therein, an essential follow-up in which the Select Committee concluded:

Your Committee have found it valuable and instructive to pursue with the nationalised industries and departments concerned the issues raised by the earlier Select Committees. They have learned that the three industries concerned have to a substantial extent followed the suggestions made in the Reports. They believe that the information conveyed in this Report and in the Appendices thereto will be of value to the House and will have the further advantage of lending a new perspective to the Reports of the three earlier Committees. (See *Report*, p. 30.)

Naturally, the subjects dealt with in relation to each particular industry have varied widely, depending mainly upon the industries' technological differences and the matters that were considered of prominent interest at the particular time. The Select Committees are concerned with information on current activities in fulfilment of their statutory requirements but not with policy matters. Yet, apart from the impossibility of determining where policy ends and execution (or administration or management) begins, it must be abundantly clear that, if such inquiries are to be of real value, Select Committees are bound to probe into and dilate upon matters that have serious policy implications, otherwise their activities would be of little value to anyone. As it is, their reports are of use not only to Parliament, on whose behalf they are produced, but to the Government who shoulder responsibility for the ultimate success of the nationalized industries, to the public for whose information the reports are published by Her Majesty's Stationery Office, and also to the industries themselves, who cannot fail to derive benefit from access to the views of such well placed outside investigators. There is also the longer term benefit to Parliament of having in its membership individuals who are well informed on the particular field.

From the investigations a general conclusion has emerged that the several Government Departments, whose Ministers have responsibility for nationalized industries, need to maintain a continuing interest in the industries concerned. This means that officials employed in the branches responsible for relationships with the industries tend to maintain regular personal contacts with their opposite numbers in the industries and to construct formal administrative machinery to an extent not visualized in the statutes. This is an inevitable administrative development, but there is evidence that it tends in practice to be overdone—as is alleged to have happened even in the case of central–local government relationships, where Ministerial oversight is by design operative only over specific services and much less continuously. The Select Committees have been critical of Ministers allowing their briefs to be exceeded in this way, and have maintained that, where additional ministerial responsibilities are desirable, they should be given specific statutory blessing.

In 1965–6 session the Select Committee on Nationalized Industries had its membership increased to eighteen and its terms of reference broadened to include the Post Office, whose metamorphosis from government department into public corporation was already under discussion. The Select Committee in its *Report* on the Post office (February 1967) endorsed the proposed change in status and organization, and the following month the Government's plans for the change were set out in the White Paper, *Reorganisation of the Post Office* (Cmnd. 3233).

It might be concluded from the unanimity with which this decision was received, including its support by both of the major political parties—or perhaps more accurately from the lack of organized opposition from any influential quarter—that the superiority of the public corporation type of administration had been proved beyond any question superior to Civil Service administration. Viewed in the light of the accumulating series of Select Committee reports on the nationalized industries on the one hand, and of the Post Office's distinguished history as a Department of State on the other, such a conclusion is certainly not justified. There have of course been times when the Post Office suffered from ineffective political decision-making, but the nationalized industries have not themselves evaded the effects of poor political foresight, nor have they been immune from uninspired managerial direction.

During the 1967–8 session the Select Committee changed its method of approach by undertaking, on lines long adopted by the Select Committee on Estimates, to examine an across-the-board problem affecting the several industries, and produced their three volume Report on *Ministerial Control of the Nationalised Industries*, already mentioned. These particular volumes will place students of government and public administration in the Committee's debt for a long time to come.

The Select Committee also produced a Special Report on *The Committee's Order of Reference* (1968) in which the limitations on the Committee's field of inquiry was discussed. It was suggested that, apart from the bodies already investigated, there were still six nationalized industries that came within the Committee's existing terms of reference (namely the British Airports Authority, the British Steel Corporation, the South of Scotland Electricity Board, the Transport Holding Company, the British Waterways Board, and the British Transport Docks Board) and the question was posed whether there were any other bodies owned or controlled by the Government that could be considered within the existing Order of reference or within a broader Order. In response to a request from the sub-committee making this inquiry HM Treasury has supplied a detailed list of thirty-six 'Bodies of a Trading Nature in which the Government has a Controlling Interest'. This list included details of the responsible Government Departments, the bodies and their functions, the method of appointment of the governing boards, finance and estimates provision, and the nature of policy control. After reducing the list by two, for reasons given, the Select Committee reported that thirteen of the remainder (including such bodies as Remploy Ltd., the British Broadcasting Corporation, the National Research Development Corporation, and Atomic Energy Authority and the Forestry Commission) fell within the province of the Estimates Committee, should they think fit to investigate them, and also that in these cases such expenditure that was provided for in the Estimates would fall to be considered by the PAC. It was also represented that a further eight bodies fell within the traditional field of the Public Accounts Committee (including the Covent Garden Market Author-ity, the Industrial Reorganization Corporation, the Sugar Board and the New Towns Development Corporations and Commission). After eliminating two other bodies for Specific reasons this left eleven bodies of which the Select Committee after detailed considera-tion recommended a majority for inclusion in their Order of refer-ence, although they were not in favour of a Treasury proposal that in any future Order of reference the bodies to be examined should be listed. The future scope of the Committee will now be determined by the decisions on the proposals contained in the

Green Paper, Select Committees of the House of Commons (Cmnd. 4507, 1970) already mentioned.

CONCLUSIONS

In examining the miscellaneous field of public administration, occupying the fringes of government and business administration, one is bound to be struck by the great diversity of the field, including as it does the public corporations, many of which are responsible for nationalized industries; regulatory bodies of various types; certain publicly controlled business enterprises; and other bodies variously patterned, functioned, and financed, but with the common element of autonomous public corporate control. Evidently such a diversity is not easily comprehended in its fullness or neatly classified. Constant changes and developments render it difficult for anyone to maintain an up-to-date picture of its shape and content. It has a complex diversity, varying types and degrees of control, and a distinct element of incoherence which renders it difficult for Government, Parliament, or public to understand what is going on within its borders.

Despite the widely endorsed doctrine, that the real virtue of the public corporation as an instrument of public administration is its comparative freedom from outside interference, the situation has changed so much since its age of acceptance before the Second World War as to weaken this apparent asset and to suggest that a return to more orthodox governmental administration might be desirable, at least in default of the invention of a better substitute.

Thus, interference by the Government has been rendered increasingly necessary (1) by the Government's expanding responsibility for the economy as a whole, (2) by growth of the substantial sector of the economy that has become responsible to public corporations and similar bodies, and (3) consequently by the need for ensuring that these bodies adopt co-ordinated economic and financial policies compatible with the overall state and development of the national economy. Another important factor, whose actual impact has not been effectively assessed—if indeed it is assessable—is the widening scope of Government patronage created by the extended use of the corporational form, and the absence of any equivalent to a public service commission for ensuring the political impartiality of the selection and the competence of the selected members of the boards (who themselves have a wide field of patronage at their disposal).

Within the present limits Parliament has had to strive hard to maintain any degree of supervision of this field, or even to obtain the minimum of information on which to reach considered judgments on the corporations' performance. Access to such information by both politician and citizen is essential to the working of democracy, especially in a highly technological age, and in meeting this particular need the Select Committee on Nationalized Industries has been effective, not only in providing the information but also in helping to keep the problem of accountability prominently before Parliament and people, thus discounting the fears of many of the original critics, both inside and outside the Houses of Parliament, who doubted the expediency of appointing such a committee. The growing problem is to know what to do with the information now it is more readily available!

FURTHER READING

Introductory

This vital but highly controversial subject is at least touched upon in the general works on public corporations and nationalized industries mentioned in the Further Reading list at the end of the previous Chapter, as well as in many of the general studies on the British system of government, although some do not extend their inquiries thus far. A very useful summary of main problems is to be found in R. W. Ennis' *Accountability in Government Departments, Public Corporations & Public Companies* (Lyon, Grant & Green, 1967) which is an expanded version of an Administrative Staff College Publication which first appeared in 1955. David Coombes in his *The Member of Parliament and the Administration* (Allen & Unwin, 1966), dealing with the Select Committee on Nationalised Industries up to 1964, provides a stimulating introduction to part of the subject of accountability.

Not to be overlooked is the first-rate summary of the development and functions of the 'Select Committee on Nationalised Industries' submitted by its Chairman as a Memorandum to the *Select Committee on Procedure* and printed in its *First Report, Session 1968–69*, on *Scrutiny of Public Expenditure and Administration*, pp. 270–3.

Historical and Advanced

A necessary text and quite remarkable discussion of the subject, supported by copious documentary evidence is to be found in the three volumes of the *First Report from the Select Committee on Nationalised Industries, Session 1967–68, Ministerial Control of the Nationalised Industries* (H.C. 371, 1968) covering respectively *I. Report and Proceedings; II. Minutes of Evidence;* and *III. Appendices and Index,* and the Government's comments in the White Paper *Ministerial Control of the Nationalised Industries,* Cmnd. 4027 (1969).

The *Reports* of the first Select Committees on Nationalised Industries, published in 1952 and 1953, and the *Special Report* of 1955 are of interest in connection with the establishment of the Committee. Apart from the massive Report on Ministerial Control, mentioned above, there have also been issued Reports dealing with general matters, i.e. the *Special Report* of 1959, which examined the experience of the Select Committees to date and suggested procedural improvements, the *Report* of 1962 investigating the outcome of the recommendations and conclusions of previous Reports, and Report of 1968 on *The Committee's Order of Reference,* considering certain publicly controlled or publicly financed bodies that might qualify for the attentions of future Select Committees.

Otherwise the Select Committees' Reports have been mainly concerned with individual nationalized industries. They are listed for reference:

1956–57 North of Scotland Hydro-Electric Board.
1957–58 National Coal Board.
1958–59 The Air Corporations.
1959–60 British Railways.
1960–62 Gas Industry.
1961–62 The Electricity Supply Industry.
1962–63 British Overseas Airways Corporation.
1964–65 London Transport.
1965–66 Further inquiries arising from Reports on fuel industries.
1965–67 Post Office.
1966–67 British European Airways.
1967–68 North Sea Gas.
1968–69 National Coal Board.
1969–70 Bank of England.

The two White Papers on the economic and financial aspects, mentioned in the text, are important: namely *The Financial and Economic Obligations of the Nationalised Industries* (Cmnd. 1337, 1961) and *A Review of Economic and Financial Obligations* (Cmnd. 3437, 1967).

PART THREE

Administration Abroad

CHAPTER EIGHT

International Administration

Although this present study has been mainly concerned with the administrative aspects of government in Britain the fact that we have been dealing with but one sector of an administrative realm of world-wide extent has never been far from our minds. In the world community there is of course a diversity of administrative patterns but, despite numerous variations in customs and structures, the similarities of means and goals in administration are often startling, as a more probing comparative survey would quickly show. With the increasing integration of the world community, through the improvement and remarkable speeding up of communications and transport, the separate national units have been drawn closer together, thus creating a continuing need for administrative co-ordination, both public and private, at the various levels. Horizontally, as it were, contacts between the national units have been developed in many ways, while vertically the web of international administration, which has been in process of development since the middle of the nineteenth century, has become more complex, both in structure and in operation, and also recognizable everywhere by the ordinary citizen, whose life is unavoidably affected by its activities and demands. An introductory work of the present type must recognize the universality of the subject and take account of international administration and the linking of the national with the international sphere. Incidentally, it soon becomes apparent that if progress towards the forming of a world community has seemed disappointing to its most enthusiastic advocates, it is within the field of public administration more than in any other, and not so much according to design as in response to necessity, that the concept of One World has been most closely approached.

GOVERNMENT OR ADMINISTRATION?

In this sphere the administrative still predominates over the political. International government as it exists is very different from the supra-national type usually envisaged by the advocates of world government. It consists in the main of action carried out co-operatively by existing national governments and the centre of power is still located in the national sphere. In supra-national government the centre of power would be shifted above the national line and supra-national institutions would exist in their own right, and not on the sufferance of the individual countries, as at present. Most of the institutions considered in this chapter fall within the normal sphere of inter-national government, though a few experiments in the supra-national type have been inaugurated.

Neither form is historically new. The city states of Sumer at the beginning of history and of ancient Greece somewhat later, to men-tion only two examples, carried out experiments in international co-operation which could be said to fall within the existing types, while forms of supra-national government have been forcibly imposed by imperial rule, often creating administrative problems for the solution of which the resources did not yet exist. Recent developments in the international sphere have tended to render the imperial type obsolete, but there is still one outstanding example of the genre in the USSR, which combines in one solid geographical block a group of national-ities whose homelands stretch right across Eurasia. The present international scheme is characterized by its comprehensiveness (until 1971 diminished and weakened by the absence of China), a comprehensiveness that has been rendered possible by the remark-able technical advances in communications and transport, bringing the nations not merely upon each other's doorstep but into each others front hall! The proper object today is to build government of the supra-national type by co-operation as opposed to force, though the emergence of the two super-powers since the Second World War, an indeterminate group of lesser powers, and a whole host of articulate non-powers, has sadly impeded development in the direction of a true World Government in which so many place their hopes for the future.

The primary aims of international government are similar to those of national government: namely, to provide security and protection for the wider community and to make the most of its collective resources through the raising of living standards to an extent, and by means, compatible with the principles on which civilization is based. The existence of the so-called 'have' and 'have-not' nations (terms as half-true and as woolly as the alternative 'developed' and 'developing') is tending to concentrate the efforts of existing international institutions upon the redistribution of resources and the development of appropriate social and industrial institutions and services in the less advanced countries. A dawning awareness of the universal nature of the adverse environmental consequences of technological 'progress' is further emphasizing the need for international administrative intervention.

The normal tripartite division of government tends, for sound basic reasons, to be carried over into the international field, where we find distinctive legislative, executive and judicial bodies, although in each case the main function is considerably modified in working. Thus the legislative bodies are largely concerned with deliberation and diplomacy, in drawing up codes, conventions, agreements, which have to be endorsed and adopted by the legislatures of the constituent nations before they can become operative within their boundaries. In adjudicating upon specific cases international courts are building up a useful corpus of case law, but even here participation depends upon the acceptance of their jurisdiction and rulings by the individual nations. Furthermore, implementation depends upon the good will of the members, for international bodies do not have at their command law-enforcement agencies in the individual countries to ensure that their decisions are carried out, as do the national governments in federal states. Certainly, sanctions can be imposed upon a nation from without with the general approval of the international authority, but in practice this has not so far proved a very effective instrument. Not only is it difficult to achieve universal application, but the effects of the sanctions often prove quite different from what was expected, largely because a state that is sufficiently united to withstand coercion can usually devise alternative ways of meeting its needs. In fact the executive agencies available in international government are not able to exercise much real power. A further weakness arises from the fact that within the democratic members of the international organization there are oppositions, who are often impelled to oppose their governments' policies in the international field as in home affairs. Thus in such agencies the strictly governmental activities tend to be minimal and weak, prominence being given to administration, which is in consequence much freer and more authoritative than in the national states.

The form of the various international arrangements and bodies varies widely. Some are general- or multi-purpose, dealing with a broad stream of activities; some are organized on a functional basis, supplying a specific service. Their scope may be (i) bilateral, (ii) regional, or (iii) universal. An example of (i) is provided by the Commission for the United States and Canada, which is concerned with the use of boundary waters on the common frontier of the two nations; of (ii) by the North Atlantic Treaty Organization (NATO) set up to give unity to the Western European defence system, and the International Organization of American States to deal more widely with the mutual interests of the member states; and of (iii) the International Court of Justice and the United Nations, whose general structure and functions will be outlined in the next section.

THE PRESENT WORLD STRUCTURE

In the international field there have been numerous developments in inter-state administration going back several centuries, although it was not until the second half of the nineteenth century that social and technological changes created a demand for inter-governmental co-operation on an ever-widening scale.

This movement had been preceded by such developments as the control of navigation on those European rivers that traversed a number of states, such as the Rhine and the Danube. A treaty agreement providing for organized control of the Rhine existed as early as 1506 and, with the termination of the period of Napoleonic conquest, a Rhine Commission was created by the Treaty of Vienna in 1815, in which many of the aspects common to international bodies were already manifested. A Danube Commission was established in 1856,

composed of representatives of the Great Powers. It was independent of local sovereignties and had autonomous control of the
river. Since the Second World War its membership has been restricted, under Russian leadership, to the East European states. With
the build up of postal services on an international basis, following
the reforms inaugurated by Rowland Hill in Britain in 1840, the
need for concerted measures of international co-ordination became
insistent. The Universal Postal Union, which was founded in 1874 to
arrange for such co-operation, covering the standardization of
methods affecting more than one country, the interchange of information, and the settlement of trans-frontier mail routes and postage
rates, was typical of the extension of such institutions and services
from a mainly European to a world basis. Today its membership
includes most of the countries of the world and it maintains the
International Bureau at Berne (Switzerland) as its permanent headquarters, although its periodical congresses meet in different countries. This category of 'international unions', as they have been
called, was found so effective that, by the end of the First World War
in 1919, they had extended into many fields of human activity and had
proliferated to such an extent that as many as 222 had been founded.
This was the pioneering stage in the development of modern international administration.

An international movement of exceptional importance and unique
interest is the International Red Cross, which originated in 1863
from the proposals put forward by Henry Dunant, a citizen of
Switzerland, to provide relief for victims of war. Its membership is
made up of those nations who subscribe to the Geneva Convention,
adopted on 8 August 1864, which lays down certain humane principles
to be observed in the conduct of war. The movement, which is
strictly neutral, works through a central International Committee
and voluntary Red Cross (or Red Crescent, Red Lion, or Sun)
Societies in the individual countries, co-ordinated through the
League of Red Cross Societies, and working today in close co-
operation with interested UN agencies.

Such developments, so important an essay into the field of extra-
national administration, were in 1919 to be greatly overshadowed by
the establishment, as an integral part of the peace settlement following the war, of the League of Nations, the setting up of its major
institutions at Geneva and of its specialist bodies, of which the
International Labour Organization has continued to afford a highly

successful example of international administrative co-operation.

The League, after a brief period of bright promise, failed, partly because of the absence from its membership of nations of world-wide status and power—notably of the United States, whose wartime President Wilson had been its foremost sponsor—partly because its actual members were in the main insufficiently imbued with internationalist ideals and purpose to achieve the modest degree of unity that success presupposed. If the League lacked political drive and power, administratively much good work was done, particularly in the sphere of social welfare and industrial co-operation, and valuable lessons were learned. The League of Nations was itself a field of experiment in the new administrative techniques needed in the international field and good progress was made in laying the foundations of a World Administrative Service, which is a crying need of the new order that is still in process of establishment.

With the replacement of the still lingering League by the United Nations in 1945, a new phase in the development of international government began. Certainly the successor of the League was fortunate in having the experience of the previous quarter century on which to build. The United Nations Organization (UNO), working through its General Assembly (representing all nation-members equally), the Security Council, the Economic and Social Council, and the Trusteeship Council, in association with the International Court of Justice, is served by the Secretariat, which is its permanent administrative body.

The four purposes of the United Nations are defined as: (1) the maintenance of international peace and security; (2) the development of friendly relations among nations, based on respect for equal rights and self-determination of peoples; (3) co-operation in solving international problems of an economic, social, cultural and humanitarian character, and promotion of respect for human rights and fundamental freedoms for all; and (4) acting as a centre for harmonizing the actions of nations in attaining these common ends.

Membership of the United Nations is open to all states, but approval of new members requires a two-thirds vote in favour by the General Assembly, upon the recommendation of the Security Council, where it must survive a veto that may be exercised by any of the permanent members. Because of this condition a few states have been excluded, including until 1971 the mainland republic of China. The General Assembly elects, or participates in the election of, the other organizations, with which it maintains varying relationships. It also controls the budget of the UN and determines the contributions of the member states. The primary responsibility for maintaining international peace and security was conferred upon the Security Council of fifteen members, of which five—extra-mainland China (i.e. Taiwan), France, Russia, the United Kingdom, and the United States—were permanent members. The Economic and Social Council, responsible for a wide range of subjects directed to the improvement of standards in the world community, has a membership of twenty-seven, elected by the General Assembly on the basis of nine annually for a term of three years. The Trusteeship Council originally consisted of those members that administered trust territories (now practically superseded), the members of the Security Council who did not administer such territories, and sufficient other members, elected by the Assembly for three-year terms, to ensure that the membership was divided equally between administering and non-administering members. It is now mainly interested in non-trust territories which have not yet attained self-government. China was voted in and Taiwan excluded in October 1971.

The International Court of Justice, superseding the former Permanent Court of International Justice, is the principal judicial organ of the UN. All members of the UN are parties to the Statute of the International Court, and a state not belonging may be allowed to become a party to the Statute. The Court's fifteen judges—appointed irrespective of nationality, except that not more than one may be selected from any one state concurrently—are chosen by the General Assembly and the Security Council voting independently. The jurisdiction of the Court extends to all cases which the parties refer to it, and all matters specially provided for in the UN Charter and in other existing treaties and conventions.

The Secretariat of the UN consists of the Secretary-General, who is appointed by the General Assembly on the recommendation of the Security Council, and of such staff as the Organization may require, the latter being appointed by the Secretary-General, under regulations laid down by the General Assembly. The Secretary-General combines the functions of chief executive and chief administrative officer. Members of the Secretariat are assigned, as needed, to the various other organizations and agencies of the UN. The whole UN Organization, which has grown more and more complex as the system of international administration has developed to meet expanding needs, includes numerous committees and commissions, as well as the highly specialized agencies to which brief reference must now be made.

Prominent among these specialized agencies, for which the Economic and Social Council takes particular responsibility, are the International Labour Organization (ILO), the Food and Agriculture Organization of the UN (FAO), the UN Educational, Scientific and Cultural Organization (UNESCO), the International Civil Aviation Organization (ICAO), the International Monetary Fund, the International Bank of Reconstruction and Development, the International Finance Corporation, the World Health Organization (WHO), the Universal Postal Union (UPU), the International Telecommunications Union (ITU), the World Meteorological Organization (WMC), and the Inter-Governmental Maritime Consultative Organization. An International Trade Organization was planned but its Charter failed to obtain sufficient acceptances, and instead a looser form of organization has emerged under the General Agreement on Tariffs and Trade (GATT), which is basically a multilateral contract with the stated objectives (a) to help raise standards of living; (b) to achieve full employment; (c) to develop the world's resources; (d) to expand production and exchange of goods; and (e) to promote economic development.

All these specialized agencies are inter-governmental bodies with wide responsibilities within their respective fields, and each usually includes an Assembly, a Council, and a staff, but the pattern varies. The ILO in particular is of special interest as a surviving agency of the League of Nations, which from its inception in 1919 has had a long and admirable record of achievement in the field of industrial relations. The Organization works through the International Labour Conference, the Governing Body and the International Labour Office headed by its Director-General. The Conference differs from similar bodies in the way its membership is constituted: besides having two governmental delegates of the normal types, each member state also sends one delegate to represent employers and one to represent workers. In this way the ILO has been able to maintain close contacts with those interests in the several countries with which its work is most closely concerned. It is significant that its activities have been characterized by a sense of realism that is not always prominent in the international field.

In 1964 the UN Conference on Trade and Development

(UNCTAD) was set up with an original membership of 132. It consists of a Conference, a Trade and Development Board, and a series of specialist Committees, together with the UNCTAD Secretariat, with offices in Geneva and New York. It has the support of the Communist countries, though the Western powers were less enthusiastic in their support. Since 1 January, 1968 GATT and UNCTAD have co-operated in establishing the International Trade Centre to co-ordinate the activities of the two organizations.

The complex international organization briefly summarized here is shown on the chart, 'The United Nations and Related Agencies', facing page 165.

THE EUROPEAN COMMUNITY

Chapter 8 of the Charter of the United Nations provides for the accommodation of regional bodies in the new system of international administration. An example of such is provided by the establishment of regional Economic Commissions, as subsidiary organs of the Economic and Social Council. These are the Economic Commission for Europe (ECE), and the Economic Commission for Asia and the Far East (ECAFE) both established in March 1947, the Economic Commission for Latin America (ECLA) established the following year, and the Economic Commission for Africa (ECA), established in 1958. The main objective of the European Commission was defined as initiation and participation 'in measures for facilitating concerted action for the economic reconstruction of Europe, for raising the level of European economic activity, and for maintaining and strengthening the economic relations of European Countries both among themselves and with the other countries of the world'. Similar aims inspired the establishment of the other regional Commissions, all of which form an integral part of the UN machinery, to which the Economic and Social Council can decentralize such functions as are best carried out in the respective areas. The scope of ECE has been badly diminished by the schism between the Communist East and the non-communist West, and the consequent abstention of the USSR and her communist neighbours.

A regional development of a rather different and more spontaneous nature has taken place in Western Europe, where a common cultural heritage, as well as an addiction to free institutions, to some

THE UNITED NATIONS AND RELATED AGENCIES

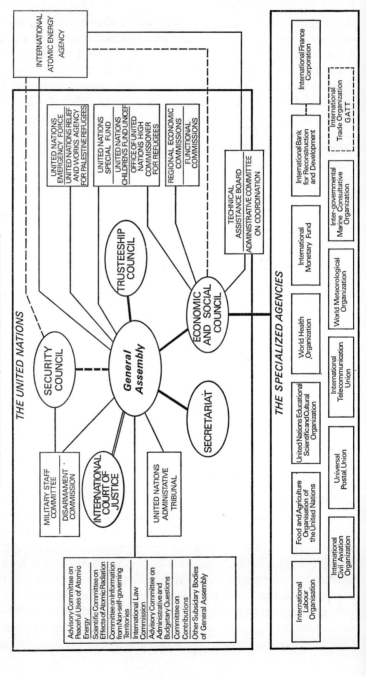

THE UNITED NATIONS

INTERNATIONAL ATOMIC ENERGY AGENCY

Advisory Committee on Peaceful Uses of Atomic Energy
Scientific Committee on Effects of Atomic Radiation
Committee on Information from Non-self-governing Territories
International Law Commission
Advisory Committee on Administrative and Budgetary Questions
Committee on Contributions
Other Subsidiary Bodies of General Assembly

MILITARY STAFF COMMITTEE
DISARMAMENT COMMISSION

UNITED NATIONS EMERGENCY FORCE
UNITED NATIONS RELIEF AND WORKS AGENCY FOR PALESTINE REFUGEES

UNITED NATIONS SPECIAL FUND
UNITED NATIONS CHILDREN'S FUND-UNICEF
OFFICE OF UNITED NATIONS HIGH COMMISSIONER FOR REFUGEES

REGIONAL ECONOMIC COMMISSIONS
FUNCTIONAL COMMISSIONS

SECURITY COUNCIL

TRUSTEESHIP COUNCIL

INTERNATIONAL COURT OF JUSTICE

UNITED NATIONS ADMINISTRATIVE TRIBUNAL

General Assembly

SECRETARIAT

ECONOMIC AND SOCIAL COUNCIL

TECHNICAL ASSISTANCE BOARD
ADMINISTRATIVE COMMITTEE ON COORDINATION

THE SPECIALIZED AGENCIES

International Labour Organisation

International Civil Aviation Organization

Food and Agriculture Organisation of the United Nations

Universal Postal Union

United Nations Educational Scientific and Cultural Organization

International Telecommunication Union

World Health Organization

World Meteorological Organization

International Monetary Fund

Inter-governmental Marine Consultative Organization

International Bank for Reconstruction and Development

International Trade Organization GATT

International Finance Corporation

extent mitigated the drawbacks of a nationalism that was largely the product of the same culture. The establishment of a real European Community has been seen by many as a desirable first step towards the establishment of a world order. By the end of the Second World War, which was, like the First World War and despite the participation of others, primarily a European civil war, it was evident that the states of Western Europe were now individually too restricted in resources to profit fully from continuing advances in science and knowledge. In fact they had reached a situation in relation to Western Europe similar to that of the German States to Germany before the establishment of the Reich and of the Italian States to Italy at the time of the Risorgimento, two important integrative movements of the nineteenth century. Now as then there are varying schools of thought to divide counsel, the opposition ranging from those who see in larger units evils that more than offset the advantages claimed by their critics, to those whose minds are too fixed in the old ways, too rooted in maintaining the *status quo*, for the essential changes to be made without painful readjustments and inevitable retreats. But despite all this the tide has continued to flow in favour of the increased integration that productivity and security predicate. The ultimate problem is to achieve unity while maintaining a healthy diversity.

The public administrator will find much in favour of European unity. Apart from diminishing the manifest inconveniences to communication, travel, and trade consequent upon the multiplicity of national frontiers, there are many European services which are sufficiently uniform to gain from closer administrative integration. Despite variations in economic productivity—and such variations have narrowed considerably since the earlier *Introduction* was first published—the several communities are reasonably homogeneous and not seriously affected by the extreme problems of backward areas that beset the world community and indeed are considerably aggravated and often in fact created by the division of areas into independent units too restricted in resources to stand on their own feet even with considerable outside aid. Despite different languages and customs, in Western Europe similar attitudes and approaches, arising from a shared history and common culture, are conducive to that degree of co-operation upon which effective administration depends.

While there has been good reason for the introduction of each piece of European co-ordinative machinery since the Second World War, the multiplicity of these developments has hardly been conducive to overall success. It all began with Benelux—the Economic Union of Belgium, the Netherlands, and Luxembourg—which virtually began with a Monetary Convention and a Customs Convention arranged by the three countries during the war when their governments were still in exile in London. The next development in this particular line was the signature of the Brussels Treaty on 17 March 1948, between the United Kingdom, France, and the Benelux Countries, with the object of achieving economic, social, and cultural collaboration and effective self-defence. The Organization for European Economic Co-operation (OEEC) emerged from a Convention signed on 16 April 1948, on behalf of the governments of sixteen European countries and the Commanders-in-Chief of the American, British, and French Zones of Occupation in Germany, with the general object of achieving 'a sound European economy through the economic co-operation of its Members'. In 1961 OEEC was replaced by the Organization for Economic Co-operation and Development (OECD), with extended functions and the US and Canada as full members, thus taking it out of the category of a purely European institution.

On 4 April 1949 the North Atlantic Treaty was signed in Washington and the Organization of the same name (NATO) was born. The objects of the new organization were the promotion of the stability and well-being in the North Atlantic area and the uniting of the members' efforts for collective defence and preservation of peace and security. The original membership of twelve significantly already included America and Canada. Yet its activities have been so involved in the military defence of Europe that, despite the overwhelming contribution of the United States, it seems appropriate to consider it as part of the system of European administration. France's partial withdrawal in 1968 further reduced the effectiveness of an institution, whose place in the European scheme had been considerably altered at least for the time being by the lessening of tension between East and West.

The next important innovation was the Council of Europe, based upon a statute signed by the governments of ten European states on 5 May 1949. This was an attempt to set up an European Parliament, consisting of a Committee of Ministers and a Consultative Assembly. As the Statute states 'the aim of the Council of Europe is to achieve a greater unity between the Members for the purpose of safeguarding and realizing the ideals and principles which are their common heritage and facilitating their economic and social progress'. A special feature of the Consultative Assembly was the weighting of its membership according to the size and importance of the member state, ranging from eighteen for the major powers down to three for Iceland. This is unusual in these international organizations, for which equality of membership is normally insisted upon, with not very happy results in the case of UN as a whole. The members of the Assembly represent the parliaments of the member states, who decide individually on the manner in which they shall be selected.

Britain was a member from the outset and has taken a foremost part in all three major organizations so far mentioned: namely, OECD, NATO, and the Council of Europe, but she remained outside the next important development which culminated in the six Western nations—Belgium, France, Western Germany, Italy, Luxembourg, and the Netherlands—signing, on 18 April 1951, a Treaty introducing the European Coal and Steel Community (ECSC), to create a common market for coal and steel within their territories. ECSC worked through four bodies, namely the High Authority, the Common Assembly, the Special Council of Ministers, and the Court of Justice, and thus constituted a complete international governing and administering system in miniature. A special characteristic of this development was its specific if limited supra-national element. For the objects of the Community actual sovereignty was transferred to it by the participating nations and the High Authority was conceived as a truly executive organ (although this aim was to be modified in actual practice). Attached to the High Authority was a Consultative Committee, an advisory body of fifty-one members chosen from among producers and consumers. Although influential opinion in Britain was at the time opposed to joining ECSC, special arrangements for close co-operation with it were subsequently brought about through the *Agreement Concerning Relations Between the United Kingdom and the ECSC* in December 1954.

The next project, arising logically out of the establishment of ECSC, was the formation by the six nations of a European Defence Community (EDC) which, organized on similar supra-national lines, would have had a much wider scope, but, when it remained only for France to ratify the Treaty, the whole scheme broke down in August 1954, with the refusal of the French Parliament to do so. As an

G

alternative, a plan to increase the scope of the Brussels Treaty was agreed on 23 October 1954, and Western European Union (WEU) was born. Its aim was to bring in Western Germany and Italy, with the object of strengthening peace and security, and of promoting the unity and encouraging the progressive integration of Europe. The main agencies of WEU included a Council, an Assembly, and an Agency for Control of Armaments, and Britain became a participant. At the time of its inception WEU had the several tasks of creating a purely European defence organization (in close co-operation with NATO), of arranging the admission of Western Germany to NATO, and of supervising the projected European Statute of the Saar. The two former tasks were quickly fulfilled but other developments prevented the third from materializing. Except for its office of associating Britain with 'the Six', WEU has had little to add to the existing system.

The main line of advance now rested with the narrower field of 'the Six'. The Members of the European Coal and Steel Community further developed their union with the signing, on 25 March 1957, of two treaties introducing (1) the European Economic Community (EEC) with the object of gradually creating a common market, to facilitate the free movement of goods, persons, services, and capital throughout their territories, and (2) the European Atomic Energy Community (Euratom) with the object of contributing 'to the raising of the standard of living in Member States and to the development of commercial exchanges with other countries by the creation of conditions necessary to the speedy establishment and growth of nuclear industries'.

The new structure for the Economic Community included a Commission, a Council, an Assembly and a Court of Justice, which parallelled the structure of ECSC. Euratom was provided with a similar set of organizations, as well as a consultative Economic and Social Committee. In practice the organs of all three authorities— ECSC, EEC, and Euratom—were closely integrated through the sharing of the same Assembly and Court of Justice. In 1965 it was decided to merge the three Communities under a combined Commission of nine members, acting individually as heads of nine executive departments (but see page 177).

Thus the institutions of 'the Six', for the three defined fields of activity, formed a nucleus government and administration of Europe, with wider powers and based upon surer foundations than the earlier and more widely-based European structures, valuable as these have most certainly been. When the Assembly of 'the Six' first met they decided to adopt the title of 'European Parliamentary Assembly'. Significantly its seating was arranged according to the political groupings and parties, on the lines of most national parliaments, and not alphabetically according to nations, as is the usual practice in international assemblies. An interesting administrative development in Euratom was the arrangement whereby the Commission was empowered to appoint inspectors with access to premises, information and persons for the purpose of verifying the accounting of materials.

In the meantime British Governments had changed their policy and evinced a desire to join the Common Market, but approaches in 1962 and 1967 were frustrated, finally through the veto of France strongly under the influence of President de Gaulle. During 1970/71 negotiations are again in progress between Britain and 'the Six', and a number of other countries are in the queue for membership (but see page 177).

Towards the end of 1959 a new European institution emerged in the shape of the European Free Trade Association (EFTA), to provide as a counterpart of 'the Six', an area in which similar free-trade objectives could be progressively developed. In the somewhat dispersed series of national communities thus co-ordinated Britain joined with Austria, Denmark, Norway, Portugal, Sweden, and Switzerland, sometimes known as 'the Seven'. The EFTA Convention, which was signed and accepted by all members early in 1960, provided for the gradual elimination of protective customs duties and quota restrictions between its members. Finland has been associated with EFTA since 27 March 1961, and Iceland became a full member on 1 March 1970. The Association, with its headquarters in Geneva, works through a Council and a small Secretariat. The chairmanship of the Council is held in rotation by each member country for six months. EFTA's achievement has been useful rather than exciting. As a makeshift means of supplementing the scope of the European Economic Community its existence cannot be conceived as other than an interim solution.

One thing that stands out clearly from an examination of the European inter-governmental structure as a whole is its over-elaboration and duplication. It calls upon the services of too many politicians and too many higher officials from the several countries and inter-linking is much too complicated. There are too many 'capital' cities and too many separate administrative units. More damning than many of the positive weaknesses is the system's failure to present a clear-cut picture to the European man-in-the-street, upon whose understanding and good-will its health and ultimate development must depend. A radical streamlining is called for, both in the interests of political effectiveness and of administrative efficiency.

Nor is the picture, given here in a much simplified form, sufficiently complete to drive home the full weight of these criticisms. Among the important international bodies not so far considered are the European Conference of Ministers of Transport (ECMT), the European Civil Aviation Conference (ECAC), the European Conference of Posts and Telecommunications, the European Organization for Nuclear Research, the Central Commission for Navigation of the Rhine, the Nordic Council and the Balkan Alliance. There is also Eurofima, a special company set up in connection with ECMT to finance the construction and provision of rolling stock for the railways in the participating countries. The United Kingdom is a participant in ECMT but not in Eurofima. The Economic Commission for Europe, has been mentioned as one of the UN's regional agencies.

In addition there are the inter-state agencies of the Soviet block, about which much less is known in the West. Foremost among these are the arrangements of the Warsaw Pact signed on 14 May 1955 by eight Eastern European countries—Albania, Bulgaria, Czechoslovakia, East Germany, Hungary, Poland, Rumania, and the Soviet Union—as a 'Treaty of Friendship, Co-operation and Mutual Assistance'. This was an answer to NATO, but the overwhelming nature of Soviet power places such Eastern European attempts at international co-operation in a category that those nations themselves, applying their own political philosophy, would term an imperialist relationship, and one very different from that subsisting within the European Community. The truth of this was decisively demonstrated when the Warsaw Pact forces invaded Czechoslovakia in August 1968.

In conclusion, if such a term can be appropriately applied to such a provisional situation, it can be said that all this hectic complexity has its dynamic, constructive, and hopeful side. The nations of Europe, in their apparent disunity, are impelled by forces that prescribe a much

larger community than at present exists: hence this, almost continuous, stream of experiments since the Second World War. Failure
in one direction does not call for despondency on the administrator's part, since from such experiments future advantages may be
expected to accrue.

The up-to-date membership position of the several European
agencies is shown in the table on page 172 setting out the 'Development of More Important European Organizations'.

ASPECTS OF INTERNATIONAL ADMINISTRATION

As a governing institution the United Nations has not been a
conspicuous success. The question of power and its deployment is a
political one and therefore outside the scope of the present work. Yet
the impact of power in the shaping of the administration is so important that the world-power pattern, which has emerged with the rise of
two super-powers, cannot be ignored in this context. Many vital
international problems fail to reach the stage when administrative
solutions can be applied, due mainly to deadlock between the two
major viewpoints and a widespread unwillingness among middle-
ranking powers to become involved unless their own interests are
vitally concerned. The application of voting principles suitable to the
selection of representatives by individual electors, such as the one-
nation-one-vote arrangement in the UN Assembly, has had the
aggravating Gresham's law effect of reducing the interest and willing
involvement of the very nations that have been foremost among those
striving for a system of world government.

Financing these international bodies presents serious difficulties.
Their continued dependence upon the financing powers of the
member states is a fundamental weakness which is not likely to be
overcome until there is a general or federal authority with the power
to assess and collect suitable taxes throughout the system. At the
moment, even where agreement has been reached as to the amount
of financial support to be provided by the member states, there is
really no way of ensuring that the agreed payments are made, or not
unduly delayed. Insistent pressure for compliance can easily bring
threats of withdrawal.

Generally speaking the developments described in the present
chapter have been inter- rather than supra-national. Apart from the

DEVELOPMENT OF MORE IMPORTANT EUROPEAN ORGANIZATIONS with membership position in 1970

Date	Organization	BELGIUM	LUXEMBOURG	NETHERLANDS	UNITED KINGDOM	FRANCE	AUSTRIA	DENMARK	GERMANY	GREECE	ICELAND	IRELAND	ITALY	NORWAY	PORTUGAL	SPAIN	SWEDEN	SWITZERLAND	TURKEY	FINLAND
21 Oct. 1943[1]	Benelux Economic Union (Monetary Convention 21.10.43: Customs Convention 5.9.44)	×	×	×																
17 Mar. 1948	Brussels Treaty Organization	×	×	×	×	×														
16 Apl. 1948	Organization for European Economic Co-operation (OEEC) (United States and Canada are associate members, Yugoslavia is represented as an observer)	×	×	×	×	×	×	×	×	×	×	×	×	×	×	×	×	×	×	
4 Apl. 1949	North Atlantic Treaty Organization (NATO) (United States and Canada are also full members)	×	×	×	×	×		×	×	×	×		×	×	×				×	
5 May 1949	Council of Europe	×	×	×	×	×	×	×	×	×	×	×	×	×			×		×	
18 Apl. 1951	European Coal and Steel Community (ECSC) (U.K. has special relations with ECSC)	×	×	×		×			×				×							
23 Oct. 1954	Western European Union (WEU) (a development of the Brussels Treaty Organization)	×	×	×	×	×			×				×							
25 Mar. 1957	European Economic Community (EEC) (set up to introduce Common Market)	×	×	×		×			×				×							
25 Mar. 1957	European Atomic Energy Community (Euratom) (U.K. has special relations with Euratom)	×	×	×		×			×				×							
20 Nov. 1959	European Free Trade Association (EFTA)				×		×	×						×	×		×	×		×²
8 Apl. 1965	ECSC, EEC and Euratom establish a single Council and a single Commission	×	×	×		×			×				×							

1 These are the dates of signing of the basic convention; ratifications followed later, preceding actual entry into force of the convention and the setting up of the...

basic power weakness, there has been restricted scope in the existing scheme for legislation and adjudication, while the intermittent nature of the exercise of executive power has meant that the administrative sectors have acquired a predominance in this field which would be quite out of character in other realms of public administration. Yet, as we have seen, the several institutions that make up the European Community have been endowed with certain powers of a supra-national type, the implementing of which is providing valuable experience for the future. The basic policies of the individual nations considerably influence the working of such powers as have so far been delegated.

International administration shares many of the conditions and most of the problems of public administration in the national field and, of course, has special problems of its own. Thus the establishment of its headquarters often depends not upon spontaneous emergence or administrative convenience but upon political expediency. The selection of New York as the capital of the United Nations was certainly influenced by a desire to discard the image of the League—a viewpoint strongly evinced *inter alia* by the powerful USSR—and to begin afresh, although in practice this was not really possible even if it was desirable. At the lowest assessment it would have been silly to discard the accumulated experience of the earlier experiment. One consequence of siting the headquarters in the United States, with its high and mounting cost of living, has been to render the running of the organization very expensive, since American standards have determined costs throughout the system.

The staffing of international institutions presents special difficulties. The language problem is vital and complicates administration, rendering it expensive, since translation is necessitated at every turn and the interchange of staff is rendered unavoidably less fluid, as well as placing special strains upon the individual official, although less perhaps where his tongue is one of the designated languages. In the case of the International Court of Justice these have been confined to French and English, but for the other UN bodies five languages have been given this special status—Chinese, French, English, Russian, and Spanish. In any case an international official will have to be able to use the language of the country in which his particular agency operates. Arabic has now been added to the official languages.

Impartiality in recruitment, coupled with the achievement of prescribed levels of competence, is just as essential but even more difficult to achieve in the international than in the national field. Educational and professional qualifications can be laid down, but even where similar labels are employed these vary considerably as between one country and another, and it is not always easy to equate them when recruiting staff members from different parts of the world. Recommendations from responsible persons and institutions have to be weighed in the balance and it is well understood that personal, political, social, and other reasons may figure in the minds of recommenders, whose own conception of the requirements of the international service can rarely be realistically based. Application, at both the recruitment and the promotion stages, of the principle of 'a fair field and no favour', difficult as it is to achieve in the national field, has in the international to cope with special obstacles, due to the need to ensure that member states have reasonable shares in the appointments. This often means the allocation of appointments to persons from countries that are ill-equipped with the skills and experience needed adequately to fill the post. To appoint such persons—and this happens unavoidably on quite a large scale—results (1) in depriving the appointing agency of the best available candidate for the job irrespective of nationality; (2) in staffing important posts with people who are below par and who not only reduce the efficiency of the particular branch but also set a bad example to the entire service; and (3) where the appointee is competent, in depriving his own state of services that it cannot afford to do without. In addition, the allocation of posts to persons of specific nationality may lead to the creation of unnecessary, or perhaps only partly necessary, posts, especially at senior deputy levels, and thus to expensive overstaffing. The filling of posts by officials who are known to be under-qualified, over-paid, and perhaps underworked, is bound to diminish staff morale and general efficiency. A natural tendency in such bodies to overspecialization and the organization of offices in too many branches and sections, is further aggravated by such staffing requirements. It is no doubt inevitable that, at the present stage of development, the staffing of international agencies should not coincide strictly with the actual needs of the work, and the international personnel manager has a nice balance to settle.

Apart from having to accept such career drawbacks as inevitable, the international official has many other problems to face. He has to cultivate a new loyalty, strong enough to neutralize his natural national inclinations. He is no more expected to give up his national allegiances than the national civil servant is required to discard his own political beliefs, but he has to learn to subordinate what are often very powerful feelings to the exigencies of his work. In either sphere only the truly dedicated man can do this and potential dedication of this sort cannot be estimated in advance. Only subjection to actual service conditions, whatever they may be, and time can achieve this, supported by a public esteem which is difficult to assess and not easily earned.

The international official, despite a normally high standard of living, has to put up with the strains of dwelling in a strange community, usually under unaccustomed climatic conditions, often without certain amenities that he enjoys at home, away from close friends, and often needing to make special arrangements for his children's schooling. Should his own country become involved in an international dispute he may have to bear exceptional stresses which render the performance of his official duties particularly difficult. The international civil servant is usually an expatriate, and history suggests that his security of tenure may often prove inferior to that of his opposite number in national services. Such conditions further emphasize his need for a strong sense of vocation, of being a citizen of the wider community. Fortunately the service of persons with such characteristics and outlook has been amply forthcoming from the days when the League of Nations was launched upon the world.

While the national civil servant who transfers to the international field usually brings with him invaluable administrative experience, in practice he will have to accommodate himself to many new conditions in his new field, and his approach will have to be flexible if he is to be as successful in his new service as he was in his old. The national civil services have their own characteristics, which will have contributed to the moulding of the international public services, some no doubt adding more than others, with the result nevertheless that the official transferring from one to the other will have a good deal to learn and to get used to.

In his daily work the international civil servant is not usually under continuing ministerial supervision, and as member of the secretariat responsible for carrying on the administration between meetings of the ruling assembly or council, he usually wields more executive authority than his opposite number in the home civil service. Where the situation warrants he will be given authority to act for the Council or Minister and thus the ministerial power in such organizations is shared in varying degrees between politician and professional administrator. Among the outstanding exceptions, pointing insistently towards the future, are, as we have seen, the European Common Market incorporating permanent ministerial bodies which establish the political appointee more permanently in the administrative picture. Another important difference between the two spheres rests in the differing impact upon the official of public opinion. While a type of world public opinion has emerged and is steadily growing, it is highly specialized and widely dispersed and the international official is not constantly harassed and called to account at the behest of the complaining citizen as is the normal lot of the national civil servant or local government official.

Although there has been a significant shift away from the predominantly diplomatic type of administration that prevailed under the League of Nations, and towards the executive type that is involved in the actual provision of services, much international administration continues to be of the former type and it is easy for the international official to place greater store upon protocol than upon actual execution, and to fail to take such action as is best calculated to achieve the international body's goals with economy and directness—in other words to stall and procrastinate. Such tendencies are unavoidably encouraged by the variety of pressures, by interests inside as well as outside the administration, which the administrator has to take into account. In all the circumstances the international public official would need to be a superman to realize the full measure of administrative effectiveness and scope of which, basically, the international bodies should be capable.

There are several peculiarities in the methods and procedures of international administration: for example the widespread use of formal meetings and conferences to satisfy the member nations that they are actively participating in the process, when the practical results of the discussions are frequently difficult to determine and often in fact amount to very little. One outcome is excessive documentation which, however valuable it may be, tends to rise to such a flood that few of those in a position to act upon it have the time to pay more than cursory attention to other than a few parts of it. Of course so much of the essence of it all could now be extracted and compressed by means of the computer, but it is to be doubted whether such extracts would have much creative potential. It is no secret that international administration exceeds the other branches of public administration in its tendencies to *paperassie*, against which French students of administration have been traditionally warned.

Yet the job of the international administrator—using the term in its widest sense—despite its manifest drawbacks, is a creative one which has its own rewards not to be nicely assessed in terms of pay and personal prestige. All public officials need to be inspired with a sense of vocation, of service to the large community, and none more than the international civil servant.

Developments in Europe (see pages 168, 169)

(1) A merger of the three Community Executives (i.e. the Commissions of EEC and Euratom and the High Authority of ECSC) took place on 6th July 1967, but the difficult process of moulding the three sets of administrative services into a single institution, as the Commission of the Community, was to take some time. Membership of the Commission was temporarily increased from nine to fourteen, mainly to improve the representativeness of the Commission. This inevitably rendered the maintenance of collegiality more difficult and made the Commission's administrative approach less flexible. A searching review of the immediate impact of the changes is provided in David Coombes PEP study, mentioned in Further Reading.

(2) Acceptable arrangements having been reached between the UK and EEC, Parliament, in a decisive vote on 28th October 1971, endorsed the accession of the UK to the Community. The further necessary action is now in hand (1972). The Republic of Ireland, Denmark and Norway are also seeking entry, to what would then become 'the Ten'.

FURTHER READING

Introductory

Works on international institutions, generally of high standard, are so numerous as to make it difficult to choose an introductory course of reading. First in the list must surely be the current edition of *Everyman's United Nations* (UN, New York), which is, however, a work for reference rather than for continuous reading. A more general introduction to the field is provided, in the Minerva Series, by Paul Reuter's *International*

Institutions (Allen & Unwin, 1958). A stimulating examination of the UN and its work is offered by H. G. Nicholas's *The United Nations as a Political Institution* (Oxford, 1959).

Andrew Boyd's *United Nations: Piety, Myth and Truth* (Penguin, 1962) looks at the development of the new system, critically but constructively, and Kenneth Lindsay's *Towards a European Parliament* (Strasbourg, 1958) discusses the European movement with special reference to the Council of Europe. European developments to date are comprehensively surveyed in Stuart de la Mahotiere's highly recommended *Towards One Europe* (Penguin, 1970).

Historical and Advanced

Clyde Eagleton's long established *International Government* (Ronald Press, NY, 1948) provides a comprehensive survey of the whole field, while A. H. Robertson's authoritative and well-documented *European Institutions* covers this more specialized area in some detail. David Coombes' *Politics and Bureaucracy in the European Community* (PEP and Allen & Unwin, 1970) is essential reading on the Community of the EEC.

Two excellent studies by Sydney D. Bailey have been made available in the Praeger Paperbacks series in *The General Assembly of the United Nations; A Study of Procedure and Practice* (1964) and *The Secretariat of the United Nations* (1964).

The practical problems of international administering are authoritatively and interestingly discussed, on the basis of long inside experience, by A. Loveday in *Reflections on International Administration* (Oxford, 1956).

Equally valuable, but rather concentrated, is Richard Mayne's brochure *The Institutions of the European Community* (Chatham House: PEP, 1968), David Coombes's *Towards a European Civil Service* (Chatham House: PEP, 1968) and Michael Niblock's *The EEC: National Parliaments in Community Decision-making* (Chatham House, PEP, 1971).

CHAPTER NINE

External Relations

Varying means have been adopted over the centuries for the conduct of external affairs, for linking the national with the international spheres. The development of the intricate network of international authorities summarized in the preceding chapter has considerably complicated and extended the problems involved.

The conduct of relations between a state and its neighbours—in other ages mainly between their respective rulers—has always constituted an important responsibility of government, although it is only in recent centuries that the function has been differentiated and diplomatic services, of a professional and specialist nature, have developed to perform these duties. The personal relations between rulers, if normally straightforward, could on occasion range over the broad field of statecraft, involving treaty-making, matters of peace and war, marriage and succession, even trade relations; but, with the emergence of the national state under pluralist leadership the less personal and more general matters began to require the ministration of specialist diplomats. To look after the peculiar interests of traders and other residents in foreign countries consular services were formed, often employing as agents nationals of the host country to supplement the activities of the professional diplomats.

With the rise of the oversea empires, either by conquest or by the settlement of colonists in comparatively uninhabited lands, the colonizing nations had to send out their own agents, to administer the territories, at least until such a time as the people of the new settlements could administer their own affairs. Consequently the several colonizing powers created their own colonial services. Notably the Portuguese, the Dutch, and the Spaniards were early in this field, followed closely by the British and the French. It is of special administrative interest that many of these overseas developments were the fruit of private initiative and organizing.

DEPARTMENTS FOR FOREIGN AND
OVERSEAS AFFAIRS

In 1945, in addition to several short-term bodies introduced during the Second World War, or immediately after, to deal with the chaos left by the fighting, Britain, as the foremost overseas power at the time, had a number of Government Departments dealing with international relations. These were the long-established Foreign Office and Colonial Office and the more recently established Dominions Office, as well as the India and Burma Offices, all under Ministers holding the office of Secretary of State. The two latter were shortly to be wound up with the granting of independence successively to Burma and India (the latter in the form of two new national units as 'India' and 'Pakistan'). These Departments were all staffed by members of the Home Civil Service, but there were separately organized Foreign and Colonial Services recruited to operate overseas, each of which was at the beginning of a series of rapid reorganizations to meet the successive changes in the world situation. Already in 1943 the Foreign Service had been reformed to span both the Foreign Office and the Diplomatic Branches abroad, in the shape of a single Foreign Service with interchangeability between the two sectors. The Colonial Service contracted rapidly with the granting of independence to many of the oversea territories of the Commonwealth.

The speeding up and broadening of telecommunications during the recent decades had completely changed the nature of the diplomatic art. At the same time the expansion of the national state on a parliamentary basis, which had converted the ambassador from personal representative of the ruler into representative of the nation, needing to practice a more open type of diplomacy than that habitually adopted right up to the débâcle of the more powerful European ruling houses in 1917 and 1918. With the expansion of the national state the needs of diplomacy have become more positive and dependent upon a wider range of knowledge and experience. Diplomats have had to adopt new methods and call upon the assistance of experts who have themselves had to understand the subtleties of the diplomatic art.

Extensive news and publicity services, operating outside official channels, have tended to reduce the predominance of the man on the spot with access to inside information, and to place the official in Whitehall in a better position to understand what was going on there. The advent of the aeroplane and particularly of the jet age since the war, by facilitating the rapid transport of minister and official literally to the ends of the earth, has tended to render much of the old protocol, to which older members of the profession continued to be wedded, a dead letter. Yet if the art of diplomacy has been modified radically by the new situation the tasks of the diplomats have had to be considerably broadened to enable them to look after the interests of government and people in the areas for which they are responsible and over which of course their employers have no executive powers outside the limited areas of their privileged embassies. The Foreign Office continued to handle relationships with foreign countries, while the independent nations of the Commonwealth remained the responsibility of the Dominions Office, which, in 1947 with the access, to the new status, of India and Pakistan, was renamed 'Commonwealth Relations Office'.

A new corps of oversea representatives had begun to develop in 1908 when the Board of Trade, which had always been concerned with oversea trade relations, appointed Trade Commissioners in Commonwealth Countries. For a time these were taken care of by the autonomous Department of Overseas Trade, established in 1917 under the joint control of the Foreign Office and the Board of Trade until its general supervision passed to the latter in 1946.

In 1962 the Government appointed a Committee, under the chairmanship of Lord Plowden, to review the purpose, structure, and operation of the services representing the interests of the United Kingdom overseas, both in the Commonwealth and in foreign countries. The *Report of the Committee on Representational Services Overseas* appeared two years later. The Committee—which defined the duties of the Representational Services as advice, negotiation, cultivation of friendly relations, trade promotion, information, protection of British persons and interests, aid and technical assistance—recommended that the services, then distributed among the Foreign Office, Commonwealth Relations Office, and the Board of Trade, should be integrated as 'Her Majesty's Diplomatic Service', with a structure which would bring the existing grades, variously classified as diplomatic, administrative, executive, and clerical, into a single inter-related hierarchy.

The new Service was inaugurated on 1 April 1966, and in the new structure the three so-called Treasury-type classes were for the first time formalized as one hierarchy, although for the time being members of grades overlapping the previous diplomatic and executive class structures continued to retain their former status and rates of pay. The amalgamation of the Whitehall Offices followed rapidly: first with the merging of the dwindling Colonial Office with the Commonwealth Relations Office, as the Commonwealth Office, in 1966, and, finally, two years later with the consolidation of the Foreign and Commonwealth Offices in a new Secretaryship of State for Foreign and Commonwealth Affairs, a consummation that twenty years before even the well-informed would have deemed extremely improbable.

The idea of affording technical assistance to overseas territories has been of long growth within the Commonwealth. Very early in the field were two autonomous bodies, originally associated with the Colonial Office: namely, the Crown Agents for Overseas Governments and Administrations (formerly the Crown Agents for the Colonies) and the Overseas Audit Departmentment (formerly the Colonial Audit Department). As Crown Agents, two Commissioners are appointed by the Secretary of State, to act as business and financial agents in this country for individual oversea governments who desire their services. The history of the agency goes back to the eighteenth century when Colonial Governors adopted the practice of appointing local representatives in London to undertake the purchase of supplies and other business on their behalf. Today the Crown Agents continue to act as agents for such oversea governments, notably in arranging contracts for the services of experts in various fields and, a reflection of the expansion of philately into big business, as agents for the production of postage stamps for other lands. The Overseas Audit Department originated in the nineteenth century as Commissioners of West Indian Accounts and Commissioners of Colonial Accounts, whose work was later transferred to HM

Treasury. With the establishment of the Comptroller and Auditor General in 1866 responsibility for the audit was transferred to the several Colonial Governments. This arrangement not proving satisfactory the Secretary of State, at the request of the Comptroller and Auditor General, in 1889 set up within the Colonial Office a Colonial Audit Branch, which was converted into the present autonomous Department in 1910.

These early developments were later joined by similar bodies with varied and interesting objectives. Thus, in commemoration of Queen Victoria's Jubilee of 1887, the Imperial Institute was established (now renamed Commonwealth Institute) to provide the people of Britain with information about their imperial responsibilities. It is an autonomous institution controlled by a Board of Governors, working through a management committee. Appointments are shared between the Secretary of State for Education and Science and the Governments of the member nations of the Commonwealth. A similarly administered body, with very different objectives, is the Commonwealth War Graves Commission, first established under Royal Charter, as the Imperial War Graves Commission, in 1917, during the First World War. The Commission, which includes representatives of the major Commonwealth Nations and also of the Republic of South Africa, continues to do admirable work in caring for the graves of, and commemorating, the Commonwealth's dead of the two World Wars. The Commission works through a Director-General and a London Headquarters, with a network of Regions and Agencies throughout the world, which cares for over a million graves in numerous War Cemeteries, as well as many memorials, in almost every country.

The British Council, established on a voluntary basis in 1934 to counter widespread cultural propaganda of Italian and German Fascism, has continued under the Royal Charter, granted during the Second World War, to pursue 'the promotion of a wider knowledge of the United Kingdom and the English Language abroad and closer cultural relations between the United Kingdom and the other countries for the purpose of benefiting the Commonwealth of Nations'. The Council is governed by an executive committee of thirty, nine of whom are nominated by Ministers and the others are representative of a wide range of cultural activities. Financed mainly from public funds the British Council operates in as many as seventy overseas countries, in language teaching and other educational work, fostering personal contacts between British and overseas people, running libraries of British books and periodicals and presenting the best in the arts of Britain.

Even more directly in the line of providing technical assistance in its modern form were the Colonial Development Corporation and the Overseas Food Corporation established under the Overseas Resources Development Act of 1948. The latter, which was appointed by the Minister of Food, was set up to concern itself with projects for the production, processing, and marketing of foodstuffs and agricultural products outside the United Kingdom. Reorganized as a consequence of the breakdown of the ill-fated groundnuts project, it was made the responsibility of the Colonial Secretary in 1951. Its operations were confined mainly to East Africa, in association with the Government of Tanganyika (now Tanzania). Under new legislation, which took effect in 1957, the Overseas Food Corporation ceased to exist when its functions were transferred to a new Tanganyika Agriculture Corporation, responsibility for which passed to the government on the spot. The Colonial Development Corporation, appointed by the Secretary of State, with a membership of a chairman, deputy chairman, and four to six others, was given the task of launching and carrying out projects for the development of the resources of colonial territories and to assist in their industrial advancement. Renamed the Commonwealth Development Corporation, this body continues to undertake numerous useful enterprises of this type, as reference to its current annual reports will show. Its supervision was transferred to the Ministry of Overseas Development, referred to below.

With the increasing emphasis placed upon technical assistance by the transformation of numerous colonial territories into independent countries, the British Government decided in July 1961, to bring together the several functions in this field of the Foreign Office, the Commonwealth Relations Office, the Colonial Office and the Ministry of Labour, in a new unit known as the Department of Technical Co-operation, under the direction of a Secretary of Technical Co-operation, who was a politician with the status of Minister of State. Under the new Labour government the Department was raised in 1965 to ministerial status, as the Ministry of Overseas Development, with extended responsibilities. According to the official statement *Overseas Development: The Work of the New Ministry*, Cmnd. 2736 (1965):

The central purpose of the new Ministry is to formulate and carry out British policies to help the economic development of the poorer countries. To this end the Ministry has assumed responsibility for the economic aid programme as a whole and its detailed composition; the terms and conditions of aid; the size and nature of the programme for each country; the management of financial aid and technical assistance; relations with international aid organisations; the British interest in United Nations programmes of technical assistance; and relations with voluntary bodies concerned with aid and development. (White Paper, p. 27.)

In the autumn 1970 the responsibilities of the Ministry of Overseas Development were taken over by the Foreign and Commonwealth Office, but continued under the control of a 'Minister for' Overseas Development, responsible to the Secretary of State.

ADMINISTRATION OF THE COMMONWEALTH

As we have seen, administration of the British Empire was at different stages the responsibility of several home Departments, namely the India Office, the Colonial Office, and latterly the Dominions or Commonwealth Relations Office, shared in varying degree with the administrations on the spot. Gradually, with the development of the dominions and other independent countries, administration has passed almost completely from Whitehall. By 1970 the remaining direct colonial responsibilities were not substantial. A characteristic of this process has been the relatively small extent to which Parliament, except when legislation was required, and the people, except when burning political issues came to the surface, have been involved. The initiative has rested mainly with the Executive, an arrangement which, if immediately convenient, reflects small credit on the democracy.

As a consequence, while movements to develop greater Commonwealth unity did from time to time attract the interest of some politicians no outstanding effort was made to evolve a coherent scheme of Commonwealth administration. Any attempt to apply a constitutional strait-jacket would certainly have been powerfully resisted not merely in the growing dominions but at home. The process of development took place largely on an *ad hoc* basis and what there existed of any co-ordinated administrative structure literally withered away, or perhaps it would be more accurate to say that it has been deformalized.

Occasional meetings of representatives from the major colonies began with the Colonial Conference in 1887, at the time of Queen Victoria's Golden Jubilee celebrations, and such meetings were replaced by the first of a series of Imperial Conferences in 1911, the last of which assembled in 1937 at the time of King George VI's coronation. Out of these grew the modern Commonwealth Conferences of Heads of Government from the several independent states, recognizing the Queen as Head of the Commonwealth.

It was not until 1965 that the Commonwealth Secretariat was set up, with a Canadian as its first Secretary-General and headquarters at Marlborough House in London. This Secretariat's main task is largely diplomatic, namely to co-ordinate contacts between the several member nations, through the circulation of papers on matters of common interest, the promotion of economic relationships, establishing liaison with several specialist bodies concerned with Commonwealth matters, organizing meetings, and other activities of this sort. It is not part of the Home Government, which merely contributes to its cost on a scale that has been determined on the basis of the relative resources of the several members. The Commonwealth Secretariat is essentially a secretarial, public relations, and common service organization, whose future will obviously depend upon the development of the Commonwealth itself.

There are many other links between the several countries: influences arising naturally from a common history and the predominance of the English language as an essential means of communication; and institutions, such as the Commonwealth Institute, the Royal Commonwealth Society and the Commonwealth Parliamentary Association, and many others established at various times for the co-ordination of specific fields of activity. An interesting example is the Commonwealth Foundation, actually proposed by Heads of Government in 1964 to promote co-operation between professional bodies within the Commonwealth. The whole field is still ill-defined and the effort at co-operation in the many spheres is probably more extensive and impressive than is usually realized. It is important, therefore, to have in existence an authoritative body, in the shape of the Commonwealth Secretariat, with responsibility for assisting in the task of co-ordinating and improving Commonwealth inter-relationships on a voluntary basis.

INTERNATIONAL RESPONSIBILITIES OF THE HOME DEPARTMENTS

Although the responsibilities of the Central Administration have been allocated among Government Departments on the basis of a broad division of function, it has never been possible to draw a strict line between home and foreign affairs. Even before the separate Foreign and Colonial Offices emerged in the eighteenth and nineteenth centuries the Secretaryship of State had been given responsibilities in both spheres, and the Departments concerned with the armed forces, in particular the Board of Admiralty, were deeply involved in external affairs. The oversea empire was defended and continually extended under the wing of the Royal Navy, administered from Whitehall, which somewhat fortuitously but with little imperialist arrogance combined its decidedly nationalist defence function with the valuable internationalist one of policing the seas in the interests of world commerce. The occupation by Britain, during the hundred years preceding the Second World War, of groups of islands throughout the seven seas was undertaken largely to meet the administrative needs of a fleet requiring a world-wide network of coaling stations. With the supersession of coal by oil fuel, and subsequently of seapower itself by the invention of the jet and the guided missile, the cancellation of one administrative need left to the Government a quite different administrative problem, which is still in course of solution.

Today the Ministry of Defence, consolidating the three branches of the armed forces into a single defence service, must still figure as a Department with major oversea functions. In a similar category was the Board of Trade, which had already existed in the form of a Standing Council for Trade and Plantations before its definite establishment in 1696, initially as a purely advisory body, but with the earlier foreign plantations functions which were soon to become quasi-administrative rather than purely consultative. Even at a time when the central administrative structure was still comparatively simple, if not very well co-ordinated, the conduct of external relations by the oversea, defence, and trade departments was beset with problems arising from varying viewpoints, and the position was to become more and more complicated with the growth of new spheres of administrative specialization with interests reaching beyond the national boundaries, and with which the accredited oversea departments were not equipped to deal. Thus the General Post Office under its ministerial head was responsible for linking its expanding postal and telecommunications services into a rapidly extending world communications network. The Department was continuously involved in the conclusion of treaties and contracts, and the exchange of technical information with oversea governments. This meant that the Post Office's headquarters' staff were constantly in direct contact with foreign governments or with such agencies as the Universal Postal Bureau in Switzerland, through which general questions of mail transport and postal charges were settled. As we have already seen, a large number of these specialist international unions were established prior to 1914, so that many Government Departments already had oversea links. Outside these formal arrangements some Departments found it important to their work to have access to foreign experience and, especially when introducing new services and setting up new machinery, surveys were carried out in appropriate fields. Thus the Board of Education, at the beginning of the present century, derived benefit from its investigations into foreign educational practices and, as is well known, the first national insurance administration in 1909 was considerably influenced by German experience, which was specifically investigated.

The immigration services of the Home Office, whose history can be traced back to Norman times, have continued to increase in importance since the passing of the Aliens Act, 1905, which empowered the Home Secretary to exclude certain aliens. Incidentally, his decision on such matters was final until the introduction of the Immigration Appeal Tribunal under the Immigration Appeals Act, 1969.

With the establishment of the League of Nations and its successor, the United Nations, in 1919 and 1945 respectively, the oversea responsibilities of the Central Administration have considerably extended and with the development of the Specialized Agencies contacts between the two spheres of administration have become continuous, so that, to deal with matters falling within their own functional fields, most of the Government Departments have had to set up specialist branches at headquarters to deal with such matters. Responsibility for maintaining contacts with these several international agencies is allocated to specific Departments. The Departments with the largest number of such contacts are those concerned with Trade and Agriculture, Fisheries and Food, as might have been anticipated, but the importance of the specific links vary considerably, and, among the important ones, are the Department of Health and Social Security with the World Health Organization (WHO), the Department of Education and Science with the UN Educational, Scientific and Cultural Organization (UNESCO), the Department of Employment with the International Labour Organization (ILO), and the Central Statistical Office (of the Cabinet Office) with the Statistical Commission (of the UN Economic and Social Council). The interested reader should consult the list in F. M. G. Willson's *The Organization of British Central Government*, bearing in mind that subsequent changes will inevitably have rendered it out of date (see the Further Reading list at the end of the chapter).

It is evident that the machinery of government in Britain has had little difficulty in realigning itself and modifying its attitudes to meet at the working level, the needs of the developing international administration, but in a broader political sense less attention appears to have been given to this trend towards assimilating the national system of public administration to the wider international scheme. Initially this is more a matter for the political scientist than for the public administrator and therefore outside our present scope but, as a beginning, the reader can be recommended to read Max Beloff's *New Dimensions in Foreign Policy*, which is offered as 'a Study in British Administrative Experience, 1947–59'.

There is, however, an important administrative activity of worldwide importance already mentioned in which all these bodies, national and international, are currently involved, namely the administering of aid to the 'have not' countries, in the form of technical assistance, to which brief further attention must be given.

TECHNICAL ASSISTANCE

From time immemorial powerful states have set out to exploit the resources of other communities and other lands, and if often such exploitation has accrued to the advantage of both participants, this result has usually been merely incidental to the original objective. Yet in a world where the exploitation of one state by another is no longer justifiable, the basic problem still remains, for the development and use of the world's resources is of interest to all. It is possible for the richer communities to help the poorer by the loan or gift of money and materials, but for those underdeveloped and backward areas of the world where the gap between them and the advanced countries is wide, and tending to become wider, these methods are not enough. The backward communities must be helped to help themselves. This is where technical assistance comes in, for it involves the provision of expert advice and of training to increase the skills of members of the underdeveloped community and thus to assist them in providing themselves with the services they lack.

The objective of technical assistance is defined in the *Observations and Guiding Principles*, subscribed to by the Economic and Social Council of the United Nations, as to help undeveloped countries

to strengthen their national economies through the development of their industries and agriculture, with a view to promoting their economic and political independence in the spirit of the Charter of the United Nations, and to insure the attainment of higher levels of economic and social welfare for their entire population.

The methods to be employed to achieve this aim had already been determined in 1948 as (*a*) the organization, through the United Nations, of international teams of experts; (*b*) the provision of fellowships for the training abroad of experts from the under-developed countries themselves; (*c*) the training of technicians within the under-developed countries through visits by experts to instruct local personnel, and to aid in organizing technical institutes; and (*d*) the provision of facilities to aid governments to obtain technical personnel, equipment, supplies, and other required services, including the organizing of seminars and the exchange of current technical information on development problems. These services were to be provided by the Secretary-General in co-operation with the specialized agencies.

Originally the responsibility of a Technical Assistance Board, organized under a committee of the UN Social and Economic Council, the provision of aid was developed under the Expanded Programme of Technical Assistance (EPTA), established in 1950, and the Special Fund, introduced nine years later, both of which have been combined since 1966 as the UN Development Programme (UNDP). This Programme is financed by voluntary annual contributions from members of the United Nations and related agencies. The resources are administered through the United Nations and eleven Specialized Agencies (ILO, FAO, UNESCO, ICAO, WHO,

IBRD, ITU, WMO, IAEA, UPU, and IMGO). There is a Governing Council of thirty-seven members exercising policy control, approving projects, overseeing operations, and allocating funds, under the general supervision of the Economic and Social Council. Management of the Programme is in the hands of an Administrator, Co-Administrator, and staff at UN Headquarters, with the advice of an Inter-Agency Consultative Board, composed of the heads of the twelve executing Agencies, supplemented as appropriate by representatives of the UN Children's Fund (UNICEF) and the World Food Programme. On the ground there is an extensive network of field offices (numbering eighty-two in 1967), headed by Resident Representatives who work closely with the governments and other international bodies with responsibilities in the area.

The vast extent of this international activity is indicated by the large number of countries and territories to which assistance has been given—as many as 140 during the first decade—and the variety of projects undertaken. These have included basic surveys of resources and the building up of administrative services; power, transport, and communications; industrial production and mining; agricultural production; auxiliary services to industry and agriculture; health services; education; community development; and other social services. During the same period advice was given in over a hundred major fields of development.

Technical assistance places a special emphasis upon advisory projects and training, the aim being to enable the backward countries to 'grow' their own experts and skills in sufficient numbers and to develop their own services. An early discovery was the impossibility of making any real advances in the absence of skilled administrators on the spot, and the result was the provision of training in public administration and the setting up of training institutions at important key-points in the participating countries. It thus came about that the under-developed countries were being provided with a form of training which elsewhere is more usually acquired laboriously by daily practice and incidentally to the performance of other activities. This by-product of the Technical Assistance programme has undoubtedly had an important influence in rationalizing ideas about public administration and has assisted the development of the subject on a world-wide basis.

*   *   *

It should now be evident to the reader that, while a detailed knowledge of our own public administration is both vital and rewarding, it cannot be fully understood without reference to the international context, to which only a brief introduction has been possible. The whole administrative complex, ranging from the simple family unit, as a spontaneous effort to manage its resources for the benefit of all its members, to the widely ranging series of international authorities with numerous specialist functions, can be seen as a single developing system, upon the continuing progress and more effective integration of which the very success of civilization itself may largely depend.

It remains in Part Three of this volume to tidy up our widely ranging exploration with a few remarks on the participation of the citizen and the future of public administration.

FURTHER READING

Introductory

The administrative arrangements are explained in two volumes of the New Whitehall Series (Allen & Unwin): namely *The Foreign Office* (1955) by Lord Strang and *The Colonial Office* (1956) by Sir Charles Jeffries. A useful short introduction to *Whitehall and the Commonwealth* is contained in J. A. Cross's contribution, under that title, to the Library of Political Studies (Routledge, 1967). A brief summary is contained in Chapter XI of E. N. Gladden's *British Public Service Administration* (Staples, 1961).

Relationships between the Central Departments in Britain with overseas organization are admirably summarized in Chapter V of F. M. G. Willson's *The Organization of British Central Government 1914–1964* (Allen & Unwin, 1968), which should certainly be consulted, and Max Beloff has provided a valuable introductory study of this developing administrative sphere in his *New Dimensions in Foreign Policy* (Allen & Unwin, 1961).

Historical and Advanced

Studies in the old Whitehall Series (Putnam) contain a good deal of relevant information, if they can be found: for example, *The Foreign Office* (1933) by Sir John Tilley and Stephen Gaselee, *The Dominions and Colonial Offices* (1926) by Sir G. V. Fiddes, *The India Office* (1926) by Sir M. C. C. Seton, and *The Board of Trade* (1928), by Sir H. Llewellyn Smith.

The nature of diplomacy and its administration are more broadly examined in J. Frankel's *The Making of Foreign Policy* (Oxford, 1963) which is highly recommended and by Lord Strang in *Home and Abroad* (Andre Deutsch, 1956).

Recent developments in the Overseas Services are foreshadowed in the Plowden *Report of the Committee on Representational Services Overseas*, Cmnd. 2276 (1964) and the whole field is further examined and important changes are recommended in the Duncan *Report of the Review Committee on Overseas Representation 1968–69*, Cmnd. 4107 (1969), which contains valuable information on the management of the Diplomatic Service.

Useful shorter texts on the important subject of technical assistance are: *Technical Assistance* (ILO, Geneva, 1954); *National Administration and International Organizations* by Roger Gregoire (International Institute of Administrative Sciences, Brussels), the Department of Technical Co-operation's *Report of the Committee on Training in Public Administration for Overseas Countries* (HMSO, 1963) and the Ministry of Overseas Development's survey *Overseas Development: The Work of the New Ministry*, Cmnd. 2736 (HMSO, 1965).

Finally two periodicals of particular interest on the subjects of the present and preceding chapters are the quarterly *International Organization*, published by the World Peace Foundation (Boston, USA) and the quarterly *International Conciliation*, published by the Carnegie Endowment for International Peace, which consists mainly of a series of studies by different authors on specific topics of which the following are interesting examples and indicate the scope of the series: *ECE in the Emerging European System*, by Jean Siotis (no. 561, January 1967), *UNCTAD: North–South Encounter*, by Branislav Gosovic (no. 568, May 1968) and *The Warsaw Pact*, by Andrezej Korbonski (no. 573, May 1969).

There is also the more widely extending *International Review of Administrative Sciences*, published quarterly by the International Institute of Administrative Sciences (Brussels) which, apart from numerous articles by scholars of international reputation, includes a valuable selected bibliography of works on public administration in the foremost Western languages.

PART FOUR

Public Administration and the Public

CHAPTER TEN

The Part of the Citizen

Government of a democracy rests upon the support and participation of the people, as citizens. The parliamentary system has been criticized as only intermittently and briefly democratic at election times, but this is surely to take a very narrow view of government which, especially in modern states, has a continuing two-way impact. Parliament's important functions include representing and interpreting the wishes of the people, and the government must be constantly concerned with public opinion and particularly with those changes in such opinion as have been taking place since the last general election, the assessment of which has been greatly advanced by the improved techniques of the public opinion poll. It is indeed vital to such a system that the channels of communication and publicity should be free and effectively serviced. Even dictatorships cannot afford to ignore public opinion. Hence their efforts through propaganda to obtain acquiescence on their own terms, or approval of their activities or tenure of power through plebiscites. In fact the plebiscite, in its particular form of the referendum, can be used in a democracy for bringing the people into the decision-making process on matters of constitutional importance as in such systems as those of France, the Irish Republic, Switzerland, and the United States, where referenda are employed for different purposes. If this particular procedure has not been adopted in Britain it is not surely because it is undemocratic but because so far a sufficient demand has not arisen for its introduction.

Local government elections are of particular importance in this context, since the candidates are not only well-known locally, but continue to operate under the eyes of their constituents, who have reasonable access to them at the town or county hall. It is true that at this level the proportion of citizens going to the poll is often very low, demonstrating a chronic lack of interest, or desire for involvement, in local affairs, a weakness that changes in the system itself would not necessarily remove.

This general lack of involvement points to one of the biggest weaknesses of democracy, which in this sense does not measure up to the better aristocracies whose members have usually demonstrated a special devotion to public affairs and a willingness to share in the onerous duties of administering. Before the modern structure of local government took its definitive form, virtually with the introduction of elected councils in the counties in 1888, effective public administration at the ground level literally depended upon the devoted service of the gentry as magistrates and in other offices, and, even at the summit, the number of unpaid posts, including of course Members of Parliament, was still considerable. The latter has since been professionalized, though such old institutions as the Justices of the Peace and the Jury continue on an unpaid basis, affording the selected citizen an opportunity of participating directly, in this case in the judicial process.

Members of the public, influenced by images in the press and party literature, are generally highly critical of public officials, whose activities, largely to meet requirements laid down by Parliament, tend to become more complicated and remote, and therefore less easy to understand. Improvement in the performance of our form of government must depend to a considerable degree upon the elimination of this serious 'misinformation' gap, calling surely for a two-way effort, on the one hand, on the part of politician and public administrator to keep open the channels of communication and to project a true and understandable picture of what public administration is currently doing, and, on the other hand, on the part of the citizen to understand the processes which he has himself ordered to be initiated. It is generally felt that, although a solution to this problem is not easily formulated, the widest possible involvement of the citizen in the administrative process is one of its essential elements.

It has been mentioned in earlier chapters that there are numerous channels through which the two sectors, administration and people, are linked. The Government publishes a good deal of information both on general matters and on specific subjects, which is distributed by Her Majesty's Stationery Office or the responsible Departments. There is the Central Office of Information to provide the Government and Departments with information media and the Department's themselves have specialist Information Officers (of various grades) to handle their public relations and information services. Those Departments whose work involves direct contact with the public usually provide public inquiry offices to handle personal inquiries, and civil servants are given training in public relations. Communications may be addressed either to the Departments themselves, who handle a large number of inquiries of all types, or to a citizen's own MP, who may himself contact the responsible Minister direct, or formulate a Question in Parliament, which may well set in train a searching inquiry into the circumstances of the case inside the Department. Recently these facilities have been supplemented by the appointment of the Parliamentary Commissioner for Administration to whom, in appropriate cases, Ministers may pass for special investigation complaints of maladministration. The meagre evidence of such maladministration that has so far come to light at least suggests how beneficial it would be to public confidence and understanding if the citizen were sufficiently well-informed to be enabled to detect the high degree of calculated misrepresentation behind much of the anti-bureaucratic comment.

It can hardly be denied that Government in Britain has long recognized the importance of keeping the people informed, a recent recognition of this fact having been evinced by the issue of the White Paper *Information and the Public Interest* (Cmnd. 4089, 1969), to which reference has already been made in Chapter Nine, Volume I.

INTEREST OR PRESSURE GROUPS

The right of individuals to band together to form associations, with the object of propagating specific ideas or of furthering certain interests of a lawful nature, is surely one of the essential freedoms of democracy. Such bodies are important agents in the formation of public opinion, particularly on issues that might otherwise be allowed by the majority or ruling interests to go by default. There are those

H

who dislike these 'interest', or 'pressure', groups as they have been alternatively labelled, but the further the modern state gets away from the simpler community, which is so compact that citizens can meet to decide policy and then act in concert (as may still be the case in small states like some of the Swiss cantons, or in the smaller parishes in England and Wales), the more necessary it becomes to encourage the formation of associations of like-minded citizens to represent the numerous group interests, whose objects and relative importance are not otherwise easily assessed in the process of governing, as they need to be. The modern trend of some of these bodies towards militancy—for which the former term 'direct action' is more accurate—must be recognized as essentially anti-democratic and treated accordingly.

Foremost among these pressure groups are the political parties, upon which modern governments of all types are based. It is their job to formulate the doctrines and shape general plans and pro-grammes for the governing of the country, to provide candidates for their support at the elections, and to persuade the electors to support them. In Britain in particular these parties do not form part of the formal machinery of government, but have the status of voluntary associations which do not acquire a special status until they have obtained sufficient representation in the House of Commons to enable them to form the Government or the Official Opposition. In single-party systems their status is quite different, since they have there become an established part of the government machine, pretending to the monopoly of state power. Even in democratic countries political parties differ from other pressure groups, less in their form than their ultimate object of participating in governing, even if only on a temporary or occasional basis.

In the wider sense interest groups participate in the political process by bringing pressure upon the Government, or upon Members of Parliament and Local Councillors. One of the means adopted is known as lobbying. In Britain this is quite a modest public relations operation whereby group representatives get together in the lobbies of Parliament with MPs, with whom they discuss their objectives and do all they can to obtain support in bringing about the changes desired or preventing those considered detrimental to their objectives. This is a two-way process which assists the legislators in getting informed on matters in which the people are interested. It is not necessarily unfair to those who do not support the particular

association, since there is nothing to prevent groups with widely con-
trasted views from pressing and submitting counter-proposals.
Lobbying derives its somewhat questionable image from its much
more vigorous use in the United States to press for a share in the
manifest advantages that Congress has to bestow. But under the
American system of government the division of powers and the existence of a plurality of state units, means that there are so many
more interests to appease, so much scope for bargaining, that the
interest groups are more concerned in sharing power than in making
a case and providing information, which is their more normal
function in Britain. Of course some British groups would like to
emulate their American counterparts, but the parliamentary system
does not usually give them sufficient rope, except when the condi-
tioning factors are consistently favourable, as they appear to have
been when commercial television was introduced.

All this has to do with the political side and not directly with
administration, but the general interest group, as a bridge between
the two spheres, deserves special attention. Alan Potter, in his
detailed analysis of the *Organized Groups in British National Politics*
(1961) divides these groups into two broad types: (1) spokesmen
groups concerned with organizing sectional interests and (2) promotional groups concerned with organizing shared attitudes. The
latter are also known as attitude groups. Even with such broad
categories it is difficult to draw hard and fast lines between the
two types, but it is not likely that a more elaborate classification
would help very much. In the course of his survey Potter does
identify a number of groupings under each type. As the several
headings at least indicate the wide scope of these groupings their
mere listing may be helpful. For examples of the several bodies thus
classified Alan Potter's book should be consulted.

The Spokesman Groups, classified according to the various kinds
of sectional interests they seek to represent, are (i) Manufacturing,
Processing, and Mining Entrepreneurial Groups, (ii) Wholesaling,
Industrial-service, Financial, and Transport Entrepreneurial Groups,
(iii) Retailing, Personal-service, Educational, and Building-trades
Entrepreneurial Groups, (iv) Farming and Fishing Entrepreneurial
Groups, (v) Governmental Groups, (vi) Employers' Groups, (vii)
Professional, Technical, and Managerial Groups, (viii) Employees'
Groups, (ix) Property-owners' and Taxpayers Groups, (x) Users',
Afflicted-persons', and Recreational Groups, (xi) Ex-Servicemen's

and Pensioners' Groups, (xii) Ethnic Groups, (xiii) Church Groups, and a miscellaneous category of (xiv) 'Mixed Groups'.

The Promotional Groups, classified according to the causes they purport to foster, are (i) Groups concerned with Economic Interests and Industrial Causes, (ii) Groups concerned with Technical Interests, Technical Causes, and Education, (iii) Groups concerned with Health and Amenities, (iv) Groups concerned with National Security, Governmental Procedures, and Private Rights, (v) Groups concerned with Commonwealth and International Affairs, (vi) Nationalist Groups, (vii) Feminist Groups, (viii) Groups concerned with Church Interests, Religious Causes, and Morality, (ix) Groups concerned with Social and Humanitarian Causes, and (x) Groups concerned with Animal Welfare. Alan Potter's classification, thus reproduced, is interesting and helpful, but a more definitive frame of reference must await further research in the subject which, in Britain at least, is still in its early stages.

It has to be emphasized that Alan Potter's convenient labels are not universally accepted, and the basic dichotomy can be interpreted in different ways. An alternative classification has recently been proposed by Jean Blondel in his erudite *An Introduction to Comparative Government* (Weidenfeld, 1969), which seems bound to have an important influence on the development of the subject. He divides the two types of grouping into (1) 'communal', i.e. those groups which embody social relationships, and (2) 'associational', i.e. those bodies which are constituted in order to pursue a goal. He suggests that the communal type can be further divided into (1) (i) 'customary', i.e. 'those communal groups which arise from the development of patterns of relationships which are "natural" in origin', and (1) (ii) 'institutional', i.e. 'those communal bodies which develop from a man-made institution, often politico-administrative, but also sometimes religious' (op. cit., especially pp. 62–70).

In a free society such bodies are voluntarily organized, depending usually upon the subscriptions of their membership for their running expenses, and their activities are not circumscribed so long as their objectives are not illegal. They depend for their management to a considerable extent upon the free services of members, although the larger nation-wide bodies may require the services of a skilled paid administrative staff, depending to some extent upon the available resources. In order to ensure the *locus standi* of such bodies their registration has been proposed, as is already required in the United

States, but so far legislation for this purpose has not been considered necessary.

These bodies are very much concerned with the collection and dissemination of information, both to assist in the formulation of policy and in extending support for their views, and in these activities they employ all the media and processes of the public relations expert and the propagandist. They seek to mould public opinion and to maintain contacts with press, local authorities, Parliament and Government, choosing the means most suitable in the light of their particular objectives and field of operations. Some concentrate upon the collection of funds to pay for their propaganda and informational activities, some actively support parliamentary candidature, others organize machinery for handling the cases of individuals requiring help. Some critics regard such bodies, especially those that attempt to exert pressures to mould or change public policy, as a menace to the working of the normal machinery of a parliamentary democracy, but in our complex society it is clear that such agencies voluntarily formed are an essential ingredient of the policy-making machinery as a means to rationalizing and clarifying an infinitude of individual viewpoints, on specific matters. Most of us, if we examine our own involvement in associations, clubs, institutes, parties, groups, and so forth, will discover that in varying degree we are supporting a number of interest or pressure groups.

ADMINISTRATIVE PARTICIPATION BY THE CITIZEN

At a time when public administration has become highly professionalized and the growth of bureaucracy hardly avoidable, it seems increasingly desirable that the participation of the ordinary citizen in public administration should be increased, when in fact, with the growth of competing ways of spending our leisure, a strong opposite trend is evident. The citizen finds administration tediously complicated and loses interest, an attitude in which he is often encouraged by the official, who, as an expert in his own field, tends to become impatient with what he considers is the interference of the amateur. Thus the general attitudes today of the local government committeeman who sees little virtue in the co-optation of outsiders to the committees and of the officials themselves who view the elected Councillors on the committees very much in the same way.

As we have seen there are many ways in which the citizen comes into the picture as part of the normal processes of democratic government, as party supporters and workers, participants in elections, particularly the local elections, as members of pressure groups, and as participants in the numerous voluntary bodies which actually provide public services, like the Citizens Advice Bureaux, the National Trusts, the Salvation Army, the St John's Ambulance Corps, and the Royal National Lifeboat Institution, to mention only a few. There are also the numerous consultative and investigatory bodies on which citizens serve in a general or an expert capacity. These include the Royal Commissions and other investigatory bodies, appointed from time to time by the Government and individual Ministers to examine and report upon some specific problem; the various advisory committees attached on a more or less permanent basis to many Government Departments, at headquarters, regional, or local levels, to advise the Minister on certain of his responsibilities or to make representations to him; and the consumer and consultative councils associated with nationalized industries and other public services. Selection in all these cases is dependent either upon membership of some authority or institution or on the individual's standing in the particular field of activity in which the advisory organization is involved. In the case of some of these inquiries, particularly by Royal Commissions and certain advisory councils, the ordinary citizen can participate by providing information in response to invitations issued by the commission or council.

There is no doubt that the practical value of the consultative and advisory committees varies considerably. Much of course depends upon the enthusiasm and abilities of the chosen members, who give freely of their services to the committee. At their best the Committees enable the administrator to keep in touch with the people and they provide an effective means of ensuring that public opinion is taken into account at a stage when such awareness on the part of the official can have its maximum impact. Here then the citizen, usually on account of his interest in, or knowledge of, the particular field or subject, comes more and more into the modern administrative picture and makes an important contribution. Throughout the country many thousands of ordinary citizens are thus actively participating in the daily tasks of public administration. It would be rash, however, to conclude that this sort of participation had yet been carried as far as was desirable. Certainly, it is doubtful whether

the best way of selecting such 'citizen advisers' has yet been dis-
covered, and this is a problem which deserves closer study. It is also
necessary to ensure that the findings of such committees are widely
publicized and that there is ample opportunity for views expressed by
the public to be given careful consideration. In this matter of informing the public the Press, in search of the snappy headline to
which even the most eminent newspapers are today addicted, could
be much more helpful than it is. It might be a good idea to insist that
all newspapers should include, not necessarily in every issue, a well
laid out section of public information selected, not by the editor, but
by an openly constituted public body or Readership Committee, and
written by a skilled journalist.

However much technology may be involved and create the
impression that the machine is poised to take over, it cannot be too
strongly emphasized that the work of the administrator has to do
with people, and unless there are means for assessing at an early
stage in the administrative process the reactions of people to his
work the administrator will be lost in a maze of uncertainty and
quite incompetent to advise the decision-makers before things have
got out of hand, or fallen deplorably below the targets planned. Only
the bureaucrat could be satisfied with such a situation and persist in
rushing ahead without let or hindrance, merely because he has
received the appropriate authority. In truth the administration of a
nation of robots cannot satisfy anyone but a dictator. Only in a
mature democracy can the public administrator find his true vocation.

It has to be concluded that this chapter has dealt very summarily
with a subject that requires and deserves much further consideration
and development.

FURTHER READING

Introductory

This is a many-sided topic whose substance is not to be gleaned from any
one source. Much information is embedded in the several text-books on
British Government already mentioned in these Notes, as well as political
science studies of wider scope. An interesting introductory survey of the
publicity aspects is provided in Francis (later Lord) Williams's *Press,
Parliament and People* (Heineman, 1946). Marjorie Ogilvy-Webb's *The*

Government Explains (Allen & Unwin, 1965) describes authoritatively the Information Services of the Central Government. There is a relevant chapter on 'Public Relations' in E. N. Gladden's *The Essentials of Public Administration* (Staples, 1964).

Pressure groups are comprehensively surveyed in Alan Potter's *Organized Groups in British National Politics* (Faber, 1961). The advisory committees of the Central Administration were examined by PEP in their report on *Advisory Committees in British Government* (1960), while for a contribution on the subject in a wider context K. C. Wheare's *Government by Committee* (1955) may be consulted.

The Story of the Citizens Advice Bureaux (National Council of Social Service, 1964) by Margaret E. Brasnett (which has already been mentioned) introduces an important institution in this sphere. Dilys M. Hill's *Participating in Local Affairs* (Penguin, 1970) provides an interesting survey of community affairs which discusses, but is by no means confined to, local government activities.

Historical and Advanced

Hugh McD. Clokie and J. W. Robinson surveyed *Royal Commissions of Inquiry* (Stanford Univ. US, 1937) to assess 'the significance of their investigations in British Politics', a subject to which little attention seems to have been given. The book is now mainly of historical interest; as is R. V. Vernon and N. Mansergh's *Advisory Bodies* (Allen & Unwin, 1940) which nevertheless is still valuable in showing how far these appendages of the central government had developed between 1919 and 1939.

Two short controversial studies of the pressure group worth reading are S. E. Finer's *Anonymous Empire* (Pall Mall, 1958), which concentrates upon the Parliamentary lobby and F. G. Castles's *Pressure Groups and Political Culture* (Routledge, 1967) which, in the space available, takes into account comparative aspects of the subject.

Contributions in this field are frequently to be found in *Political Studies*, the quarterly journal of the Political Studies Association of the United Kingdom, and in *The Political Quarterly*.

CHAPTER ELEVEN

The Future of Public Administration and its Study

As public administration does not stand alone, but depends directly upon government, of which it is part and for whose service it exists, a forecast of its future structure and content would have to follow an accurate assessment of the government of the future. Formerly this would not have been so difficult, but, in view of the extraordinary acceleration in government changes during the last two decades, and the many further developments in prospect, any forecast of the form and shape of government in Britain and the world in, say, ten to twenty years time, would be subject to too many imponderables to inspire confidence. How much more difficult, therefore, would it be to sketch out in any detail the new public administration, remoulded as it must be by the technical changes in civilization as a whole and the Government's extending responsibility for the nation's affairs, coupled with its increasing need to fit into an emerging pattern of international administration?

The whole outlook is enormously complicated by the need for the maintenance, or indeed the extension, of democratic participation in affairs at all levels. The situation is further influenced by the need for humanity to take more effective charge of its destiny, in curing or evading the terrible side-effects of technological changes, rather than to go on accepting the fatalistic attitudes to invention and science, so prevalent in print and broadcast—the immemorial philosophy of the Gadarene swine *en route* to a fulfilment they were incapable of comprehending and therefore of forestalling! With so many vital matters

at issue in the near future—for the time margin is diminishing rapidly
—how can administrative forecasting amount to much more than
guesswork? The administrator has to carry on as best he can and can
only advise, quoting precept and example, within the major scheme
which is properly for determination by the politicians and their aides,
however blind. Those who counsel otherwise—and they are many,
though of several minds—are in fact advocating a different type of
polity, shadowing perhaps a new Super-Bureaucracy!

It is the task of public administration to follow the Government
and to reshape itself in order to serve the Government's needs with
maximum effect and efficiency. But there are trends in public administration, especially in the rapidly developing technical services
that are becoming available, which will obviously condition its
shaping in the future, and there are policy matters within the
administrators' own sphere, correct decisions on which will go far to
ensuring effective results. However, in times of radical government
changes it would seem desirable that there should be maximum
administrative stability, compatible with such adjustments as are
needed to facilitate those changes. The administrative machinery
should be flexibly designed to accommodate reshaping as required so
as to reduce the need for periodical radical reform in this sphere.
Where there is instability in both spheres, as we seem to have at the
present time (1971), the community will be called upon to pay the
highest price for such benefits as are offered, even though those
benefits may often not in fact accrue.

Administrative amateurism on the part of politicians in power,
aided and abetted sometimes by poor forward-planning by the
professional administrators in their own sphere, can lead to excessive
chopping and changing in the administrative machinery and procedures. There have been a number of instances of this in Britain in
the sixties when the machinery of government, established over the
centuries, has been torn apart in numerous ways. No sensible person
would deny that the emerging situation called for radical readjustments, but much more administrative forethought, and much more
searching public comment, was needed than was apparently forthcoming. Perhaps in fact more was forthcoming, inside the administration itself but was rejected by the politicians because it did not
flatter their political purposes, inevitably looking to the short term
rather than seeking the longer more statesman-like solution. We shall
not know until more information is available.

Examples of this, already mentioned in this book, were the emergence at the end of 1964 of the Ministry of Land and Natural Resources and the Department of Economic Affairs and their disappearance in 1968 and 1969 respectively. It was pretty obvious from the very beginning that the tasks which these new, expensive organizations were designed to perform could have been handled within the existing structure with suitable, but not necessarily extensive, rearrangements.

There is evidence that changes of this sort are made with insufficient forethought. It has become the habit of new governments to overturn the administrative arrangements of the old, causing unnecessary administrative dislocation whose costs could be high and which, in any case, the public has a right to be spared. Of course the administration must be sufficiently flexible to cope with the Government's policy, but the task of ensuring that it develops rationally and effectively on a long-term basis needs some new constitutional machinery to ensure that both Government and Opposition participate in ensuring that the Government's administrative arrangements have a high degree of stability.

In a broader sense there are certainly going to be radical changes in the form and practice of public administration. Apart from the sophisticated new techniques that are being developed in administration in all spheres, there is the over-riding portent of the computer, which is already reducing, if not eliminating, the need for much routine and sub-standard labour, creating new social problems and widespread needs for retraining. A possible, indeed highly probable at least for the time being, surplus of unskilled and only marginally retrainable, labour will have serious implications for the State services, which have in the past often acted, as a matter of policy, as sponges to absorb into the public working force persons of reduced capacity, and particularly those to whom the State acknowledges special obligations, e.g. for military services rendered or those disabled in its service, as well as other disabled, especially the blind, and perhaps the aged, to whom special opportunities for employment are given. At rather higher levels there is likely to be a greatly increased demand for personal services of many kinds, for coping with the new social complexities or the special psychological stresses of the New Society, as well as for meeting demands created by the increase in leisure, which, in the early stages at least, many will find something of a mixed blessing. Those who forecast the early advent of a wonderful leisure-filled arcadia, from 2001 onwards, too often in their utopian dreams fail pathetically to visualize the social problems that would inevitably arise as a result of such a sudden change-over to a state of widespread boredom, if it actually did occur as they predict. New types of social service will be called for, preferably outside the normal State apparatus, but there can be little doubt that the great problems with which the New Society will be confronted will be more easily taken care of if there already exists a highly flexible, public spirited, and professionally expert system of public administration, whose first priority will be to organize and run, with high skill and efficiency, the services upon which the community's health and even survival will certainly depend.

PUBLIC ADMINISTRATION AS A SUBJECT FOR STUDY

When the original work first appeared in 1948 the image of public administration in Britain was both primitive and decidedly hazy. In the universities and higher schools which taught politics and government, the administrative aspects of government were given little specialized attention. If considered at all, public administration was the preserve of the officials themselves, and even with them interest did not penetrate very deeply into the hierarchy. Of course this does not mean that administrative practice in Britain was backward or ineffective: on the contrary British administration, in both public and private spheres, had achieved empirically a high reputation throughout the world. Published materials and scholastic support, however, were meagre compared with what was available in other fields of activity, although this was a British weakness not duplicated everywhere. For a considerable time in Germany, for example, and more recently in the United States, appreciable interest has been paid to the study of public administration at university level.

Illuminating the subject at numerous points there were certainly the incidental references to administration in works on the British system of government, in the memoirs and biographies of statesmen, and in the detailed treatises on local government which had for long been available to students and practitioners in that field. On the work of the Government Departments there was the pioneer Whitehall Series of individual volumes covering most of the main offices, published by Messrs Putnam.

A few universities provided instruction in public administration, sometimes leading to a Diploma, but their syllabuses were largely concerned with the machinery of government in a somewhat broad sense, so that a sound knowledge of the Cabinet and its working in the context of central government would suffice to carry the student a long way towards success. There was a good selection of supporting subjects of course. Most popular among these qualifications was the University of London's Diploma in Public Administration, which was widely available to external students at undergraduate level. Revised after the war and given postgraduate status, it was thus placed beyond the reach of many serving officials who would have profited by undertaking the necessary studies. The changes seem to have been infused with a desire less to producing a qualification of practical value to the administrative novice, than to boosting the prestige of the faculty, although there was probably present a too optimistic estimate, in the immediate post-war climate, of the subject's potential attractive power, an expectation in which the University was not alone.

The officials themselves already had their (now Royal) Institute of Public Administration, launched in the early twenties by a band of enthusiasts who believed in the need for extending and deepening the study of public administration and improving the professional competence of its practitioners. However, such support among the practitioners in the three branches of public administration for which it caters—central government, local government, and public corporations and other autonomous public bodies—had not extended as it should have done, while since the war, during a period of unexampled expansion in government and the public services, its individual membership has remained pathetically small in relation to the total numbers employed. It has, however, strengthened its financial support by the introduction of corporate membership, which has been taken up widely by Government Departments, Local Authorities, and other Public Bodies. Good work has been done in research and the provision of courses in subjects connected with public administration in its several branches, notably for groups of overseas students. The Institute's most enduring contribution has probably been in providing inspiration for the establishment of similar bodies in many parts of the world, and in the issue of its quarterly journal, *Public Administration*, which has been of great help to English-reading students in many lands.

Staff training in the public services had for long been based upon the less formal type of instruction at the desk and, except in a few branches, mainly those in which more ambitious types of training were absolutely essential, it was only after the publication of the Assheton *Report on the Training of Civil Servants* in 1944 (Cmd. 6525) that more formal methods of training were generally introduced and a forward-looking policy on staff training gradually developed. But the tradition of paying little attention to the more general and philosophic aspects of public administration continued until the post-war extension of higher education had got well under way.

PROGRESS REPORT: TRAINING THE OFFICIAL

Since that immediate post-war period the place of public administration in society has been radically altered. The main factors have been due (1) to the substantial extension of the scope of government and the growth of the nationalized industries on the fringes of government, and the proliferation of administrative agencies in many fields, including the rejuvenation and substantial extension of public services in the international sphere, and (2) changes in the complexity and techniques of administration engendered by the impact upon it of vastly improved communications through the rapid conveyance of information, persons and goods in several ways and the introduction and extending use of the electronic computer, which, almost overnight, has speeded up the automatic control and channelling of production, and the tremendous increase in scope, rapidity and accuracy in which the information required by the decision-maker and administrator can be made available to him. The development of jet propulsion for the aeroplane has brought the world's governing and administering institutions into much closer working relationships, putting widely distributed areas into almost instantaneous contact, if need be.

Inside the public services changes were already in train which would in any case have had an impressive effect upon the art of administering. In Britain, for example, under the influence of the war-time Select Committee on National Expenditure of the House of Commons, the new efficiency approach, widely known as 'Organization and Methods' was being developed under Treasury leadership and, stemming from the Assheton Report which was one of the outcomes of the Select Committee's findings, internal staff training had been given a boost and new objectives, the attainment of which the normal attacks of cheeseparing on the score of economy were subsequently unable to do more than to slow down for the time being.

In local government, mainly under pressures from the officials themselves through their associations (in particular by National and Local Government Officers' Association—NALGO), a movement was launched to raise the status of the administrative and clerical staffs *vis-à-vis* the professionals and technicians, by introducing examinations leading to the award of a professional Diploma in Municipal Administration, which it was intended should constitute an essential requirement for appointment or promotion to higher posts of an executive or administrative nature. The Diploma is largely achieved through spare-time studies and its introduction, an admirable development in every way, was an advance in further education rather than a movement to improve in-training on Civil Service lines. The new public corporations were much better equipped than the established government services in matters of training. They were not only well-placed to encourage further studies of a professional or academic nature but also to provide the sort of in-training needed within their specialist spheres of activity, and these were substantially oriented towards the study of technical subjects, industrial expertise, and business management rather than to public administration in a specialized sense.

In the Civil Service a widespread prejudice against the academic approach as a means to the improvement of administrative competence had first to be broken down, less in the top ranks, which were packed with first- and second-class honours graduates (though not usually in relevant subjects)—although they often harboured unspecified objections to the rank and file cultivating a professional interest in their work—but more openly among the older middle-grade supervisors and managers, who saw in their own modest advancement sufficient proof that practical experience was the golden route to such advancement, and among the rank and file who were dead against any system that permitted a dedicated colleague to steal a march in the promotion stakes as a result of burning the midnight oil, an attitude strongly reflected by the staff associations at the time. It was therefore nothing less than a revolutionary change of front when, in the late fifties, the Official and Staff Sides of the Civil Service Whitley Council agreed to support the introduction for civil servants of a Diploma in Government Administration, of degree standard and for spare-time study, in parallel with the existing Diploma in Municipal Administration. Its organization was in fact undertaken by the same examining body.

Unfortunately, the old attitudes were to die hard and indeed are still far from buried. Not only was it officially emphasized that the holding of the Diploma would not be regarded as constituting a promotional qualification, but the work attitudes of most existing supervisors and managers in the several Departments were to ensure that, in the main, minimum encouragement should be given to those members of the staff who planned to undertake study for the Diploma. Facilities were certainly made officially available to such students and in this sense a useful step forward had been taken.

During its first decade support for the Diploma in Government Administration cannot be assessed as other than disappointing. For the time being the impulse from the official and staff interests, which had supported the new development, seems to have died down and insufficient encouragement had been given to induce working civil servants to give up precious spare time to such studies. In the field of formal staff training a more hopeful development has taken place. Plans have been put in hand to establish and develop the new Civil Service College, which the Fulton Commission proposed. At the outset it seems that most emphasis is being concentrated by the new College upon the training of the more senior ranks in the mysteries of higher management, but it is to be hoped that concern with such important studies will not impede the much more urgent and difficult, not to say expensive, task of improving the professional training of the middle and junior ranks, among whom there are many more potential leaders than the system has hitherto troubled to cultivate. In this age of extensive educational advance it is important that the emphasis on paper qualifications should not dam up advancement to the worker ambitious to make his way up from desk or bench.

TRAINING FOR THE POLITICIAN

The trend to separate public administration from politics, necessitated by administration's expanding tasks in meeting governmental needs of growing complexity and the parallel development of professional non-partisan public services, has not been without its drawbacks, drawbacks such as accompany all specialization in human affairs. The simpler world is always to be preferred, providing it copes adequately. Specialists inevitably employ and develop methods of working that are not easily understood by the non-expert, and too often choose the complicated solution when a simpler one could be worked out. It is not necessary to go back beyond the early Victorian period to discover Government Departments which were so compact, in their primary function of secretarial office, that the political heads were able to know all their officials personally and to understand, if they were so minded, about all that was going on around them. At this same period Parliament itself could still concern itself with the detail of its law-making and so keep its delegation of the rule-making powers to a minimum. The Government machine was still simple enough for the ordinary civil servant, often a direct appointee of the Minister, to function very much as a copy clerk or office auxiliary, though there were exceptions of course, notably in taxation offices, where special knowledge had to be acquired and procedures learned. In the modern phase all this has changed and the changes have been cumulative. The organization and procedures of the Departments have become so complicated that even the long-established insider finds it increasingly difficult to see the picture as a whole, to fit his own particular operations and responsibilities into the wider administrative context, or relate them to the broader ends they are intended to serve.

The Government itself is made up mainly of persons whose training has been in practical politics, as distinct from statecraft; in the formulation of policies and the construction of programmes for the party to which they belong; and of course to all the mundane and often burdensome tasks that the basic constituency work involves. Some will have had previous inside experience of administering in ministerial posts, but many will not: most will certainly have had outside experience in the organizing and administering of other bodies, but too often the ordinary politician's knowledge of these processes will not amount to much, and much essential knowledge will have to be acquired after he has actually received his appointment. Clothed with his new responsibility the new political executive will discover that everything is so different inside from what it appeared from without.

The practical politician is concerned with interpreting the needs of the community and with finding ways of meeting the wishes of the people, in particular of the supporters of his own party. He has to devise practical and practicable schemes for implementing the required changes, as and when the time comes for his party to take over direction of the nation's affairs, or, when he, as an individual, is elected to Parliament and, as member of the ruling party, is selected to be a member of the Government. All such schemes for political, social and economic improvement have to be administered, and unless their sponsors have practical knowledge of the capabilities and limits—particularly the limits—of administration in the particular context, it is certain that they will encounter unexpected, and possibly insuperable, difficulties when they come to implement their schemes through legislative and executive channels. It can easily turn out that what the politician wants most eagerly to achieve is not administratively practicable with the resources and techniques available to the government in the existing circumstances, or is achievable only at the expense of other developments which are more urgently needed, or so regarded. Every government has its scale of priorities which, even in an autocracy, is not easily determined, but which is too often completely ignored until the time for the implementation of policies has arrived.

It is on such matters that the administrator's professional advice is invaluable. At this stage, when the politician has become statesman, he will depend very much on expert advice from many quarters, for all projects are extremely complex, but from no one more urgently than from the administrator who is responsible for the mechanics of the projected changes. This is where the confidence of the statesman will be greatly strengthened by the knowledge that he has the support of a corps of professional administrators who are habituated to giving impartial advice and application to the government's business, without permitting their own predilections for or against the particular solution from affecting their diagnosis or subsequent performance.

It is in any case essential that the responsible politician should have sufficient knowledge and experience to be able to appreciate the administrative assumptions of the advice that he receives, as well of course of the criticisms levelled against it. It is often alleged that because of their ignorance of the inner working of the administrative machine Ministers are frequently completely in the hands of the administrators. This seems very unlikely, when one considers the sort of qualities that are required to win ones way to the top in the political struggle. No doubt there are exceptions, where a weak Minister falls under the control of an exceptionally strong administrator, but it is one of the important tasks of the Prime Minister to discover and take steps to liquidate such situations. He has the power to do so, and if he has not the competence or the will, then it is there that the real weakness lies.

Nevertheless, so varied and multifarious are the duties of Ministers that it would be unreasonable to expect them to acquire the requisite administrative understanding at the last moment. It has already been conceded that many will already have acquired the right sort of experience in the course of their political careers and in other spheres, but under modern conditions sufficient grasp of the position is not to be acquired merely by sitting upon committees or even taking charge of bodies that are being effectively run by others: some basic training in public administration is desirable and, if the present trends continue, will become essential.

The position of local councillors is even more precarious since they often have little or no previous experience before election, although it has to be conceded that one of the virtues of the committee system of management of the councils' affairs is that they have had more opportunities to pick up the job as they go along. Both types would profit from attending courses in public administration, suitably tailored to their needs. Some steps have already been taken to help local councillors in this way, and with the adoption of the new management methods that are advocated such training will be even more necessary than ever. In the case of Ministers the training would need to be acquired during the earlier stages of their career. In due course, it could well be considered whether newly appointed ministers should not attend suitable courses at the Civil Service College.

TRAINING FOR THE CITIZEN

The ultimate success of democracy will depend to no small degree upon a high level of understanding of the processes of government on the part of the ordinary man. The ignorant are much too vulnerable to be able to sustain an effective system of representation and, despite our many decades of universal free education, it can hardly be doubted that the pool of ignorance, in this field among others, even if it is getting proportionately smaller—which some experts honestly doubt—is still much too large for the health of a free society. Unfortunately the task of understanding the running of our affairs is itself becoming increasingly difficult owing to their growing complexity. Not that the particular problem is confined to the short-comings of a citizenship endowed with responsibilities that at current levels of comprehension are clearly beyond its capacity. One of the major problems of an age of increasing complexity is to prevent the amateur, whose unique enthusiasms and special insight are even more than ever needed, from being crowded out by the specialist, whose impressive knowledge of his own small world is often offset by an astounding and frightening ignorance of almost everything else. But, with the need to avoid the onset of a new authoritarianism, it would be wrong to discard the possibilities of building an informed demo-cratic citizenship adequate to the tasks by which it is confronted, without at least making a better effort to solve the problem of wide-spread involvement and participation than we have yet managed.

It would be difficult to substantiate a claim—were anyone so optimistic as to make it—that our educational system, with all its brilliant ideas, and bright new gadgets, is securely oriented towards the production of the complete citizen, capable of fully participating in the running of the sort of polity that is emerging before our eyes. To be effective the mere casting of a vote, upon which at present so much of this participation rests, depends upon a much deeper knowledge of statecraft and the responsibilities of citizenship, than the average citizen today commands. He needs to know much more about the workings of society, and of the machinery of government and how it operates, if he is to be equipped to make his proper contribution, and to be in a position not only to improve it but to devise and support new ways of extending it.

Education for citizenship should therefore be the first requirement of any civilized society, and one that can be adopted without political bias, except by those autocratic schools of thought and action that see the common people merely as dupes for the achievement of their own peculiar goals. To suggest what should be the content of such education-for-citizenship would take us beyond the scope of the present work, but certainly a good deal of attention should be given to, the working of public institutions, in particular as it affects both the citizen's duties and his rights. As a minimum, it seems that to be able to play his part as a responsible citizen he should be expected to qualify in civics, while all those who aspire to take an active part in the conduct of public affairs, in the broadest sense, should undertake a more searching examination of public administration and social affairs. There would be no case for the prescription of a narrow or illiberal syllabus.

Probably the vital step would be taken with the teaching profession itself formulating new educational ideals, directed to the formation and equipping of the citizen of the future. Broadly one can visualize the individual's education as having three distinct aspects: education for life, education for citizenship, and education for vocation, to each of which the study of public administration contributes.

PUBLIC ADMINISTRATION STUDIES IN 1972

Since 1945 the education system, in its several branches, has taken an increasing interest in the teaching of such subjects as Civics, British Constitution and Public Administration. More and more Universities provide diplomas and degrees in Public Administration and relevant specialisms, while the schools in general are paying more attention to the basic subjects, which can be offered for the General Certificate of Education (GCE) and similar examinations. The contribution of Further Education in this field has been extended by the recent introduction of Ordinary and Higher National Certificates in Public Administration, which, however, are hardly yet off the ground.

For serving officials (in Local Government) there is the Diploma in Municipal Administration (DMA), and (in Central Government) the Diploma in Government Administration (DGA), both of which are organized by the Local Government Training Board, Alembic House, 93 Albert Embankment, London, S.E.1. Papers in Public Administration and related subjects are often included in examinations set by other professional bodies.

A useful series of single-subject examinations (which the unattached student can undertake without committing himself to concurrent study of a group of subjects which may place too great a strain on his spare time) is provided by the Royal Society of Arts, Examinations Dept., 18 Adam Street, Adelphi, London, W.C.2. The subjects in question are, in ascending order of importance, Civics

(Stage I), Central and Local Government (Stage II) and Public Administration (Stage III). Each Stage is independent of the other but in the nature of Public Administration, as a higher level subject, it is desirable that the student should first acquire a sound knowledge of the relevant supporting subject at Stage I or II.

In the Public Administration field the supply side is evidently extending, although as a whole the picture is still somewhat scrappy. The main problems rest in the sphere of demand. What is needed is a widening realisation on the part of the authorities, the individual officials and the citizen that such studies are not only important to society but of considerable interest in their own right. Only with such extended interest can the educational authorities hope to provide instruction of the quality needed and encourage a supply of the type of inspired teacher required to put it over.

Index